THE

SAINT

NEXT

DOOR

THE
SAINT
NEXT
DOOR

DAN JASON

**PRACTICING HEAVEN BY LIVING LOVE &
DISCOVERING GOD'S HOLINESS WITHIN**

atmosphere press

This message of hope was written to share the love of Christ with every person in our world. It's especially for my brothers and sisters of faith. Know that your life, your faithfulness, and your love are great gifts to be celebrated and shared! Each of you plays an important role in the Church. You have a specific mission to carry out, which will help build up the Kingdom of God. You are called to be a Saint because love and holiness are within you.

My prayer is that you work hard to strive every day to impact the lives of others, live out your faith boldly, and walk humbly with God. This approach will inevitably better your community and the earth. Your faithfulness is essential and answering God's call will come through generous acts of service, heartfelt compassion, and by sharing the love of Jesus with each person you encounter. You are the light the world needs! It's time to recognize the Saint within you and to be the *Saint Next Door* for others.

CONTENTS

DEDICATION

This book is dedicated to my godson, Leonardo. Being your godfather is the greatest honor. Watching you grow up has been life changing. Your love and the way you impact everyone who knows you is remarkable. By embracing and reflecting the love of Jesus, you bring such great hope to us all. It's so powerful and tremendously beautiful to share this journey with you.

This piece of literature was written as my offering and prayer to the faithful followers in our world. I especially want to encourage young people who are the present and the future Church. You have the ability to leave your mark on society and blaze a new trail that provides renewed hope. Always remember to stay true to who you are and who God is calling you to be. Your love for Jesus and for the body of Christ on Earth is both beautiful and inspiring. Nothing you say or do to bring hope and joy to others goes unnoticed.

Remember, as Saint Paul said so powerfully in his letter to the Romans, "All things work together for the good for those who love God" (Romans 8:28). Keep walking boldly by faith, run your own race, and stand firm in what you believe in. Wherever the journey of life leads you, and to whatever capacity you are called, walk humbly with the Lord. You have what it takes and you are well equipped. Pick up your cross daily no matter how heavy it might be and forge on. God has blessed you with gifts, talents, and treasures to share with the world. Be brave, be iron tough, and be different. The world needs heroes and it needs you. You are a Saint! You were not made for comfort, you were made for greatness. Trust, spread your wings, and soar. It's time to summit to new heights and to share the love of Jesus. It's time to uncover the Saint within you. By living out your faith and by spreading great love, you will truly change the world. Now, go out and set this world on fire!

FOREWORD

"To fall in love with God is the greatest romance;to seek him the greatest adventure; to find him, the greatest human achievement." –
St. Augustine of Hippo

I feel I've known Dan Jason for much longer than from when I met him. Perhaps this is the paradox of encountering an "old soul." Dan was my host at a FOCUS convention I attended in January 2020 in Phoenix, Arizona. FOCUS missionaries bring their love for Jesus to campuses, evangelizing through accompaniment, just being there and discovering how God shows up in prayer and word, work and sacrament. That's what Dan does with his many lives. One would never guess his age was 31 from reading his books, which are packed with the wisdom and experience rarely found in men so young.

In the common lexicon, "old souls" are folks for whom material possessions matter little, focusing on meaningful connections. Drawn to others, they still treasure time in prayer and meditation, but only to think on how to make a difference. A deep empathy for those the world ignores, the poorest of the poor, moves them outward, much like the Spirit driving Jesus into the wilderness.

To hear Dan tell his story or give advice is to find yourself motivated. His enthusiasm is contagious, whether he is speaking to children—he writes children's books!—or giving pointers to post-collegians or families seeking to be debt free and to acquire financial independence. Yes, he has published a book on dollars and sense. The great read in your hands, however, is a depth charger: it will pierce your soul to its core and plant seeds to fire it up for this life and beyond.

Dan is a man who has felt life by embracing it. Born into a family that provided him the love and security we hope for every child of God, little in his early years would seem to presage the fire in his belly that began to set him on his chosen path to maturity. He will tell you how he came to a crossroads, questioning his life's meaning, heading as it was to comfort and security, but lacking purpose and joy. He became convinced any life not Christ-centered was worthless to him. The book you are about to read reveals why.

Absent in the narrative is any trace of an angry young man. The hunger is deep and the passions aflame, but this is fundamentally a book about love. I would, in fact, recommend it especially for anyone in a serious relationship, or who is contemplating a decision that involves a long-term relationship, whether that be to marriage, priesthood, religious life or, for that matter, any major trajectory in life, a new job or a career choice.

Dan is something of a man for all seasons, having traveled worldwide to many countries in diverse economic and sociocultural conditions. I will spare you details, but you will be as enthralled as I was to learn how present God can be in both the sublime and the ridiculous, the contrasting circumstances in which human life is lived, or partly lived. The face of Christ can be clearer in suffering and squalor than in the paintings of the masters and in stained-glass splendor.

Much peace and beauty, however, awaits you if you make the journey and stay the course with Dan. He sees himself as a coach, not a guru. In order to make a connection with the reader, he shares much from his personal struggles, discoveries and graces so that the reader will feel a connection, even a friendship.

Perhaps that is what best describes the style of the author: an offer of spiritual friendship. One traveler along the road to Heaven offers himself, not perfection, but his honest self. It is an Emmaus. What exactly were those two companions discussing on the road? Seems they were disputing, even arguing the hearsay about the demise of Jesus of Nazareth, sharing hopes, disappointments and dismay. Little matter who was right or wrong. They were talking about Jesus and, lo and behold, Jesus showed up!

It would not surprise me if at times, the reader might stop and pause at a phrase or a chapter just read. You might not agree, understand or feel particularly comfortable with it. Take the time to pause. This is not a book to be rushed. If you do give it the time and attention that I believe its gravity and sincerity deserves, I guarantee you will feel that Jesus has certainly shown up and touched you with his love.

As Dan says so many times and shows in so many ways, when you are in love you cannot keep it to yourself. You will not come away from reading this book without being changed and learning something about love. And you will be so much better for it.

– Bishop Edward Scharfenberger
Diocese of Albany, New York

INTRODUCTION

by His Excellency, Most Reverend
Bishop Scharfenberger

*"To one who has faith, no explanation is necessary.
To one who lacks faith, no explanation is possible."*
– St. Thomas Aquinas

It is recounted how a curious admirer, fascinated by how a 24-year-old Michelangelo Buonarotti went about sculpting his *Pietà*, was emboldened to ask him one day just how he managed to tweak such exquisite beauty out of the unsightliest mass of marble. Recall that the artisan would typically accompany the rock hunters on the trek to and from the quarry. That was part of the fun, part of his mission. Traveling to the Carrara caves in Tuscany he oversaw the painstaking extraction of the hoard, dormant for millennia, awaiting liberation so that its true purpose could at last be revealed. Or so legend depicts how a figment in the mind of an expectant visionary engaged a dead block to release its hidden treasure.

Already previsioning the outcome, his anxiety must only have grown as he witnessed the cutting and the chiseling, the hoisting and the hauling, feeling every bump in his stomach, no doubt, as rickety wheels rumbled over the slow road to his craftsman's shop. So to the original question, how did the sculptor manage to extract such a magnificent masterpiece out of an ugly chunk of rock? Michelangelo famously quipped, "I just chip away the excess stone."

Fact or fiction, it well presages the process of the making of a Saint! What God the artist does to free the thirsting heart, yearning to be turned—the body and soul it inhabits—into the image which God always beholds from the depths of the divine heart. Nothing delights God more than to enjoy each and every one of us. In the sunlight of grace, love allows love to be perfectly human, in all its incarnate glory.

The thrust is forward, outward and upward—that the Saint within is released to be the neighbor who becomes the presence of God on the journey to Heaven. Love is distorted by secular anthropology because it focuses blindly on me and excludes the author of love, the One who lives for love—is indeed Love itself as Jesus is Love Incarnate. Living Heaven on earth is what Love Incarnate looks like. Journeying with God to Holiness is then attending the prep school to Heaven, being educated towards Sainthood. Playing in the love manual genre by injecting Heaven, the divine, God, blows up the purely sex-oriented, self-centered secular distortion of true love.

Body-souls, incarnate spirits that we are, as the theologians speak, we cannot really be our true selves unless we yield to the gentleness. The loving hand of the divine sculptor carves away what does not belong there. From all eternity, God sees the creation inside. He knows the Saint that lives in us, the Saint we are each meant to be.

This is a book about how to become a Saint. It's written by a self-confessed seeker, who only knows and wants you to know better who it is that makes Saints and how he finds him doing it. When you are in love, you have to sing about that love. So this is a hymn about a love our author has come to believe in, that is ours to enjoy and ours to share. It is not because of what we do, but because of what we are—who we are. Each of us is, in a word, a chip off the old block of the one who made us through love and for love.

God is all of that—an artist, an architect and a sculptor—a lover willing our existence forever, our eternal life. The shell of excess material is to be chipped away, to fall to the ground. In life, however, the original masterpiece that God created and that he longs to restore and to perfect, becomes damaged or tarnished.

The beauty God creates, molds and extrudes out of us sin-sick human subjects is intended. All beauty is intentional. We can accept this destiny, to be human beings free and fully alive, the call to be holy,

Sainted, "of God," or we can strive to wrestle with God, tying ourselves into a knot—a "not-of-God"—denying, rejecting what we truly are, what and whom we are made for.

God's vision always sees the Saint within. Why? Not only because we are made in the image and likeness of God, but because the Father sees and loves in us what he sees and loves in Christ, his beloved Son, the second Person of the Blessed Trinity Incarnate. Why? Because the Holy Spirit, who is the Love between the Father and the Son, lives within us, who are baptized in the name of the triune God. As the Evangelist proclaims, that Spirit teaches and reminds us who we really are despite what the world may fling at us or even what we may have told ourselves or been talked into.

All that tarnishes or disfigures us comes by what we allow our senses to absorb or consume. The bad seed of temptation injected into our veins, sown into the field of our hearts, does not, however, alter our spirit-driven DNA. If we cling to the weeds that sprout, they will weigh us down and choke us, even to the point of drowning. If we let go and let God, the divine sculptor will take over and strip the waste away, with an axe or scalpel, whatever is required by the weight and nature of the blight.

What the author offers in this book is a gentle artist's hand, however, not an axe, to chip away in each chapter, our fears, excuses and pretenses, so as to release the opportunities that grace provides so generously. St. Augustine once pleaded, as he came to discover the relentless press of the source of all sanctity, "Lord make me holy, only not yet." Are we afraid of becoming what we truly are, what we are meant to be, what we are made for? This is a very good question. Am I resisting God?

In the end, we come to the beginning, where God made us in the divine image and likeness. We come to where God, seeing us as we truly are, shows us what we may have become, where we are going, and what we are meant to be. We receive him loving us with the same love as he had for the only Son, begotten of the all-loving Father. For to become a Saint is to be Christified, made like Christ. This is God's original plan: that what we will be in Heaven becomes visible even on earth, even as we pray each day in the "Our Father" that God's will be ours. Heaven on earth. Is that possible? That is what Saints come to believe in as they live it. That's what by God's grace they find themselves living and loving. To "practice" Heaven, to live in the here and now as if we were already in Heaven, now and here.

By grace we become who we are! A Saint is that beautiful image that God sculpts out of the substance of our mortal flesh, in which he has planted the seed of eternal life. Incarnate spirits, we are made for Heaven. And so, practicing Heaven. We become perfectly human, for a Saint, after all, is a human being who becomes, by the grace of God, nothing more than whom God wills—and nothing less.

On every page, in every chapter of this book, our author will accompany you on a journey into your future in Heaven. He will give you pause to take time to reflect on where you have been, what you learned, what you know and what you might need to unlearn and "unknow." Be prepared for many surprises! You may discover what you think is your present reality is, for better or worse, a shadow, an illusion that haunts you and holds you back from the glory that lies ahead. And it will all be for the better. You will find every page lifts you up to a new height you may not have imagined. God has ways of doing that as we become more aware of his presence in our everyday lives.

Do not rush this book. It is full of jewels to be discovered and savored. There are twenty chapters, each one building upon what has been proposed in the ones before, each to be pondered and each with its own set of challenges. But if curiosity impels you to read ahead or to skip around, because something in one of the titles attracts you or speaks to you, you will not spoil any punchlines. For what you will find is that the theme of this book is love and love to the full. God's love for us, each and every one of us, the love of Jesus who would have died for you and me alone, even if you were the only person in the world.

A word about the title of the book: The *Saint Next Door*. You will not find an explanation in any one chapter of the book, but you will know the answer without doubt by the time you have completed it. I do not want to play the spoiler here, and I think you will discover the meaning yourself even when you are only into a few chapters.

It is entirely possible that there is a Saint living next door to you, speaking literally. Novels are full of stories of people whose lives are transformed, undetected by those around them, even inside prison walls. As our author relates and many of us have experienced, Saints are found everywhere. Many times we just do not notice, in part because we are accustomed to look for them. Graham Greene's novel, *The End of the Affair*, is about just a transformation where, tragically, time is wasted and lost looking the wrong way for the love thought dead that is only growing. It is the pattern of the cross. What we thought lifeless has risen.

Yes, the *Saint Next Door* to you might be praying for you, loving you and sacrificing for you, even to the point of death. Parents will often undergo incredible hardships for their children. But the *Saint Next Door* may also be you!

It could be that there is a Saint within you that is yearning to be released, like the figure inside the marble block that the artist set his hand to. God is with you to let that Saint emerge and shine. You may discover as you read and reflect, that the joy of being a Saint, what lets the Saint in you grow—hatch and thrive, is the awareness that the light glowing in you is meant to be released and to let the world around you shine. Does it not seem that Jesus had something to say about that? Light shining in the darkness. Not hiding it under a bushel basket.

One of the most insistent themes that the author returns to throughout the book is that to be a Saint does not mean to be perfect. This mistaken notion, perhaps more common even than any other caricature of what a Saint truly is, has done more than other misunderstandings to discourage so many from striving for holiness. In fact, Heaven is the rightful home of everyone who believes in Jesus and becomes his disciple. It is the universal destiny of all human beings! God wants us all in Heaven.

What the Lord invites us to do is to be perfected, refined like gold, to grow in grace and holiness. It does not happen overnight. Baby steps. St. Thérèse of Lisieux grasped this perhaps better than any other theologian. Considering herself to be so small and insignificant, such a little person, like a small bird hardly able to soar. Seeing herself unlike the eagles of spirituality in her Carmelite order, such as Teresa of Avila and John of the Cross, she humbly accepted her littleness which, she believed, was her guarantee to become a great Saint. This was precisely because of her smallness.

Like that small bird she would envision herself slowly taking, halting small steps up that great stairway to Heaven. Barely able to crawl, she continued slipping and sliding up those huge steps. What gave St. Thérèse of Lisieux such confidence was to just keep trying— and try we must, she insists! Her tiny steps are what made her so irresistible to God. God cannot refuse those tiny creatures who are so helpless. It just brings out the "God" in him and down he comes to sweep us up into his big arms.

Doing small things well. What Matthew Kelly calls "holy moments," are the stuff of sanctity. The little martyrdoms we suffer each day as we let the slight slip away and, if we are a little courageous, we may even let the mountain dissolve into a molehill. It's what Kelly calls "the biggest lie in the history of Christianity"—that we are not all called to be Saints and that Sainthood is only accessible to the high and the mighty. On the contrary, Sainthood is for sinners, too. In fact, mostly all Saints were sinners!

Do you remember what Pope Francis said, early into his papacy? One reporter asked him, "Holy Father, how do you describe yourself? What can you tell us about yourself so that we may get to know you better?"

Without hesitation, Pope Francis said that the one thing about himself that he was absolutely sure is true and that describes him better than anything is that, "I am a sinner." Wow. A pope admitting to us what we know is true! Wait a minute, I mean no disrespect, but of course we would not expect even a good pope to be perfect and sinless every day. Otherwise we would not have to pray for him. Anyway, I felt so good when I heard he had said that. It gave me hope! That is, I can confess my sins and still know that I have so much room to grow.

In this book you will learn how, contrary to being repelled by sinners or, worse, ignoring the poorest and lowliest among them, Jesus is attracted to them! What? You mean if we are miserable and suffering from sins and vices, God does not just let us stew in them because we brought it all on ourselves? Well, exactly. Jesus is drawn to sinners because that is the reason he came into the world and why he stayed to the bitter end of his mortal life right up to the cross. As it has been said in so many ways, Jesus took upon himself the punishment that we deserved, so that we could have the reward he deserved.

You will see as you read not only that this is possible—to struggle with sin yet grow into a Saint—but how it is possible for you, even if you feel you are beyond redemption. Cheer up! You have company. The company of Saints! And you are invited to be in that number. And do not give in to discouragement. The most diabolical of all temptations is the temptation to discouragement. Satan's favorite. Don't be fooled.

I once began a homily during one of my parish visitations where I got the strange urge to ask an unconventional question. I hesitated a moment to ask it because I was not sure how it might turn out, but I overcame my momentary doubts and just blurted it out. I said, "Will the worst sinner in this congregation please stand up!" Without a moment's pause, one middle-aged woman in the center of the church stood right up. Then an old man in the last row. Then another woman, and another man—a young man. It caught on like wildfire until almost the entire church was on their feet. I had to say, "Cut it out," but it proved the point.

It was kind of a reverse example of the time when the crowd was set to stone the woman caught in the act of adultery (the man scurried away, I guess). As everyone picked up a stone, Jesus asked would the one without sin please cast the first stone. One by one, they peeled away.

None of us is worthy. None of us deserves the reward of Heaven. But God just wants to give it to us. And to get us there he has to make us holy. God knows how to do it and, if we trust in him and his promises, he will get us there. Even the worst among us can become the greatest Saint, by the power of God's love and mercy.

I mentioned that the *Saint Next Door* might actually be what each of us is meant to be to the person who lives next door. In other words, the mission of every disciple is to become holy not only for our own sakes but for the sake of our neighbor. What we learn as we contemplate the road to Heaven is that it is like the story of the man beaten by the side of the road that the priest and the Levite passed by. Only the Samaritan—the outcast presumed to be a sinner—noticed the poor man and looked after him. He was the *Saint Next Door*, the one who was the true neighbor.

We know that we have great aids in growing on our path to holiness, the sacramental life of the Church, and especially the Holy Eucharist. Often we go to Mass out of habit or obligation, because of what we have been taught. And we may assume that just by the practice of attending Mass that we automatically get a "Get Out of Hell Free" card. Well Jesus has paid the price of our admission into Heaven and it is not just dusting a church bench that will validate the ticket.

In this book, the author makes a sports analogy of the Mass in a way I never thought of, that also helps us understand better the connection between Mass and our daily lives as disciples of Christ. Rather than seeing church as a kind of spiritual gas station, a drive-in operation where we just get refills so we can drive off alone in our vehicles, he compares it to a pre-game rally or huddle.

In the locker room, the coach calls the team together. He gives them a pep talk, goes over the rules and game strategy, calls players by their nicknames and rehearses their positions and moves, reminding them of the other team's tactics and weaknesses. The team will probably stand up and shout a motto, maybe even chant their song and do a little pre-game victory dance—but the game is on the field!

Thinking of Mass as a pre-game rally, to rev us up for the game is not to take away its majestic significance at all. In fact, without the prep and the rehearsal—the warm-up—the team will never go on to victory. In many ways, it is that meeting in the locker room which is absolutely essential for the team's spirit and ultimate victory. It's when the team huddles together before taking the field, where they will take their positions, relying on one another, but without the security of the close presence, the intimacy of the embrace. This is like the game field of our everyday lives.

The Latin Mass ends with the exhortation, "Ite missa est," which literally translates, "Go, the Mass is." I've heard some say this means get out of here because the Mass is over, but just the opposite is true. The Mass continues as we leave, bearing the Lord's real presence within us and, because we are united by the one Lord, we remain connected until we meet again at Mass. You mean that slow poke I just cursed out for short stopping before the light turned red and was sitting in the pew behind me? Yes, it's true, players on the field commit errors, sometimes even bumping into each other. Remember, we are still a team. And we are on the road to victory. We don't reach our common goal fighting with one another.

What gives us courage and strength in the vineyard, confidence on the road, grace in the field, is the knowledge and assurance that the team is behind us. What our Eucharist affirms is that Jesus himself is always with us. When we are alone, he is there and yes, there may even be more than a few angels in the outfield!

Enjoy this book, savor it, and feel the love. Know that you are God's beloved child, chosen, called, and embraced by God whose very essence is love itself. Take all the time you need. Let the good news sink in. Let it make you good news, too, so that everyone you meet can feel the joy in your heart. Trust that this is found in the peace the world cannot give, it's discovered in the presence of a Saint that is the God in your heart.

HEAR ME KNOCK
CHAPTER 1

*"Hope is being able to see there is light
despite all of the darkness." – Desmond Tutu*

Neighbors are what we are, Rose used to think about Amelia. She would see her across the street cradling her coffee cup and struggling down the driveway in heels every morning. Then zipping away in her car, barely buckled in, with the rosary hanging from her rearview mirror swinging all over the place. If Amelia was to look up and catch Rose watching her, she would flash her a quick smile, an exasperated wave, then be on her way.

They lived in a loud and busy neighborhood. One filled with lots of families and children constantly on the move. It seemed each day there was a new child Rose saw riding their bike down the street or being pulled by their dog on the sidewalk. She was surrounded by people. Just neighbors, really. But that night standing outside Amelia's house, Rose could hear the faint sound of the television coming from inside and knew she had no choice but to knock. *Of course, the rain had to come tonight,* Rose thought. She tapped two knuckles on the door. Their houses were across from one another and from Amelia's house, Rose could see hers from a different perspective. She looked at her house, the one she had lived in for two decades now. She saw her welcome mat that said, "A spoiled dog lives here!" from when she and Jack used to have Beau and she saw her garden out front, drenched in the rain.

She observed her home as if she was not herself but instead was someone else looking into her life. She thought about this a lot. What it would be like to have someone else's mind, feel someone else's problems. She often thought of moving to a new neighborhood, perhaps with less kids, less houses, maybe less pain. She'll even get a new dog or maybe a cat, who won't know her for any other reason than the fact that she feeds it and pets it and won't care about her looks or her sadness. Often, Rose will walk right into a thought like this and get stuck in it. That's what happened the night she found herself at Amelia's front door.

Amelia heard the knock at the door and hurried over to the small window of her foyer to see Rose huddling beneath a heavy raincoat. She opened the door right away and could sense something was wrong. Amelia had noticed a change in Rose. As much as a friendly neighbor can notice a change. She knew it was none of her business, really, but she did check the paper every morning. In fact, it made her late most days and she would end up running out to her car, practically falling down the driveway. But five months, eleven days ago, she opened the obituaries section to see that another neighbor of hers had passed, Jack Evers, Rose's husband.

Before Jack's passing, Rose hadn't felt such grief in years. As a young girl, her parents passed away in a crash. She was old enough to remember but young enough to be able to move on. But when Jack died, this was a different kind of pain. She felt it every morning when she would wake up and for a few seconds forget that he was gone. Some mornings she could even feel him there on his side of the bed before realizing he wasn't actually there. Her mourning hovered over her life like a fog, clouding the day. She couldn't make toast without seeing him. Couldn't drive down their street without hearing a song on the radio that made her burst out in tears. She had no one else. No other family. She ached with loneliness. And that night, with the rain and the darkness, she looked across the street. Rose saw Amelia's house, realizing it was the only place with the light on and was where she had no other choice but to go.

Walking into Amelia's dimly lit living room, Rose thought maybe she had made a mistake. They were neighbors, that's all, and this wasn't Amelia's problem. It wasn't her job to help her, Rose thought.

"Is everything alright?" Amelia asked.

Rose was looking around. She looked at her chipped red fingernails clutching the maroon couch, at the crucifix over the front door, at the toaster on the kitchen counter.

"Yes. Everything is fine. I was just looking for something," Rose said.

"Looking for something?" asked Amelia.

"Yes. Do you have any mulch?"

"Mulch?"

The two women just looked at each other for a moment, pausing to see if one would speak before the other.

Rose broke the silence first. "Yes. Mulch. For my garden. I'll need to replant some of my flowers after this storm passes."

"Oh, I see. Well, I'm sure I have some in my shed but I don't think now is a good time to get it."

"Right. Tomorrow then." Rose got up off the maroon couch and left just as quickly as she had come, back out into the rain.

The next morning, Amelia went out to her shed, grabbed a bag of mulch and made her way across the street. She liked Rose's house. It was small, but looked like it was right out of the Better Homes and Gardens magazine. She walked up the steps and stood on the "A spoiled dog lives here!" welcome mat. Before she could knock, Rose swung the door open.

"My mulch!" she said. "Fabulous."

"Do you have a dog?" Amelia asked.

"Not anymore."

"Oh, I'm so sorry. I didn't know."

She handed over the mulch and felt Rose staring at her for a moment. She realized she was looking at her necklace; a silver cross her mother had given her for her birthday several years ago.

"Does that stuff work?" Rose asked.

"Necklaces?"

"No. The praying."

"Hasn't failed me yet," Amelia said with a smile.

Rose nodded then walked down her front steps to her garden. She already had her tools waiting for her. She had been alone for a while now but she could sense Amelia's certainty, the trust she had in God. She wasn't sure the first time she noticed it or felt drawn to it. Maybe it was the rosary or her necklace, or the light, gentle way about Amelia. But Rose wanted to feel that way too.

"What do you think? Want to help?" she asked Amelia, holding up a pair of gardening gloves.

"Oh, I would. It's just I don't actually know how to do any of that."

"Then how come you had mulch?" Rose asked.

"I don't know. I figured maybe I would start my own garden, or maybe a friend would need to borrow it sometime."

Rose realized that her neighbor had been watching her too, and that she knew far more than Rose realized.

"Well, how about I give you some gardening tips and you teach me what you know."

As time passed, Rose started to fully pour out her heart to Amelia. Their friendship blossomed like flowers in their garden that sprouted afresh each spring. With each new flower they planted, Amelia taught Rose a new prayer, psalm, and a special bible verse. Tulips for the *Our Father*. Violas for the Rosary. And slowly, Rose came to learn that Jesus asks us to receive his love and to share that love with our neighbor. Amelia had been waiting with her door open all along, perhaps it was because God wanted Rose to first learn love herself.

Rose no longer had to contain her heavy feelings of being lost and confused. For years she had buried them in the desert of her darkened heart, but now she was free from the slavery of heartache. Storms had weathered this young girl drastically to say the least.

Amelia suspected things had been troublesome for Rose who had kept a distance since moving to the neighborhood, but all along she could sense a great beauty that was inside of her friend. The road Rose traversed had been rockier than most people experienced and the thorns in her garden, which once had choked her own growth, were now being pruned thanks to Amelia's loving friendship. Agony and grief had left Rose searching for answers since her parent's accident. This had been compounded by the tragedy of her husband Jack's death. Life had carved an enormous hole in her bleeding heart. The cheerful little girl she remembered looking at in the mirror from her childhood had withered into a pathetic flower whose roots were dried up and dead. The seeds of faith that had been planted in Rose's heart from years ago, hadn't been watered until now.

As she planted and conversed with her beautiful friend Amelia, the broken cassette tape of her life that had replayed in Rose's mind was no longer stuck on repeat. There was a new song and tune in her heart. Rose's spirit felt wild and was free again! Like a flower that lacks sunshine and the sweet rain that quenches its thirsty roots, Rose hadn't realized who she was missing all along. Her parents, yes. Her beloved husband, unquestionably. However, *the who* went even deeper...Something or perhaps someone put it in Rose's heart and that had led her to knock on Amelia's door. She was there in her friend's presence because God knew that Rose needed a listening ear and was crying out for help.

Amelia was patient and calm. She had a deep faith and knew how to keep things in perspective. Rose saw the beauty and peace in Amelia's heart right away. She longed for what her friend had, but she didn't know why and surely did not know how to attain it. What Rose didn't grasp was that mulch and a garden would be the answer. Moreover, she hadn't noticed *who* she was actually longing for—Jesus.

Amelia was someone who poured into the lives of people and her divine spark attracted them to her like a magnet. Her deep compassion led her to be patient, to listen, and to love Rose back to life. In the eyes of those who knew her, she was a "Saint." After that initial stormy night, Rose and Amelia continued to garden. They grew together through the seasons of life.

Certainly, Amelia greatly supported Rose. She helped her get through another treacherous part of the journey. Ultimately, she found more than a friend. The gaping hole in Rose's heart had been filled. Jesus had been the missing piece to her puzzle. The Lord had never stopped seeking her. He never had stopped loving her. As the days flew by and the calendar turned, Rose came fully alive. She now had renewed hope like the tiny bulbs that burst through the soil stretching toward the sunlight. Amelia had planted, they both watered and tended the garden together, and God caused the growth. Rose's joy was back and her smile turned as radiant as the morning sun!

The two women who were once detached neighbors, formed an

indescribable bond as soul sisters. God had fused them together both as Saints the next door down. Rose and Amelia grew holiness in the garden of life. Seasons changed and storms came and went. New mulch was brought in every spring and replanting occurred time and time again. As Pablo Neruda put it, "You can cut all the flowers, but you cannot keep spring from coming."

Long Awaited Answer

See, it all began with a knock and a door being opened. The same holds true for you and me. For many people out there, the door of faith has been shut. Even harder to accept, the door of the heart might have been locked. As long as the key to the door hasn't been thrown away, hope remains. Pain, turmoil, difficulty, the list goes on. At times, life has gotten the best of us. It can cause us to leave our garden untended or cause it to die. Others have drifted, becoming disconnected from the vine. The things that really matter have often been replaced with mere placeholders of temporary happiness. What our hearts need and crave most is to find rest in Jesus. The human soul longs to be filled with God's love and a life in Christ. Stephanie Laurens put it like this, "Love truly is the most transformative power on Heaven and earth."

Regardless of which side of the door you are on today, hear the knock. There is a Rose and an Amelia out there in each of us. That's a great thing to acknowledge because it reminds us that there is a Saint inside waiting to bloom. Ultimately, God is knocking on your heart. He is unceasingly searching for you. The Lord desires for you to open up your heart to him so you can receive the greatest life which is found in the love of Jesus. Faith and God's grace will transform you. God wants you to uncover the beauty that has been inside of you from the beginning of time. Jesus will reveal the Saint that is within you if you allow him. God is calling and he asks you to listen. This is not just any call. It is the call to become great! The Lord is calling everyone to become his loving Saints!

As we begin traveling this road to Sainthood, it is meaningful to take account of where you are in your faith. The current place is different for each of us and the depth of our relationship with the Lord is so vast. This makes the human experience and the call to Sainthood even more special. It is specific, and each person that walks this earth does so in a unique manner. What holds true for all of us is that we are called to Sainthood and are on the journey together. At various times in our lives we are called to different people, particular places, and periodic pathways.

However, through it all, you and I have the most important and universal vocation to live out and that is to holiness which comes through love. Cullen Hightower once said, "Faith is building on what you know is here so that you can reach what you know is there." The evidence is not always seen completely until we trust boldly by taking the next step and journey on.

Everyone in this world needs a ray of hope and a light of inspiration. Amelia was that for Rose and you can be the sunshine for others during dreary seasons of life. Humanity eagerly awaited Christ's coming for centuries. Now, our world, in its brokenness and complexity, waits for you. Friends, family, co-workers, and those strangers you have not met yet, all crave love. God's love working in our lives and being shared through us has no limits.

As his vessels, we change the narrative from darkness to light and from death to life. Together we are invited to enter into the renewed hope found in God alone. Hope is like the sun, namely it is found in the Son. As we journey toward Jesus, the shadows of life's burdens are cast aside. The Lord opens our hearts so we can receive his love to be shared with all, entering into the marvelous light of the resurrected Christ. The reality is that you are a Saint. You are walking the road to holiness. The crux of it all remains in the love found on the Cross.

So as we take the first major steps of this journey together toward Sainthood, it is paramount to at least try to conceptualize the depth of God's love. The Cross is powerful beyond measure and with it comes great hope for those who believe. Whether young or old, rich or poor, black or white, man or woman; no matter what our differences might be, we are being called to be the *Saint Next Door*. The human soul was formed in the same manner—all people created in the image and likeness of God.

Therefore, one thing remains central for everyone, to come to accept that we are loved by God and holiness is found within. By your faith you gain endurance to take on everything life throws your way and through it all Jesus carries you. God has a great plan in store for your future. It's time to let go and to trust a little more deeply. The Lord is knocking on the door of your heart. Jesus is awaiting your answer and he's asking you to start his knocking for others. Take his outstretched hand today. Follow Jesus and know that we walk this road of love and holiness together. Our final destination is Heaven as his Saints!

Challenge 1

Throughout the course of this book there will be a series of challenges, 20 in all, to help you stay focused as you grow closer to Jesus and experience God's love. The main objective of each of these is to deepen your faith. For your first challenge, please write down the things in life that you're wrestling with. Jot down anything that comes to mind that has been harbored internally or is leaving you feeling empty. Meanwhile, record all the beautiful things that have brought you the greatest fulfillment, joy, and inner peace. Think of the ways that love has impacted your heart. Write down the times you have received or cultivated God's love. Prayerfully reflect on both of these lists and invite God to speak to your heart. Listen and wait. Jesus is knocking, listen. The Lord knows there is a Saint the next door down within you. Hear him knock. Open that door and receive his grace.

LIFE TO THE FULLEST

CHAPTER 2

*"I came so that they might have life
and have it to the full." – John 10:10*

Purpose & Joy

What does your perfect day look like? Picture yourself doing what you have always desired. You're on cloud nine, living it up and soaking in every second. Perhaps you're on a majestic beach looking out at aqua blue water. You are reclined underneath the umbrella while sipping a cold drink with your toes submerged in the white sand. Or maybe you are stepping foot off the plane in an unknown city, ready to take on the bright lights and see all it has to offer. No matter where you want to be, you are having a blast because your best friends are with you and those closest family members are there making memories to last a lifetime. Soon you will be headed to your favorite restaurant and ordering anything you desire. The world is your oyster. Life is so good! You are walking around with some serious bounce in your step and the biggest smile on your face.

Think about your ideal month and now imagine your optimal lifestyle—the dreams of your childhood coming to reality. All this sounds great, but we pinch ourselves to hit the reality check button. Certainly we are not here to feel empty or to simply pass time. The very essence of life is a great mystery. So why are we here on this planet called earth? What is our purpose and how do we discover it? Many important and complicated questions flood the mind when contemplating the meaning of life. What is evident is that we are present, an opportunity has been afforded, and an energy flows within us. Joy and purpose go hand and hand.

Surely, life is a gift. Have you ever sat down and thought about the chances of you existing? Most people have not. Afterall, air fills our lungs without effort, our hearts beat automatically, and we wake each morning naturally. The functionality of the body and all of its extraordinary characteristics is bewildering. Science can explain a lot, however it cannot fully reveal how the human person and all its profound complexities has a soul that never dies. Did you know that the chances of you being born are about one in four hundred trillion! If that isn't a head scratcher, I don't know what is. The point here is that mere chance isn't the reason you are alive, you were written in God's book of life.

You were on God's mind since the beginning of time as the great prophet Jeremiah reminds us, "Before I formed you in the womb I knew you,

before you were born I dedicated you, a prophet to the nations I appointed you."[1] From the moment the first breath filled our lungs on the day you were born, until your final hour here in this world, you have life. Blood pumps through your veins. There is an energy, aura, and personality in you that nobody can replicate. Your DNA is unique and your life can only be explained as a gift from the Lord. However, there is a great distinction between having life and being fully alive. It is my hope that you understand that we were all made for more. Each man, woman, and child was made to have life and to have it to the fullest!

---

[1] Jeremiah 1:5

Co-Creators with God

In comparison to the magnanimous nature of creation and the history of the world, let alone eternity, our individual lives are a mere blip on the radar screen. Here one second and gone the next. Yet, each of us is here for a reason and our time is meant to be filled with abundance that we can share. God does not want us to just go through the motions during our lifetime. No, that is not what was intended. We are told very emphatically that Christ said, "I have come so that they might have life and have it to the full."[2] Life to the fullest has become my personal mantra. So what does life to the fullest mean anyway? How do we achieve this and what steps do we need to take to get there? The answer to this question remains within each individual person. Arriving at this answer and understanding the abundance and how you can become the best version of yourself that you can be is a journey of faith. Imagine it is summer time, you are on the boardwalk after a fun day at the beach. The warm sun is shining down on you and the cool ocean breeze is felt as you hop on.

The tandem bicycle that you are riding is something new to you. Of course you have ridden a bike a thousand times as a child, but this is a little different. Do you get on the front and have the ability to steer, or do you jump on the back and commit to pedaling. The former involves great control, while the latter requires trust. Life is like a tandem bicycle and you can live it to the fullest when you get on the back and trust in God to steer and navigate along the way. Your effort, cooperation, willingness to listen, and perseverance are extremely important. If you stop pedaling the bike slows and eventually will stop. Not to mention you could fall off. Meanwhile, as you go even though you do not know completely where the Lord is taking you, the path you are on is filled with great promise. Certainly there will be bumps along that boardwalk, even obstacles that will have to be maneuvered around. You are wearing a helmet in case there are any crashes.

Over the course of time you come to realize that collaborating with the driver works the best and communication is key especially going around turns and changes throughout the ride. While in unison it is as if you are seamlessly riding together and there are no hitches. You

---

[2] John 10:10

have inner peace and you can see the sunset ahead. As you coast to your final destination and the bike slows as you stop pedaling, you look back and see the terrain you have traveled. The highs and the lows, the enthralling moments and the hardship along the way...They all shaped and made you who you are. Most of all, you did your part. Not only did you enjoy the ride and live fully, your route, although so unique, showed others how to ride.

See, each of us is on the road to Sainthood and the first step is to realize that God desires to ride along with us. The solo trip will not leave you fulfilled because you were made for more! Listening is key though. There is a reason why Jesus took Peter, James, and John up to the top of the mountain to pray. Yes, Christ was transfigured before them. This is a remarkable and significant event in salvation history. However, what God said to the three apostles, he says to us all, "This is my chosen Son; listen to him."[3] Certainly, witnessing the Lord's transfiguration and him shining in all his glory was a beautiful expression of the transformation that God would do for the early followers.

It also demonstrates his power and what he can do for you and me in our lives. Holiness and Sainthood are most definitely not pure white bliss all the time though. That goes without saying and we would never attain Sainthood without grace. The words that the apostles not only heard, but took to heart, are what I want to emphasize here. Listening is far different from hearing. Listening involves receptivity and then turns into direct action. Later in our journey we will uncover the noises of life and learn more about how to strain out the things that are unnecessary. For now, let's understand that listening is a necessary trait of a Saint. The road to holiness becomes more manageable when you listen to God who loves you most and when you walk hand in hand with Jesus.

No matter who you are, where you are from, or what might be different about you, every person belongs equally to the human family. This is a beautiful thing because that ultimately means you and I are part of God's family. Since we are all members of the body of Christ, we each have a special and unique calling on our lives. The world often tells us that we cannot have fun, enjoy life, and be happy

---

[3] Luke 9:35

if we follow all the rules. We are told it is impossible to adhere to the Commandments and live a moral life, while experiencing enjoyment.

A Better Way

Culture today suggests that surely we cannot obtain fulfillment through religion or spirituality. It is a sad situation that so many young people are growing up without a foundation set in solid faith. The "religion of the nones" is growing at an all-time high. What is even more alarming is that people continue to wander without faith and stay distant from the shepherd of their soul. Many remain lost for a lifetime and continue to search aimlessly amidst the lures of the world for satisfaction. Emptiness, loneliness and a lack of joy rob people of life. However, there is a better way—*the way*. A relationship with Jesus and fostering faith is essential. Tapping into the recesses of our heart and uncovering our spiritual nature is fundamental to our human existence, let alone our arrival to Sainthood and holiness.

Faith must be the bedrock which our lives are built upon. Jesus was very blunt when he said, "Everyone who listens to these words of mine and acts on them will be like a wise man who built his house on rock. The rain fell, the floods came, and the winds blew and buffeted the house. But it did not collapse; it had been set solidly on rock."[4] Our Lord then went on to say that ignoring him and the spirit that lives within us, is like building on sand. We all know what happens at the beach when a hurricane blows through. It is cataclysmic and everything is swept away. My hope is that you will build your life and faith on rock and can be like the palm tree. If you and I have deep roots that go way down below the surface of the beach, we will be anchored to bedrock. When the inevitable storms of life blow through, we will stay connected to the Lord. Because we are anchored to God, we receive his grace and blessing.

Therefore, we will also have the inner ability to bend, having the ability to adapt because of Jesus' power in us. The flexibility and strength of our roots will allow us to survive. Although this is good when facing tumultuous periods along the way, we were made for so

---

4 Matthew 7:24-25

much more than mere survival. You and I were created to thrive. For me, the palm tree is a sign of flourishing. Ponder this for a moment. Palm trees thrive in the most exquisite places on earth and they provide shade on scorching days in the sun. Life is assuredly not a vacation all the time, however God made us to be fully alive! So how do you get this fullness and abundance of life that Jesus speaks about in John's Gospel? You might be wondering what is in it anyway? What measuring stick are you using when it comes to assessing your life? The course to arriving at a full and abundant life is by doing one thing and doing it well. You become a Saint. Wow! Stop! You are asking me to do that? What if that is impossible? What if I don't want that responsibility even if it is a possibility?

The thing is, not only is Sainthood possible, God wants us to become holy and he wants to infuse us with his presence in our lives. A relationship with him and becoming a Saint is what you were ultimately made for! You are called to be Saints. By answering this call to Sainthood you will receive life to the fullest. Now you might be thinking, "Me a Saint?" Yes, you. You are truly called to be a Saint. See, there is a common misnomer that being a Saint is out of the realm of possibility, that it is unattainable. How can we, mere humans achieve such allure and elevate to such high scale holiness. The answer is found in the fact that we were not made for comfort, we were made for greatness.

When we strive to lead a life as God's faith filled people and we give our best to love others by sharing Christ with the world, that is the first step toward Sainthood. Becoming a Saint is not about perfection. Saints are actually the least perfect people. The only thing that the Saints did perfectly who came before us, was they embraced their imperfection. So accept God's invitation. Allow his mercy and grace to fill in all the gaps. When most people think about Saints they begin to call to mind the men and women who did the holiest of things in life. The characteristics and lists are composed of the miracle makers and those who radically changed the world. Heaven is filled with the likes of Saint Peter, Saint Paul, Saint Teresa, Saint John, St. Jude, St. Anthony, St. Catherine, the list goes on. Although this is taught to us and believed to be true, we still don't grasp that we are called to be Saints also.

Additionally, you might think like I once did, that Saints and miracles existed a long time ago. Thousands of years ago when Jesus was around and shortly thereafter, these powerful people—Saints and the experiences they lived out are what we read about in books. Certainly, no one today becomes a Saint, let alone is Sainthood a universal calling by God to his people. Wrong! We are all called in this manner to holiness. Heeding this call is our greatest responsibility. In fact, as the faith filled men and women of the Church it is the surest road to fulfillment—life to the fullest. Sainthood is the fastest way of reaching Heaven!

Why do we believe that we cannot reach Sainthood and why are there so many feelings of unworthiness? The truth is that God calls us and showers his grace upon us. God brings holiness to our lives. The Lord will continue to work in your life if you allow Him. As long as we say small yesses along the way, the path begins to open up. When we realize that we are a people set apart—that we were made in the Lord's image and likeness, things start to materialize. I have learned that when I put aside my own desires and really build a relationship with Christ, his love transforms me from the inside out. It is not by our own doing, but rather by the love and mercy of God that this is even remotely possible. There is always more to be found in the Lord. Never do you reach the end or the "I made it" stage because it's not about what is simply good for you. With God it goes far beyond the good as our lives in Jesus transcend the natural world and its implications with hearts on fire for him.

This journey of Sainthood calls us to discover what is better, namely the ever progressing best soul and intimacy with our Lord every step of the way. Surely, many things are good in this life, but our call to holiness is about choosing what is greater in the sense of what God leads us to that provides lasting peace and freedom found only in him. Recall Martha and Mary. What did Jesus say? Well, he tells them and us that Mary chose the "better part" and that is what we are asked to do also. We will examine this again with more complexity later because this idea of choosing what is better is paramount. However the thing to hone in on is for you and I to always seek the greatest place where our hearts are fullest and we overflow with the heart of Jesus' love because in doing what is better we chose to become who we are created to be—Saints!

The power that exists in walking by faith daily, striving to love

God and others, and living with great conviction does something within each of us. As you navigate through life, divine connections take place, encounters and experiences unfold, and you will discover who you truly are. It is in the midst of this journey and living life fully that we become totally alive. In our humility and our willingness to forgive ourselves and others of our shortcomings, God infuses his holiness within us. No longer do we live and move and have our being on our own, we are filled with the Holy Spirit. The Spirit, named and sent by Jesus as our Advocate, is powerful beyond measure. For peace comes to the soul in knowing, "Where the Spirit of the Lord is, there is freedom."[5]

Christ came so that you would have an overflowing abundance. There is no better way to have life to the fullest than to answer the call of our lives to Sainthood. No one comprehended the call to Sainthood or professed it more accurately than Saint Mary Teresa, better known as Mother Teresa of Calcutta who said, "Do small things with great love." That is what Sainthood is about and that is what life to the fullest exemplifies. How we climb the mountain is by stepping on the rungs of love all the way to the top.

First we must humbly receive the love of Jesus Christ, who took the Cross to die for us, so that our sins could be forgiven. Our Lord did this so that He could open wide the gates of Heaven. Afterwards, when we realize that God has no limitations and his power is endless, we can begin to conceive how Sainthood can be reached. When we conceptualize that the Lord will bless our lives and has given us such great gifts that must be shared with the world, then we will take another step closer toward Sainthood. Then, when we understand and accept that perfection will never be reached, we grow in faith all the more. God never asks us to be perfect, he just simply requires that we do our very best daily. Going all in and genuinely striving to be better will get us even closer to the Sacred Heart of Jesus.

Finally, when you and I embrace our sinfulness, when we ask God for his grace, and we say "yes" to daily holy moments we impact our world in a profound manner. There is only one you in this world and there will be only one you for all eternity. God is calling you to be the best version of yourself that you can be. Remember, God doesn't make

---

[5] 2 Corinthians 3:17

any mistakes. The Lord surely did not make a mistake by creating you, his Saint!

Now it's Time

Today is the day that we journey together toward Sainthood. The world truly needs heroes and it needs you. Will you answer the call and give your all? Do you have what it takes to live boldly, without abandon, and with true authenticity? Love is your guide to Sainthood and receiving and sharing Jesus with others is the key to life to the fullest. So what are you waiting for? Our existence on earth is short and there are no guarantees. You have been blessed with life, now it is time to stop putting limitations on what God can do through you. Believe and know that it might seem impossible for human beings, but "nothing is impossible for God."[6]

No matter where you are on this faith journey, whether you are at the very beginning or you are someone who has a close relationship with the Lord, God loves you and needs you to build up the Kingdom. On your grave it is going to have your name, your date of birth, and the date when you died. However, the good news is that Saints always live. The thing about Saints, who embody life to the fullest, is that they are focused on what comes in between those dates on the tombstone. The strongest person the world has ever seen, the most unselfish, and the most loving cannot do it alone.

When we invite God into our lives, when we ask him to show us the way, and when we say "yes" to where he leads us, then we begin our journey toward Sainthood. As Father Michael Gaitley beautifully articulated in his book *33 Days to Morning Glory*, "Total Consecration to Jesus through Mary is the surest, easiest, shortest, and most perfect means to becoming a Saint." Father Gaitley explains that when we say "yes" to Christ and ask the intercession of Mary, it allows her to help us become Saints. The Blessed Mother was closest to her Son and can help us receive Christ's Sacred Heart. It is when we give ourselves completely to the Lord that a great transfiguration happens in our lives. We are made holy because he is holy. We are made Saints

---

[6] Luke 1:37

because that is what the Lord calls us to.[7]

Sainthood is not for the faint of heart, but it is what God asks of us. The Lord asks that we tackle every day by putting on our armor of faith and spreading his great love. Joy is there to be shared. Just as we have been blessed with the gift of life, we have a present to unwrap every single day. It is like Christmas morning as my friend Greg explained to me. Life is the perpetual gift we find beneath the tree every day we open our eyes. When your feet hit the floor in the morning, you have a choice to make. What are you living for? Who are you living for? Will you rise to the occasion and take the road that is less traveled and blaze a new trail or will you settle for mediocrity? Never forget, you have what it takes. There is a fire burning within you right now. Your faith and God's love are the greatest gifts you have received and your faith and the heart of Jesus are the greatest gifts you can share with the world.

At the end of the age when our life here on earth comes to a close, my hope is that we will be able to say we did all we could with our time on this planet. However, the greatest blessing will be what you leave behind, your legacy. The legacy of a Saint is all about how he or she impacted the lives of others in a positive manner and the ways in which they loved with great ferocity. That is what the dash on the tombstone is all about. We will dig into this concept even more later on. Living with purpose and conviction will ensure you are fully alive and that will not only fill you with the greatest joy during your journey on earth, but I believe it will be what leads others to Heaven.

Beyond everything, you and I are challenged to do our personal best to build up God's Kingdom one person at a time. Saints...Why not me and why not you? As Jesus told his disciples, "'Take nothing for your journey, neither a staff, nor a bag, nor bread, nor money; and do not even have two tunics apiece'... Departing, they began going throughout the villages, preaching the gospel and healing everywhere."[8] Just go! Do not worry and allow God to lead you every step of the way. Our Lord encourages us to come and follow him. As St. Irenaeus put it, "The glory of God is man fully alive." It is time for us to journey on the road to Sainthood together! Now is the time to live life to the fullest!

---

[7] Father Michael Gaitley

[8] Luke 9:3

Challenge 2

Reflect on what Jesus is trying to tell us in John's Gospel when he said, "I came so that they might have life and have it to the full." What does LIFE to the FULLEST mean to you? Be honest with yourself and think about what is holding you back from taking a quantum leap in your faith. How can you reinvigorate your life, trust God more deeply, and tap into your full potential? What is holding you back from starting today? Know with full confidence, you are loved. Pray on the fact that God calls you and needs you as his Saint in this world. Tell yourself that you are a Saint and allow the Lord to lead you to holiness. Joy and your purpose lived out awaits you!

WALKING THE NARROW ROAD
CHAPTER 3

*"The world offers you comfort, but you were not made for comfort.
You were made for greatness." – Pope Benedict XVI*

Setting Out on the Journey

While traveling to Dallas, Texas, a number of years ago, I met a retired couple named Mike and Jill Lawrence. These folks from the deep south amazed me. As I got to know them more on the lengthy flight to the lone star state, Mike said they had a fun practice to spice up their life. Quarterly, he and his wife would spin a globe and wherever either of their fingers landed that is where they would head off to. It was a continuous adventure with no telling where each spin would land them. Imagine catching the next plane to an unexpected and unknown territory. Sounds exciting to me! Traveling and being immersed in a different culture is amazing and life changing.

Everyday billions of people around the planet travel. Airplanes, cruise liners, trains, automobiles, bicycles, and walking on our own two feet carry us to so many destinations. Whether it be driving to work, stopping to visit friends, or going places out of necessity, movement is inevitable. The interesting thing is that there are innumerable ways to get to our desired location and a variety of methods or vehicles we can take to arrive. Such is life so we walk the road ahead of us. As God's faithful people we are on a pilgrimage on earth that ends in Heaven. Journeying to get there happens on a road that was made for travel. All are welcome and there is no limit to the space on the highway. Some of us arrive more quickly than others on this road to holiness and Sainthood, meanwhile others take a more circuitous route. As the scenes of our lives unfold, it is important to remember that the road to Sainthood was made for people like you and me.

By definition a Saint is a person acknowledged as holy or virtuous. Saints are typically regarded as people who have done something miraculous throughout their lifetime, have passed on from this world and now their souls are in Heaven. Within the Catholic Church there is said to be more than 10,000 Saints. So maybe the road to Sainthood isn't as unattainable as one might have first thought. It might be the road less frequently traveled, but the one that was made for everyone to take. Certainly, Sainthood is something special and not a mere handout. It doesn't come automatically. We will see that our effort and God's grace is a recipe for growing in faith. What must be known is that we are all called to step foot on the road toward Sainthood. Some people might be thinking, I don't want to be a Saint. That is way too much pressure and there is nothing I could possibly do that is so impressive or meaningful to get such acclamation.

The thing is that it is not so much about what we do, but what we allow God to do through us. How you invite the Lord into your life and open up your heart to his will is a tremendously powerful thing. This is not something to take lightly, yet we do not have to have all the answers. And most importantly, you do not have to be perfect by any stretch of the imagination. Sainthood is a word that carries tremendous allure and majesty. The modern world tells us that most people never think about Sainthood and for those that do, it is usually connected to asking for the intercessions of a favorite Saint. What we must come to understand is that this is not a foreign concept at all and it is not something that has faded away as an old school religious notion of the past.

How the Road Begins

The first step on the road to Sainthood is embracing our own sinfulness. In order for us to be filled with God's mercy and grace, we must admit our wrongdoings, shortcomings, and imperfections. Each of us was born into a fallen world where human nature is flawed due to the sin of Adam. But we must not forget that our defective tendencies and our tainted human nature was made whole. Therefore, we are holy thanks to Christ Jesus. Saint Paul reminds us of this in his letter to the Romans, "Therefore, just as sin came into the world through one man, and death through sin, so also death was passed on to all men, because all sinned...But the gift is not like the trespass. For if the many died by the trespass of the one man, how much more did God's grace and the gift that came by the grace of the one man, Jesus Christ, overflow to the many."[9]

God sent his Son to us to be the redeemer of all and to open wide the gates of Heaven. Saints are on the road journey to the promised land of Heaven which eagerly awaits them. This is your call. That is what you and I were made for. Anything less than this and any life not striving for holiness is a life that is incomplete. Gaps exist and there is no doubt we could never try hard enough or do enough for others to become Saints. The beauty lies in the reality that God will never stop calling people to Himself and his love for humanity lasts forever.

Regardless of what we have done and how unworthy we might feel, the road to holiness was made for us. On the other hand, despite how much good we have accomplished in our lives or the loving acts of service we have completed, we are all sinners. We all fall short of the glory, but in Jesus we are made complete. You should find some comfort in knowing this. Understanding your brokenness as a human being not only will allow you to better grasp this call to Sainthood, but it will allow you to grow in compassion and love for others. This holds to be especially true with regard to forgiveness. You are made worthy by the redemptive blood of Jesus Christ on the Cross at Calvary.

It is all about grace. In order to embrace the invitation to Sainthood from our Heavenly Father, you must embrace the way of the Cross. So you mean suffering is the way to Christ and through it

---

[9] (Romans 5:12, 5:15)

we get one step closer to Sainthood? Yes. Actually, we must fully come to terms with and accept an essential invitation from God. The signs on the road are pointing us in the right direction. You and I have an important role and mission in life. There is not one particular thing we must do or a specific task we have to achieve before our final breath. No, instead, it is a way of life.

The way of the Cross is the way of love. It is striving daily to share the love of God in everyone we encounter and in all situations. As Adrian Rodgers once said, "Holiness is not the way to Christ. Christ is the way to holiness." Jesus makes us holy. That is because Jesus alone can make us whole and complete. Without God in our lives we are empty inside. The fire within you must be stoked by the Lord as he sends so many experiences, opportunities, people, and life-giving events your way. The road you travel on might be the one less taken, but it is your calling to go out there and make disciples by leading others closer to Christ.

Think about all of the powerful parables that Jesus shared with his followers in just three years of ministry. Reflect upon his stories, sayings, and teachings. When we do so and then we come to recognize that Christ's last statement during his time on earth was, "Therefore go and make disciples of all nations, baptizing them in the name of the Father and of the Son and of the Holy Spirit, and teaching them to obey everything that I have commanded you. And surely I am with you always, to the very end of the age."[10] So why did your Lord and mine share these direct and very specific words with his disciples before he left?

Additionally, why are these the last recorded words of Jesus before he ascended into Heaven where he now awaits us? I believe that it is because this great commission is exactly what each of us is called to in our own unique way. God has blessed us with life. He has granted us talents and abilities that no one else can replicate. As his chosen people, we have the opportunity every day of our lives to go out into the world and impact others. By sharing our faith, loving and serving his Church, namely the Body of Christ—we carry out what He has asked us to do. By doing so, we travel the road paved to holiness, a road made for us to get to Heaven.

---

[10] Matthew 28:19-20

The English word Saint is derived from the latin *sanctus* which means, "to make holy." There is only one that can make us holy, that is Jesus. Since I was about twelve years old, I have worn a bracelet with the inscription W.W.J.D. Many people know that these letters stand for "What Would Jesus Do?" What would he do? We know because he has revealed so much to us through the scriptures, how he lived his life, the ways he healed the sick, cared for the poor, and welcomed sinners. The Gospel message to spread the good news is what we are asked to do.

God has designed every person in a special way. We are all different. The best part is he just simply asks us to show up and the Lord promises to fill in all of the gaps that might exist. We will fully dive into this heartfelt matter later on, but for now it is key to understand that we just need to show up. I know that when I first heard of this concept that I was called to Sainthood, I just simply shook my head. How could I, so feeble and mortal, be asked to summit a mountain top so high? What I didn't realize then is what God has continued to make so clear to me and his people now. He is journeying with us. The Lord is journeying with you.

Winding Road to Holiness

God only knows what you and I have been through and what you face today. He alone understands what you are in need of in order to get to the next stage in this life. The best part is that we are never called to perfection; we are called to try and to just give our all each day. If you go all in and live with great vigor, you will be surprised what God will do through your life. Understand that we are workers in the vineyard. Like the parable suggests, some people will show up right away and work the entire day, while others might come into that vineyard toward the tail end of their lifetime. No matter when we enter, the reward and pay, as the parable suggests, is the same for all of the Lord's workers. I mention this because many times people get stuck on something that they did in the past and they haven't forgiven themselves. In essence, they have written themselves off already. Remember, God fills in all the gaps and he will continue to do so. Even if we are the ones at times creating gaps or causing the road to holiness to become more bumpy, his grace and mercy are unending. So long as you have at least a small measure of faith, whatever you ask for and whatever you need will be granted.

Having experienced frequent highs and lows throughout my lifetime, it has become very clear that God is in complete control of everything. The sooner you choose to collaborate with the Lord the better. If and when you come to the point where you are uttering arguably the most difficult, yet most powerful words, transformation will occur. Saying and living the message, "Not my will, but yours be done," is nearly impossible at times, but God will help us go get there and will forever change us. Sainthood might seem scary to you. I know it did to me at first.

However, when I began to read about the lives of the Saints and understand that they were common people and sinners that lived in an uncommon way, it wasn't so daunting. These were ordinary people. God called the average of the world to do incredible things. Looking at who He worked with, it becomes easier to grasp. As I read about the men and women who said "yes" to God's call on their life, I began to think, "Why not me?" If God can transform Saul from the most heinous enemy of the Church and such an intense persecutor of Christians to a man on fire for Christ, He is capable of anything. After all, God formed Paul into the one who wrote over two thirds of the New Testament.

The Lord certainly can shape you and me into vessels of his love. If the Lord can take Augustine, a great womanizer, thief, and fornicator and renew his spirit, turning him into a great evangelizer, then why not you and me? It was this man, St. Augustine, who emphasized the human desire and need to find rest that only God can provide. This comes through love, through praise of God, and an open heart. Augustine explained how eternal life for humankind is the perfect fulfillment of desire for the soul. Certainly our reward and the pinnacle of this journey on earth awaits us in Heaven because for the soul, only God can fulfill it completely.

St. Augustine's words beautifully portray the longing of the human heart and the yearning of the soul to be one with the Lord in saying, "No man can fill his desires, nor can any creature satisfy a man, for God alone satisfies." Human relationships involve risk. They often lead to disappointments or hurt. Many things can happen and

great unpredictability exists. However, God transcends and transforms all the aches of life that we experience and he can turn
everything to joy. Jesus has the power to surpass man's desire and
that is why Augustine taught this message of soul connection with our
God by relaying that man is never at risk accepting God. Augustine
went on to say, "You have made us for yourself, oh Lord our heart is
restless until they rest in you."[11]

It will be in Heaven that all Saints will receive the fullness of life
with God. As a Saint, know with full confidence that you will receive
God perfectly. You will be satisfied and enter into the glory which will
surpass all of your expectations. See, the Saints of the Church and the
everyday Saints of today are people who never gave up and keep
striving to get closer to Christ one moment at a time. In doing so these
men and women have been granted abundant graces that lead to a
transfiguration. The road to holiness is a road that is paved through a
relationship with Jesus Christ. When we unlock the door of our hearts
to the Lord and invite him into our very souls, then we receive a gift
that has eternal rewards.

Living within us, God can take our brokenness and weakness and
turn it into his greatest strength. He gives us the heart of his Son and
we are turned from sinners and transformed into Saints. Never forget
that at your baptism you were clothed with Christ and made new. The
scriptures remind us, "So whoever is in Christ is a new creation: the
old things have passed away; behold, new things have come. And all
this is from God, who has reconciled us to himself through Christ and
given us the ministry of reconciliation."[12] Every day when we wake up
we have this newness of life and it is important for us to remember
that we are clothed in the light of Jesus.

Just Start Somewhere

The greatest commodity and blessing of life is time. Saints learn to use
time well. Each morning when your eyes open and your feet hit the
floor you have the opportunity and ability to use this precious gift of

---

[11] Magnificat Vol 22 No. 11, page 391
[12] 2 Corinthians 5:17-18

life. Saints understand this concept well and they maximize time in order to use each day as their present back to God. How you begin your day is imperative. It is what shapes your entire outlook and it sets the precedent for how you will respond to everything that will come your way. When your alarm clock rings, are you like the majority of people that hit the snooze button numerous times struggling to get out of bed? In your call to holiness, be unlike the majority of people in our world. Be different and be uncommon.

A number of years ago when I was on mission in Macy, Nebraska I spent a week on the Winnebago Reservation. I had the privilege of serving the Native people alongside some dynamic college students led by a young priest named Father Chris Stanish. Being immersed in the beautiful culture of the Natives taught me so much, especially with regard to tribal bonds, being one with the earth—God's creation, and having a heart for others in a quiet and humble way. We ended up bunking together at the rectory at St. Augustine's, the local parish while on mission. Each day Father Chris and I would drive in from the rectory to a local school and community center on the reservation. That was where we met up with the rest of the group and spent time with children and the poor.

Over the course of that week Father Chris and I had some really meaningful and memorable conversations. One of the major topics that we discussed was how we engaged in daily prayer. I shared my prayer routine with Father, which often included an act of gratitude for the day, a rosary, reading of some scripture, and intentions for loved ones. After listening to me, Father explained how his life began each day. There are some things that you will never forget. These moments are stamps on our life timeline, being etched into the stone of our history in such a concrete manner.

As my great grandfather used to say, when it clicks it sticks. I had a particularly epic moment during this car ride with Father who shared from the heart. When I had started my day all I was thinking of was how I could bring some joy to the elementary school kids who our group would be spending time with at St. Augustine's School. That did happen and it was very good, however God had a different message for me on that particular morning.

During that brisk and sunny drive, Father Chris and I continued to chat. I began to listen. Father Chris explained to me that he began each day with the *"heroic minute."* He talked about how he gave himself and his life as a complete offering in service to the Lord wherever he would be called to that day. I was captivated and inspired. I wanted to hear more. I had heard of this phrase known as the *heroic minute* maybe once before, but had thought nothing of it. Little did I know that implementing the *heroic minute* would change my life. It sets an important criterion for you daily.

Father explained to me that the *heroic minute* involves the initial 60 seconds of our day from the time our alarm clock rings to us beginning whatever is to come. Instead of tapping the snooze button, we open your eyes, shut off the alarm and thank God for the day. Envision yourself doing so. You are awake and out of bed. Your bed is neatly made. You are now ready to crush the day and are enthused to get after it! Sounds pretty awesome and clearly a tone will be set for our day. But there was more Father Chris shared and we will get to that in a moment. The *heroic minute* was initiated by St. Josemaria Escriva, an all-time go-getter, priest, and man of God who was daily working full throttle to build up the Kingdom. Sam Guzman had this to say about the *heroic minute*:

> The *heroic minute*. It is the time fixed, literally 60 seconds, for getting up. Without hesitation: a supernatural reflection and ...up! The *heroic minute*: here you have a mortification that strengthens your will and does no harm to your body. If, with God's help, you conquer yourself, you will be well ahead for the rest of the day. It's so discouraging to find oneself beaten at the first skirmish.

Along with the *heroic minute,* Father Chris explained there was something else he did every morning to start his day and to achieve victory right out of the gates. My ears were wide open when he told me that he gets out of bed and bows his head to the ground, uttering one word, "Servencia," which means "Servant," or another translation is "I am here to serve." After expressing this one word power prayer offering to the Lord, Father explained that he kisses the ground, the very earth that God created. Wow! From that day on through today, there has not been a morning that has passed that I do not recite that dynamic prayer shared to me by this young holy priest.

This calls to mind how important prayer is. When people think of Saints praying they probably are visualizing hands folded, kneeling by one's bedside with eyes closed. The uttering of memorized prayers and stained glass windows does have a place and can bring great meaning to the lives of the faithful. However, prayer is simply communicating with God. Prayer is hanging out with Jesus. It's telling the Lord what's on your mind and what's in your heart. There do not have to be great formalities to it or any at all. Instead it's the communication with God that takes place on the day to day in any location, while doing anything or nothing at all. Like all solid and positive relationships, the person who desires to grow closer to Jesus and further in their faith must spend time with him. It's that simple. Nothing complex is required, no strings attached, and no pressure at all. Just talk to Jesus like you talk to your best friend. Maybe in time you will stick around long enough to hear him talk to your heart.

Niali was on the train headed home from a long day at work. She was exhausted and her family would eagerly await her, especially those two sweet children. Overwhelmed, she needed some rest. Her eyes closed as the rattling of the subway car seemed to rock her to sleep. She paused, took a deep breath, and for a moment quieted her heart. Niali opened herself up and laid some truth onto Jesus and said, "I'm tired and I give my heart to you. Please give me rest." She would be at her final stop before a three block walk and a four story climb to her Midtown Queens apartment. As she scaled the final section and rounded the corner she could hear Jamal and Jasmine's little voices. They were excited to see mom. Niali closed her eyes one more time and uttered, "Thank you Lord for my babies and for getting me home after a long day."

Unfiltered, raw, and honest talking to Jesus is prayer. The Saint learns often that it's sharing your heart and experiences with the Lord that matters most. God doesn't care so much about what we tell him, but that we spend time with him daily. After a while he works on us and we grow closer, trust is built, and then we are pouring out our dreams, hopes, and desires to our loving Father. Talk to him like you talk to your best friend. Just be in his presence and receive his love. Like her children who ran to Niali after that arduous day of work, so does our Lord want us to run to him so he can embrace us with the purest love.

Father Chris reminded me yet again that prayer is not mundane and every day must begin with a sense of thanksgiving because it truly is a gift. Each morning I now do the same thing as the young priest, I kiss the day into being, lifting up all that I am and have to the Lord. As I reflect on this, I realize that our lives and our time is to be filled in service to God; this is the living prayer. Is this not our highest calling? You and I were made to dedicate all we think, say, and do to God. You do not know the day nor the hour when your time on earth will be up, however you do control how you use it. Giving it to the Lord could never be a better investment, as his return will be exponential when it comes to the great blessing and love that is shared with God's people.

Saints and *everyday Saints* for that matter are those people who maximize time and utilize it as a blessing which they give away to better the world through love. Victory is either won or lost in the mentality that we set and the expectations that we implore for our lives. We all have 24 hours a day, 7 days a week, 365 days a year. Time does not discriminate and it comes down to maximizing the 86,400 seconds we are gifted with per day. How are you using it? Who are you spending time with and what are you doing? Undoubtedly, like the Lord said, "Where your treasure is there will your heart be also."[13]

Time is a matter of the heart. So spend it wisely, be present, and use it to the best ability you possibly can as your greatest offering to God. It is often said that successful people rise early. Success however is subjective and the beauty of it lies within the beholder. What I can attest to is that time is precious and a gift to be used and used wisely. From the day you were born you were in a race against time. But I believe that when you use it with a clear perspective, time as finite as it can be, will turn into your greatest ally. It's extremely important to live in the present moment—the now, and focus on what is ahead, versus what already occurred. Time affords us the ability to get stuff done, work toward what we desire, achieve our mission in life, and ultimately reach our destiny before moving on from this world.

Another special encounter and time that I want to share is a conversation I vividly remember while serving at the Capital City Rescue Mission. I was speaking to James, a resident and programmer

---

[13] Matthew 6:21

at the soup kitchen in Albany. James and I had never met prior to the night I am referring to. However, since then we have developed a trust after serving countless dinners to help feed the homeless. James, along with other residents of the *New Life Program*, was rehabilitating. The Mission allowed for men like James to get away from the negative factors of life and have the time and space while being assisted to overcome drug addiction, substance abuse, or incarceration. James and I talked about repatriation—renewal.

We called to mind and to heart that God leads us to increased hope for the future. It was by the end of our conversation that we both realized that only God in due time can reshape our perspective through his grace. Driving over to serve dinner that evening I did not know that we would engage in a deep conversation. Actually, I had no clue what the Lord had in store as James was a stranger who I had not known. This man who I would soon talk to frequently as a brother in faith, has since become a spiritual friend. James seemed troubled and I listened. He opened up to me for some reason and talked about his past. I heard all of the difficulties that he had faced. Clearly it was a tough journey thus far.

The willingness of James to share and his vulnerability enabled solid trust to be gained and a relationship was built. On that particular evening, James and I spoke about mindset. The topic was specifically on the concept of a windshield. See, James had been like me and like many people for the majority of his life. He kept looking backwards, staring out the rearview mirror. The next time that you are in your car, take notice how small the rearview mirror is. Meanwhile, recognize the huge windshield that is in front of you. I explained this analogy of life and the windshield to James.

The rearview mirror represents everything that happened. It encompasses the things you did, and the fabric of your past. This includes the good, the ugly, and the indifferent. You cannot ignore it, just like you don't want to ignore cars you see in the rearview mirror while driving on a highway. That would be dangerous to do. Ultimately, what you have passed in life and the things you have gone through has shaped who you are today. But again, look at the massive nature of the windshield. There is a specific reason that it is so humongous in comparison to the rearview mirror.

See, the windshield is a symbol of all that is happening now and all that is ahead of you to come. It serves as a constant reminder that you have to keep the windshield of your life clear, so that you can see well and drive with God to your next destination. Therefore, by focusing on what is before you and not dwelling on the past and that which lies behind, you are able to move forward and advance toward your destiny. It fires me up to think that God has so much in your future and that you have a choice in it. We are co-creators and co-drivers with the Lord.

My hope is that you and people like James will keep the windshield mentality. Learning from the past, forgiving ourselves and others, and moving forward is key. By doing so you can keep your eyes on the prize, namely Jesus Christ and everything that God has for you to receive both now and in the days to come. As St. Paul emphatically tells us in his letter to the Philippians, "...Just one thing: forgetting what lies behind but straining forward to what lies ahead, I continue my pursuit toward the goal, the prize of God's upward calling, in Christ Jesus."[14] As the conversation with James came to a close, both of us had been impacted. The encounter and the time we spent conversing about things of the heart mattered. James then told me that he now understood what Paul meant in his letter to the Thesselonians when he said, "Rejoice always. Pray without ceasing. In all circumstances give thanks, for this is the will of God for you in Christ Jesus."[15] James shared some tough life occurrences with me that day, rearview mirror things. He also told me how excited he was to start living in the present to build his future with the Lord. The road looked brighter and the days ahead in that windshield kept James going. Oftentimes we just have to start again, somewhere.

TIME: Our Greatest Gift

Along with perspective and a windshield mentality comes choices. The things we do daily all take time. Time is a great asset and when we use our lives as a gift to God then we essentially pray without ceasing as Paul suggests. In essence we offer our total being up to the Lord as

---

[14] Philippians 3:13-14
[15] 1 Thessalonians 5:16-18

a present in thanksgiving and in humble service. When you do this, whatever you are doing becomes an act of holiness and takes on some new meaning. I challenge you to try it and I hope that you can live looking through that windshield of life mindset. With renewed hope in the promises that lay ahead by God for your future, along with maximizing time there is nothing you can't do.

Whether in the extraordinary moments or amidst the mundane, keep going and in all you do use your time as a prayer to God. The next time the dishpan is overflowing or you have to mow the lawn on a scorching summer day, offer that labor up to the Lord for a family member who is sick or an important intention that is in your heart. There is great power in prayer and offering up ordinary moments can create a powerful ripple effect within creation. No matter what you are doing, you can grow in holiness if you allow God to infiltrate your life. When we invite him into what we are tackling during the normal, those events through the grace of Christ will allow us to grow in holiness.

Furthermore, by offering up ourselves, our livelihood, and everything we engage in up to the Lord, we are essentially calling Him our best friend. Jesus wants to be your best friend. As the famous t-shirt says, "Jesus is my homeboy." The Lord desires to be close to you. Think about this for a moment. I want you to call to mind the person you are most connected with. Why do you have such a great relationship? What kinds of things do you discuss or activities do you engage in together? Undoubtedly, as time goes on we grow closer to those people we spend the most time with. We conversate with them and enjoy their presence. Now, as you and I grow in holiness and as we strive to become Saints for God's Kingdom, this must hold true in our relationship with Jesus.

You probably have heard that God cannot fit in a one hour box that the world has decided to call "church" on a Sunday morning. If we try to shove Jesus into this single limited dimension, we will be on spiritual life support in no time. Don't get me wrong, going to mass or to your place of worship is an important part of our call to Sainthood. We will discuss this more later on and uncover the importance of participating in the sacraments. However, what I am getting at is that one hour a week is not what I would call a "best friend." Surely, God does not expect us to be kneeling beside our beds all day or having our nose in the Bible 24/7. What he is asking us to do is to allow him to be part of our lives throughout the day. The Lord desires to hear of your plans. He wants to know what is exciting you or bothering you. You and I have a good Father who loves when we ask him for help. It makes God smile when we praise him for his faithfulness, and it is good for our souls when we show gratitude in thanksgiving for the many blessings we receive.

Walking the road to holiness and taking steps toward Sainthood is not about miraculous events or doing the unthinkable. Actually, it is quite the opposite. It is slowing down, being present, and recognizing God's presence. During the many situations of life, he is there with us. By means of the people we encounter and in sharing the love of Christ with those we meet, we come face to face with our Lord. Remember, God is the potter and we are clay. The potter spends 95% of his time working the wheel continuously shaping and reshaping the clay. This is a reminder to us to remain malleable so God can form us and continue to work in our lives. If we shut him out or if we become hardened our life falls apart.

Similarly, when clay is brought to the oven too quickly, it cracks and breaks. This analogy holds true in life because flexibility leads to betterment, meanwhile rigidness often limits us. The former is so good and the latter so dismal. Many people never become who they were truly meant to be. The best pottery is a work of art done over a very long period of time. The clay is extremely flexible, bending and contouring to new angles as the hours march on. This is what the Lord is asking of you and me. As we journey on through the course of life, he wants to shape us and our hearts. Even after the soft clay has been fully hardened in the red hot kiln, it is not permanent art. It can be much more difficult to reshape the solidified pottery, but it is not impossible.

This is a reminder to you and me that we must remain open because God will work on us even if we harden our hearts. Jesus finds a way to get in between the cracks and inject us with his holiness. He permeates our hearts and his love is the necessary formula which tends to soften us a bit. Our Lord, the holy master of our lives, chisels away at our hearts. He is always working and willing to chip away and get to the very essence of souls. So don't settle, but remain open to where God is leading you next. When you understand that where you are called to is an ever evolving capacity, it creates space in your life which allows you to be more free. This not only will reduce the stress you feel during the ebbs and flows of life, but most importantly, it will help you stay focused on your true North. Living out your life mission and purpose is key. The answer is found in Jesus who knows your heart.

We zig and we zag. We go two steps forward and then retreat five steps back. Three steps sideways and then meander in a circle. The route doesn't matter and should not be compared to anyone else's road. Just remain open, flexible and willing to go where the Spirit leads you and peace will fill your heart even when things are not particularly clear during various points in your life. It will be after the fact when you are sitting in the quiet, chilling with God, resting in his presence that he will whisper something. During these moments when we settle ourselves and truly listen, this is when we are given that calm that tells us we are right where we need to be. Just keep in mind, we cannot ever get there if we do not take a leap of faith. And after all, isn't becoming whole or growing in holiness on the road to Sainthood all about faith?

As disciples, we are certainly not a *one and done* type of people. We are journeying and we remain on the road to holiness because we are journeying with Christ. Yet, the crucial question is do we see God and do we allow him to be seen by others through how we live? Jesus was present with those who walked on the road to Emmaus. As Cleopas and another disciple traveled through the byways toward the city they conversed and even spoke to the Lord. He was disguised from their presence because "their eyes were prevented from recognizing him."[16] They were amazed that the man (Jesus) had told them that he didn't know what had taken place. Cleopas and the other disciples grew very animated and they started proclaiming how this man who was supposed to be the Savior was professed by some other disciples to have risen from the dead.

Imagine being in that conversation for a moment. We aren't talking about shooting the breeze or passing some time with small talk here. This moment is part of salvation history. The biggest point for us to recognize, as we explore our own road to Sainthood, is that

---

[16] Luke 24:16

Christ was with them in their midst. However, they did not see him. So I ask myself, why? Why was it that Cleopas and the others journeying toward Emmaus didn't recognize the Lord? Why is it that I can be face to face with God and not see him working in my life? Well, life tends to blind us and there are experiences that we have that we suggest are coincidental, luck, or a random occurrence.

My hope is that as we travel toward Sainthood together and get to know the Lord more intimately we won't be blinded by the ideas of the world. On the other hand, my prayer is that our hearts which are set on fire for the Lord will remain vigilant. Let's keep our eyes wide open so we can see Him at work in a special manner in our lives. Like the men on that road who later would have an experience of Christ when He broke the bread with them that evening, my hope is that you too will ask the Lord to stick around as they once did. The fact is that the Lord is not leaving you and never will. The big looming question that remains is if you will stay by his side.

The Saints have had their hearts turned inside out and the scales of blindness peeled from their eyes. Similar to Paul during his conversion experience, you and I must see differently. I pray that our eyes be given a new sight and a vision for holiness so that we can see more clearly. I hope your heart is stirred up so you can understand the calling of the Lord in your life. In doing so, God will provide answers to you and his great call resounds like a trumpet blast across the whole planet. In a world where many people do their best to pretend that God does not exist and in a country that is the so-called greatest in the world, how can it be that the "Nones" continue to be the most rapidly developing sect in society? Atheism or "Noneism"– not believing in anything at all, is rising like a tidal wave ready to wipe out the next generation.

It is up to you and me to defend and spread the faith. The scripture says plainly, "The harvest is abundant but the laborers are few."[17] That is why God calls us to be laborers and he calls his laborers as Saints. We know that we reap what we sow. With that said, what better and more fertile ground than to sow and labor in the vineyard of the Lord on the road to Sainthood. If not us then who, and if not now then when? So maybe becoming a Saint is a big deal after all.

---

[17] Matthew 9:37

Consider this, the world has billions of people. We each play a part in the important role of building up the Kingdom. Why not you? Why not me? Crazier things have happened for sure and remember that God will never expect us to be perfect. His only ask is that you keep getting back up and you give your all every single day.

The real heroes are not the ones who get it right the first time, but they are the people without the cape that keep going. Sainthood requires this type of zeal, positivity, endurance, and boldness as we travel the road to holiness. It's your call at your baptism. Nearly one hundred times scripture references Saints. This is because you are called to this lifelong pursuit. It is not a far off dream or a mirage. You and I were made to be Saints. The best part is that in order to be a Saint you have to be common. Yes, you heard me correctly.

By the power of God and your small yes, his grace and love flow in and through you. Holiness is what you will receive. A transformation takes place and the common becomes uncommon. Then, the uncommon person transfigures into a great Saint. The caterpillar is an average creature, yet when it enters the chrysalis the metamorphosis turns it into a beautiful butterfly. Like the butterfly that spreads its wings and soars through the air, people can be transformed into a masterpiece. After all, we were not made for mediocrity in this lifetime. God did not create you to be anything less than spectacular in this world. You are called to greatness. You were made to be a Saint!

Challenge 3

Reflect on where you are in your spiritual walk with God. Where might you need a metamorphosis to take place? How can you enter the chrysalis to allow God to help you become the radiant person that is inside of you? Today, think about and dream up your wildest scenario. Think about what excites you most and what the road to Sainthood means for you. Take the next step on the road made for you and travel closer to God. He will show you the way.

SINNERS, YET SAINTS
CHAPTER 4

*"I am not a Saint, unless you think of a Saint as a sinner
who keeps on trying." – Nelson Mandela*

Born Into a Broken World

It was 11:17 pm on the evening of January 7th. Snow was lightly falling as downtown Minneapolis was becoming a winter wonderland. A loud cry came echoing through the hallway as little Joshua was embraced by the loving arms of his mother Jamie and his dad Marcus. The proud parents beamed with excitement over welcoming their first son into the world. All was good. This evening was a significant moment that was stamped in their minds as the date and specifics of the 6 pound 7 oz little boy's birth were engraved on their hearts forever.

Chances are you don't remember your own birth, but for those who have children or will experience this joy, you are probably glowing at reminiscing the time your kids came into the world. Surely this is a tremendously beautiful experience. Each of us enters the human situation by the grace of God. We are born into a complex universe. At any given moment if you turn on the news, negativity and destructive things fill the television screen. The innocent presence of your angelic child can be corrupted with a mere flick of a switch. Crime, hatred, discord, tragedy; the list goes on. In a splintered world it can sometimes make us feel absent from goodness and positivity.

Perhaps you might even wonder where God is and how he is allowing so many horrific things to transpire? We even come to question our own lives and at times go down the rabbit hole of wondering if God exists at all. Not to mention, we question who we are as people. This holds true for even the most faith-filled people. We hear and believe that God is here, but actually, where is he?

It's important for you and I to take notice of these thoughts. It's necessary to assess the feelings we have and address the issues we wrestle with in our hearts. They are natural and it is okay to have them. When I am feeling overwhelmed by life and the situation that looms around me, I try to slow down and look back at the life of Jesus and the Saints. Our Lord faced turmoil in his life. He wept when Lazurus died because he felt the heartache of losing a friend. He called out to God, in the garden questioning God's presence before the events of the Passion. Jesus suffered greatly, hanging on the Cross bearing the sin of the world. Not to mention, the agony Jesus must have felt when he gazed into the sorrowful eyes of his Mother before he exhaled and gave up his spirit.

A Battle Fought By All

When I think about this, it brings comfort and hope to me. Certainly Jesus never sinned because he was God incarnate and completely holy. Yet, he was fully immersed in a sinful world that needed forgiveness and love. Afterall, that is why he came to heal, save, and restore a sinful broken humanity. We know this, however it can be hard to relate or understand how the Lord's life is similar in many ways to our own. I get that. He came down from Heaven and fully understood the plan and mission that was to be accomplished for the sake of the world. But what about you? So in these moments when you see evil, experience death of a loved one, battle your own vices, or struggle to keep faith, how can you relate?

We must not look any further than those Saints who walked this earth before our time. Take Mother (Mary) Teresa; she continues to come to mind because of her example. Mother's steadfast faith and purest heart to love as Jesus and do whatever he asks of her impacted the world for decades and her legacy shines forth years after she is gone. From the outside and even amongst the sisters who knew her best, she had unwavering faith and the closest relationship to Christ that one could have.

It wasn't until recently, years after her death, that the letters and secret struggle she faced including a great doubt in God was made known. In the collection of diary entries and compilation of personal letters entitled "Mother Teresa: Come Be My Light," 66 years of internally deep thoughts, heartache, and darkness reveal that even the greatest of Saints are searching for God's existence. Read her words carefully and slowly. These revelations about Mother's life, as shocking as they might seem, are filled with truth and rawness of what it means to be a human being who desires to seek God wholeheartedly in a troubled world. Below are some snippets of her letters and outpouring of her hurting heart as she deeply struggled to keep the faith. But even though these questions and doubts lasted for years, her light of faith never fizzled out completely:

"Jesus has a very special love for you. As for me, the silence and the emptiness is so great that I look and do not see, listen and do not hear."

"I spoke as if my very heart was in love with God—tender, personal love. If you were there, you would have said, 'What hypocrisy.'"

"Please pray specially for me that I may not spoil his work and that Our Lord may show himself—for there is such terrible darkness within me, as if everything was dead. It has been like this more or less from the time I started the work."

"Such deep longing for God—and ... repulsed—empty—no faith—no love—no zeal. Saving souls holds no attraction—Heaven means nothing—pray for me please that I keep smiling at Him in spite of everything."

"I utter words of community prayers—and try my utmost to get out of every word the sweetness it has to give—but my prayer of union is not there any longer—I no longer pray."

"If there be no God—there can be no soul—if there is no Soul then Jesus—You also are not true."[18]

Many people might argue that these letters should have been destroyed, which is said to have been Teresa's request before her death. However, I believe it is a true blessing that they were not. The raw authenticity of her life and relationship with the Lord speaks volumes to us. What a gift to leave the world with. Years upon years of heartfelt and sacrificial service was done in devotion for her love of Jesus as his most humble of servants. Then, Mother passes on from this world and Mary Teresa's letters come to light. The contrast that exists is massive.

The point here is that despite her holiness and drive to do the loving works of charity and to actually be the hands and feet of Jesus, she felt God was absent. Meanwhile, in the darkness and amidst the desert of her soul's journey, she never gives up hope and still believes. Love wins and faith comes out on top. This is good for us today because of the richness and authenticity. It shows you that God will continue to be at work in your life, even if you don't feel his presence. Questioning the Lord and even having doubt happens, but the most important thing is that we keep going. Mother Teresa did that. She was a 20th Century, modern day apostle. Her life portrays that faith doesn't mean full understanding, but it is paved with great love and commitment.

Additionally, Mother's life exemplifies the fact that only God knows what we have been through and the struggle we face today. To uncover the intense darkness and contrast within the soul of a woman

---

[18]Mother Teresa: Come Be My Light.

so dedicated to being the hands and feet of Jesus is profound. These words above should comfort us and bring some encouragement to our tired souls when we face trouble, darkness, or have our own doubts. Although these feelings were real, the agony seemed to never end, and she went so far as to doubt the very existence of God. Mother Teresa kept the faith and did not allow darkness to win. She became the light and in doing so Christ was brought to the suffering. Her love for Jesus triumphed over the sinfulness she witnessed in the world, the isolation the lepers endured, and the brokenness in her own life.

Clearly St. Teresa of Calcutta did something beautiful for God. Mother's private vow known as A Folly of Love states, "Ask Jesus not to allow me to refuse Him anything, however small. I [would] rather die."[19]

Mother Teresa's vow did the supreme justice to take all limitations off of God. So often people limit God and what he can do in their life. Through joy and by remaining open to where he is asking them to go, there are endless possibilities. How we respond to the nudges of the Lord in our lives both small and large is essential. As Saints it is our ideal to come to full spiritual maturity by God's grace so we too can pledge as Mother did "not to refuse him anything." In doing so the doors will fly open, the call will become clearer, and we will set no limit because God is limitless![20]

Mother answered the call within the call and did respond to Jesus telling her to "Come be my light." For her, the call within her vocation of religious life was to be with the poor. Mother literally became the hands and feet of Jesus by dedicating her entire life to service of the poorest lepers and most disenfranchised humans on the planet. She sought out the rejected because she accepted God's calling wholeheartedly. She is famous for hearing the words of Jesus, "Will thou refuse?" And although we will most likely not have this intense experience and encounter to audibly hear Jesus, he does speak to our hearts. The question is are we listening? Are we open enough to allow Jesus to do something really beautiful with the life he gave us?

---

[19] Mother Teresa: Come Be My Light, 28.
[20] Mother Teresa: Come Be My Light, 38.

Redeemed by Grace to Love Completely

The hope is that you and I can answer that with a "yes" in the best manner possible. By answering the call within the call on a train when she heard God's voice and knew what had to be done, Mother Teresa joined the limitless nature of God. The governor was taken off of her life. Her humanity was no longer hindering her ability to serve but it became the vessel with which the love of Jesus flowed to the poorest of the poor in the slums of Calcutta. The world saw dirty, disgusting, and repulsive people who were so sick and dying. Mother Teresa saw the face of Christ and smiled, bringing the poor the love of Jesus and in doing so she radiated joy.[21]

There is a reason why Jesus went to the well. It wasn't because he needed water. He needed to satisfy another thirst, his thirst for the heart. Mother Teresa said that the single most important reason for Missionaries of Charity to exist was to "satiate the thirst of Jesus Christ on the Cross for Love and Souls."[22] So in the same fashion and spirit, yet in our own unique way, we too have a calling as Saints to quench the thirst of Jesus. Now you might be thinking that is some heavy lifting? Certainly, I am no Mother Teresa, and perhaps you don't even want to be. That's okay. God isn't concerned with us trying to stack up to do miraculous things and I believe that isn't even what it's about. Let's not lose sight of doing the smallest acts with the greatest love.

By walking with the Lord daily, we will share Christ's light. Satisfying the soul of a person through sharing love with them is the greatest gift and it can be done so simply. Right now in the present moment we have the opportunity to give a drink to others and to Jesus simultaneously. How will you decide to do that today?

Day by day when we love by seeing Jesus in others we tap into the springs of that life giving water that the Lord spoke about at the well. Sometimes our own well might seem to be running dry. Who do we turn to but the *Saint Next Door*? We go to the person we know that is loving and doesn't judge or count the cost. We are drawn to the people who care and exude kindness with a smile. Holiness is all around us

---

[21] Mother Teresa: Come Be My Light, 40.
[22] Mother Teresa: Come Be My Light, 41.

and it starts with small acts. One cup of spiritual water at a time, perhaps just a single sip. Remember, God's grace and infinite love is more than enough for all souls to be satisfied. Lest we never forget it is not only about who Jesus wants to be for you, it's also about who Jesus wants you to be for him.

The thoughts we wrestle with individually can be taken further and often lead us to pressuring ourselves to overload our schedules with "good things" and "good tasks." People often attempt to generate or revitalize faith through doing things. Certainly action is required and faith is fostered when we serve. We will discuss the call to loving service later on. For now though, it is crucial to realize that God desires to have your whole heart. Living a Saintly life is about receiving the generous heart of the Lord and then loving Jesus back by spending time with him and his people.

Our Lord wants you so greatly. He desires that you crawl back to him. This is especially the case when your heart needs to be glued together due to significant troubles faced, sinfulness, or the imperfections of your life. The great modern day philosopher, Eckhart Tolle, who is super conscious of the present as well as the inner being of the human person said, "You do not become good by trying to be good, but by finding the goodness that is already within you and allowing that goodness to emerge."

God brings out this goodness and he is the light that shines in our darkness. Mother Teresa found the light that carried her on and you must do the same. When we choose to step into the heart of the matter, we come to realize that although society has its great flaws and humanity is indeed broken, it is also full of so much goodness. Ostensibly, we see this in Mother Teresa's selfless love of the poor in India. You have your faults and I have mine. These exist and come with being human. What must be realized is that there is so much good on the inside of you already. Your goodness, your greatness, is already there. The Saint is within you. God looks right past your shortcomings. He walks with you in the darkness even when you might think he is not there. You just have to tap into your faith and continue to believe.

When asked about his life and being chosen as the Pope, the Holy Father responded, "I am a sinner." Strong words from the leader of the faith, Pope Francis. Even the man chosen to shepherd the Catholic

Church realizes he is full of holes that only Jesus can fill. Undoubtedly, we are all sinners and have our struggles. Some of the crosses you and I bear are greater than others. Certainly the path of various people is more sequitous than the journey traveled by some.

However, the fact that we are all sinners is something that we should and must embrace on this road to Sainthood. It might seem strange or even out of place to you perhaps, but it is in our favor. So how could anyone's sinfulness be of favor? Well, if Saints had to be perfect then none of us would ever be able to get there. It would be truly an unreachable pinnacle. Unfortunately many people believe that to be the case when even hearing talk of the Saints.

As Bishop Scharfenberger put it, "Usually we think of Saints as being somewhere else, far away, up 'there' or in some altered state, not the real world." When referring to the idea that the Saint is next door and within us, he went on to say, "This brings Sainthood uncomfortably and tantalizingly closer. It does not only mean that literally the Saint might be closer than you think, but that YOU are called to be that *Saint Next Door*." This is so true.

Most people think of Saints as being somewhere else, distant, or fictitious. The 21st Century notion is that Saints are certainly not part of this world, but reserved solely for God in Heaven. So how can you relate to them and the life of holiness the Saints lived, let alone be a Saint in your own life? Although you might not yet recognize the Saint within you, it is truly right next door. Since God has called us each by name and accepts us into his fold just the way we are, this is a huge and pivotal concept to digest from the onset. Take some time to look back at the holiest men and women who blazed a trail for the faith.

As great Saints from the time of Christ to the present day, you cannot but notice the amazing contributions of these influential figures. Meanwhile, it is clear that each one of them had their downfalls. The important thing to keep in mind is that God overlooked the flaws and imperfections and saw their true potential. He tapped into who each of these great Saints were at their core. Only God knows one's full capacity. A zeal for building up the Kingdom, a passion to live life with the utmost intentionality, and a desire to lead souls to Christ through the mission of life is what sets Saints apart.

Jesus came to this world to interact with and call upon the lowly and downtrodden. He had and still has the power to make the seemingly average person into a great masterpiece. The truth is, however, that greatness lies deep within each of us. As the scripture says so powerfully, "I did not come to call the righteous, but sinners."[23] Will you allow the Lord to heal your brokenness, forgive your sinfulness, and shape you into the clay masterpiece that he has planned? My thinking is what do you have to lose...Rather, the benefit will be unexplainable. Trust and take his hand. The Lord is calling you and he is calling me. God sees the Saint within!

Jesus could have lived as long as he desired, after all he was fully human, yet totally divine at the same time. However, God came down to walk on earth with us and to fully enter into the human experience not in a grand manner, but in the most humble of circumstances. After all, the Lord came and was born to a poor young girl from a small town and entered the world in a stable. Let that resonate for a moment.

Then Jesus grows up the son of a mere carpenter. Nothing extraordinary about that. Yes, the majestic nature of his ministry, all the miracles, and the remarkable components of Christ's three years of carrying out the plan of salvation did leave its mark on the world in grand fashion. His life and time on earth changed humanity for all eternity. This is essential to our faith and the promise found in God's sovereign plan. We can lose sight though of some other crucial pieces along the way.

Called to Discipleship Just as You Are

What must be emphasized and continuously recognized is that Jesus called the unrighteous, the common person, and the unlikely to be his twelve. I often wonder how many people Jesus asked to follow him throughout his lifetime before the twelve apostles said "yes" to his call. The number could be thousands. Imagine Christ walking on the beach near the Sea of Galilee and going up to a man or woman and asking them if they would follow him. Picture Jesus inviting them to be his disciple, only for the person having been asked to tell the Lord, "Nah, I am good, no thanks."

---

[23] Mark 2:17

In one regard it seems crazy to think that anyone would deny Jesus, especially if the Lord were to ask them to follow him and that person being summoned knew what we understand now. Although, what an immense responsibility to sign up to be the Lord's apostle. On the other hand, one might think that the twelve were crazy to have agreed to follow him. At that moment in time there was not much evidence at all that pointed to the fact that Jesus truly was the Christ— the Messiah. For us future Saints, we need to focus upon how *the ask* of Christ relates to our own personal lives and calling.

The words Jesus uttered to Peter, Andrew, James, and John, as well as the others being called are central to the faith. Those words expressed by the Lord carry such tremendous weight and are powerful beyond measure today as we live in the 21st Century. Jesus said, "Come follow me and I will make you fishers of men."[24] Average fisherman, tax collectors like Matthew, and many others who from first glance weren't anything special received and accepted the call. The world would argue what good could come of them. But it makes sense in a way.

After all, Jesus himself was discounted from the beginning by many from his hometown. When told about Jesus of Nazareth, Nathanael responded, "Can any good thing come from Nazareth?"[25] So that brings you and I to where we are now. No matter what your career is, no matter where you currently stand on in this journey of faith, no matter what you have done or failed to do, Jesus is calling you. He called the sinners to be his apostles. He called them to be his right hand men and the ones to not leave his side. They answered the call initially. Lest we not forget that they also denied him three times (Peter), sold Jesus out through betrayal with a hateful kiss (Judas), and upon his time of arrest they "all left him and fled."[26] It is said that only John, the beloved disciple, was with Jesus through it all and remained by his side during the crucifixion. John was there with Mary and with Jesus at the Cross.

The good news is that Christ believes in second and third and fourth chances. He ended up giving the keys to the Kingdom to Peter,

---

[24] Matthew 4:19
[25] John 1:46
[26] Mark 14:50

asking him to build up the Church. See, Jesus overlooked the denial and saw untapped greatness in the once broken fisherman named Simon. Jesus can see past our flaws and inwardly notices the highest potential we possess as well. Whether we come today, tomorrow or even years down the road, God longs for us and loves us the same. Turn your back like Peter, the vicar of Christ and first Bishop of Rome (Pope), Jesus is still there waiting. Not only is he waiting for a full return, but our Lord is expanding his reach to love us back into his gracious presence. So there is more than hope for you and me. There is a path to holiness and Sainthood. You must not get in God's way, but instead just say, "Yes," when he asks you to follow him. As the Lord called the first apostles by name, so too Christ calls you and me.

Picture yourself in a small sailboat rocking back and forth on the sea of Galilee. You are toiling day after day trying to make a livable wage by fishing. This laborious task is not glamorous by any means and what is even more challenging is that it was the trade of thousands of people in that area. Day after day you go out on the open waters hoping to reel in the big catch. Simon (Peter) and his brother Andrew were behind on their taxes. Some gambling, unsound financial decisions, and a lack of catching fish led them to be in "hot water." The Romans wanted their tax money and these brothers didn't have it.

So Simon goes out all night to fish and in the morning is met by Andrew. Their friends James and John come along with their own father, Zebedee. The three arrive on the scene to help Simon and Andrew because they got wind of the trouble these brothers were in. Compassion moved their hearts. You don't want to see your close friends be arrested, let alone killed for tax evasion. A steep penalty for, but that was the case in those days beneath the iron-fist rule of Caesar in Rome. Net after net was cast and nobody caught a single fish. How would you feel at this point? I suppose Simon and Andrew would feel a little more comfort knowing that Zebedee and his sons were there to help them. It cannot go unnoticed and is a beautiful example of Sainthood, as they showed up to help their friends in dire need. However, the situation didn't change. Along comes a stranger who is watching from afar. Jesus is there on the shore observing what is taking place. The fishermen had heard about Jesus teaching as a new

Rabbi, but didn't know much else.

Being a Rabbi or teacher in those days was nearly as common for Jewish men as being a fisherman. He tells them to throw out their nets one more time. I could only think about what these five men must have been thinking. They had been there together for hours tossing out their nets into what seemed like an empty sea. Most of all, Simon had been there all day and all night fishing. He probably was ready to give up and face his fate with the Romans. They might have been thinking this guy doesn't know how long we have been here and that we have caught nothing. They might have been wondering who he was anyway or perhaps, why listen to him?

After all, Jesus was a rabbi, not a fisherman. Maybe it was the encouragement of Jesus that stirred up something in Simon Peter to lead him to toss the net out one more time. So he does and the rest is history. Teems of fish flood the net so much to the point that it is in danger of tearing. The catch is the best of Simon's lifetime and the Lord spares them. Shortly thereafter, Jesus asks Simon, Andrew, James and John to follow him. They say "yes." He called them each by name and took these average fishermen and turned them into great apostles that the Church was built upon.[27]

Underdog Story

We all have an underdog story when it comes to our faith. The presence of God in our lives empowers us, changes us, and leads us to impact the world in a profound way. We will discuss the importance of being fishers of men with unfinished business more at the end of our journey together, but the point here is that we are all called upon by the Lord. He makes us great and Christ's power in you changes everything.

Will it be easy, no. Then again nothing worthwhile and life changing is ever easy or typical. Can we do it? If the apostles could, we can too. Let these words of our Lord sink in for a moment. When Jesus was about to go to the Father and ascend he had this to say to his followers and to us, "Amen, amen, I say to you, whoever believes

---

[27] Matthew 4

in me will do the works that I do, and will do greater ones than these, because I am going to the Father."[28] Chew on that thought and try to digest it. Seems almost impossible. How could we be called and then carry out even greater works than those of our Lord. This shows the power of his Holy Spirit and the great way that Christ works through us. It also explains how important it is to heed the call and be soldiers in the Lord's army on the road to Sainthood. I hope you are starting to see and believe that the Church and world needs you.

Oftentimes in our lives, our greatest adversary is our own self. We tend to get in the way and hinder our own growth. It is not bad to be your toughest critic in order to maximize your desire and ability to improve. Bear in mind, you are on the road to Sainthood and striving for holiness. I often contemplate why we stop our progress and are the hindering block from obtaining the next level in our faith. Even if we doubt our own abilities, we must realize how mighty the Lord is. Perhaps we are humble enough to understand that we cannot do it on our own, this is good. It is crucial to stay the course and keep the power of God in the forefront of our minds and written on our hearts. He alone has big plans for you and will do marvelous things in your life.

The one who loves you beyond human comprehension can make anything happen and desires that his people and Church are well able to do what God has planned from the beginning of time. God knows the secret desires of your heart and he understands what will bring you lasting joy and peace. We might think we know what will give us that lasting fulfillment, but God only knows the depths of our inmost being. This is why Jesus emphasizes joy to his disciples by relaying a profound message, "By this is my Father glorified, that you bear much fruit and become my disciples...If you keep my commandments, you will remain in my love, just as I have kept my Father's commandments and remain in his love...I have told you this so that my joy may be in you and your joy may be complete."[29]

So what is this part of John's Gospel trying to relay to us? I believe it is that life with Christ and becoming a Saint can be found in about three things: 1) Producing fruit for the Kingdom through discipleship,

---

[28] John 14:12
[29] John 15:7, 8, 11

2) remaining in God's love through the power of salvation, and 3) having lasting joy which comes through faith and grace. Growing up in a small town I participated in so many sporting events and various community competitions. I often remember traveling to different towns across the Northeast and my grandparents saying, "Jeez, what do they feed these kids?" This funny reference to big kids for their age comes to mind at this juncture because it reminds us that what we feed our souls is essential for us to grow closer to the Lord and stronger in the faith. Our soul food and the graces we receive from above are what well equip us for Sainthood.

The Saints fed the body, but most importantly, they fed the soul. That is what you and I must do on a daily basis and it has to be a practice that comes so ingrained in us that it is embedded in the fabric of our Christian DNA. Your mindset must go even further. When you switch from wanting to be a Saint to believing and receiving the gift that there is a Saint with you—this opens up a new realm of possibility. You and I are Saints and we need to work to plant more seeds. In doing so, the sinner is made into a great Saint and can produce the fruit by toiling in God's vineyard daily. There are no limits with Jesus. You are never too far gone and you are never not good enough. As Oscar Wild put it, "Every Saint has a past and every sinner has a future." The Lord has placed a great call on your life. Now it is up to people like you and me to answer that call and to take positive strides in faith with God into our future. Cast the net out one more time and allow God's love to overflow in your life. Saints are willing to receive the Lord and they radiate the joy of Jesus to others. I assure you, by doing so, your life will never be the same.

Challenge 4

Each of us can struggle from time to time with self-doubt, our own sinfulness, and things that we want to change. Have a heart to heart with God. Ask him to help you with whatever it is that seems to be hindering you from living out life as a Saint. If you can, do an examination of consciousness and reflect on your shortcomings. Try to get to confession and lay down all the burdens at the foot of his Cross. Know that Jesus is there to receive you with his arms outstretched wide. His great love is never ending and he desires to walk with you. Trust that you have greatness within you. God sees the Saint within you right now and wants you to tap into your spirit because you are a true gift to the world!

NIÑOS DE DIOS
CHAPTER 5

*"You are a child of God...You are wonderfully made,
dearly loved, and precious in his sight. Before God
made you, he knew you. There is no one else like you."*
– Psalm 139

Lost, then Found

Envision yourself in a crowded shopping center. Meandering through the aisles, browsing the array of offerings is something you have done countless times before. You are hoping to find a meaningful gift in time to put it under the tree for Christmas. You notice a mom with her younger daughter. She seems to be around five or so and they are picking out a special present for grandma. All of a sudden, the crowd in the store is growing more and more dense and people are everywhere. The small child's eye is on something shiny and she wanders. A little more time passes, maybe ten seconds or so and then mom lifts her eyes up. Her daughter has disappeared. The problem is that there is no sleight of hand of a magician in the making. This stage is real and her princess is gone. Put yourself in the shoes of that mother. How are you feeling? What thoughts begin to race in your mind? You go straight into turbo mommy mode and begin to race around the store like an Indy stock car hitting the accelerator at full throttle. Frantically you search for your little girl. Your heart is pulsating uncontrollably and you cannot stop sprinting up and down the different aisles calling Jasmine's name. You call it out louder and louder. You begin begging other shoppers and store employees to help you find her.

Has anyone seen this precious child? Where could Jasmine possibly be? You are praying that your most prized possession will magically show up around the next corner. Simultaneously, your little girl notices that mommy is not there. She realizes that she is lost. Jasmine is alone and there are many grownups that she doesn't know. She quickly becomes a fish swimming upstream. She sees many other kids clinging to their parent's side as holiday shoppers storm the store looking for last minute deals. The little girl begins to cry and tries to run back to where she believes her mother was. Her cries grow louder and louder. She is beyond scared and real worry sets in. Mommy's precious angel is afraid and doesn't know what to do. Jasmine desires the comfort of her mom like the baby chick who left the nest and who is not ready yet to fly. All she wants to do is be held safely.

After great searching and calling out her name louder and louder, time and time again, finally the little girl hears her mother's voice. Renewed hope enters Jasmine's heart and the waterfall of tears begins to subside. She cannot see mommy yet, but her mom's voice grows louder. She knows that mom is right around the corner. Her daughter yells loudly, "Mommy!" When they catch sight of one another they lock eyes and the biggest smile comes across Jasmine's face. They run towards each other and engage in the warmest embrace. Mommy hugs her beautiful princess and holds her tight. She kisses her daughter and squeezes her again, feeling her baby's warmth and thinking to herself, "I will never let you go." The little girl gazes into her mom's eyes and the deep connection they share is a moment that seems to last forever. "I was so worried about you," Mom says. "Never leave my side honey, I was so nervous that you were lost." The little girl learns a valuable lesson that day to always keep close to her mommy. Mom exhales deeply, falling onto her knees in the middle of the store. She utters a silent prayer of gratitude to God. Wow, was that a close call.

Jasmine's mother was searching for her and thankfully she found her. While lost, the small child kept looking for her parent and called out for her mom. Love was the magnetic force that eventually led them back to one another. This is the way that God pursues you and me. You are his beloved daughters and sons. He is constantly on the search for your heart and desires to find you. Jesus will never stop looking for you. No matter how far you drift away like that little girl did from her mom's side, the Lord will relentlessly seek you out just like that mother did.

The same must be true for us in searching for Jesus in our own lives. If we pursue God, as the lost child did, we will not only find him, we will find new life. This is all because of love. We can learn from the child and the way that she was calling out for her mommy. When you cry out to God when you are lost, He will find you. When you search for him and run to his loving arms, He will embrace you completely. What you have done, whether it be falling into some sort of sinfulness, choosing to stray, or any other thing that has separated you from God, this is forgotten at once. Just like the response to the Prodigal Son's return home, our Father embraces us and welcomes us back. Jesus awaits you with his arms wide open, desiring nothing more than to shower you with his unconditional love. God is patient and waits for us as it says, "For this son of mine was dead and is alive again; he was lost and is found."[30]

Drifting away or even completely having turned your back on God doesn't matter at all anymore. The mother never ceases with the search for her missing child and will do anything to get her baby back. God loves you and searches for your heart with a full and never ending pursuit. Jesus wants to hold you close. He desires that you come to him like a child with the trust of a little one. Our Lord is calling your name. He desires you to be fully in his presence. God wants you to give yourself completely to him and to come just as you are. No matter what your circumstances might say or how bleak the outlook might be, he is ready to welcome you back. Regardless of how distant your faith is, God keeps searching. Whether you have made mistakes that are hard to forgive yourself for or you have experienced tragedy or ache, Jesus is calling. He is chasing you down because he loves you with an infinite, never failing, and tender love. When we learn to run to him instead of from our Lord a radical change happens internally.

---

[30] Luke 15:24

Seeking Jesus without abandon opens up our hearts to allow Jesus to fill our souls with the pure joy experienced by the mother and her little girl when they were reunited. That joy that filled the Prodigal Son who was once empty inside and lost his soul, will come bursting in and love us back to life! You and I know that feeling because it is much more than a feeling. The soul-filled connection is deeply rooted as it is an eternal matter of the heart. Rest in these words from the Prophet Isaiah which beautifully articulate God's unceasing search for you and his perfect love He has for you because you are his child:

> *But now, thus says the Lord, who created you, Jacob, and formed you, Israel: Do not fear, for I have redeemed you; I have called you by name: you are mine. When you pass through waters, I will be with you; through rivers, you shall not be swept away. When you walk through fire, you shall not be burned, nor will flames consume you. For I, the Lord, am your God, the Holy One of Israel, your Savior. I give Egypt as ransom for you, Ethiopia and Seba in exchange for you. Because you are precious in my eyes and honored, and I love you, I give people in return for you and nations in exchange for your life. Fear not, for I am with you...*[31]

Being childlike with unwavering trust, a positive outlook, and a joy-filled spirit is something that adults tend to struggle with. Getting lost in the beauty and moments of the world where time seems to stand still is a great quality of a child. They can play and run outside with such imagination for hours on end. Kids have the ability to go freely through their day never thinking about all that has to be done. They are fully there in the present moment. Embracing the present and being immersed totally with the people or situation we are in is often forgotten by adults. We get caught up in busyness and amidst the lists, agendas, and calendars we tend to forget the big picture. Staying on schedule and checking the boxes off becomes our reality. Distractions are endless and time races by.

The business transactions of life often rob us of what is most important. We tend to miss the holy moments. We overlook and don't

---

[31] Isaiah 43:1-5

recognize the beautiful times when God shows up on the scene. He appears to us through the generosity of another person, an unexpected event, or a dazzling occurrence in nature. Let's face it, you and I struggle with balance for a number of reasons. Many of them are legitimate. After all, God only knows what you have been through and he alone sees everything in your heart. There's a powerful saying in Spanish which goes, "Niños de Dios que están hechos de amor," meaning *Children of God who are made of love.* For all of us, we are called to be wrapped up in God's arms and enter this childlike state because we are truly the Lord's children who are made to exist in love.

So far during our time together we have touched on and will continue to uncover how to navigate the road to Heaven. It is important to know who you are and that answer is deeply rooted in *whose* you are. The Lord is known to ask his first apostles very thought provoking questions and this remains the same for you and me. He desires that you contemplate them and look deep down into your heart. Jesus desires that you seek him like a child. The Lord is seeking you and so is your Heavenly Father. The Saint is the person who not only allows God to seek them out, but is also looking for Jesus.

Who Do You Say I Am?

One of the most profound and intriguing questions Jesus asks us is, "Who do you say that I am?"[32] Imagine being on the other end of that loaded question. It's just you and the Lord, one on one. Who is Jesus and who is He for you? I believe that we might have an advantage in some regard over the first followers of Christ. Jesus appeared out of the blue, coming onto the scene in the lives of the Twelve in an unorthodox manner. Their deep trust from the start in Jesus was quite impressive. Certainly, he believed in them and knew what they were capable of all along, as the power of God has no limits when at work in the lives of his faithful.

They didn't know too much about Jesus, yet they gave discipleship a legitimate shot. Still, the apostles weren't completely sure of who Jesus was. Others spoke about Jesus in a variety of ways and the early

---

[32] Matthew 15:16

followers echoed what they heard. The apostles responded with many different answers as they were told numerous things about the Lord. Some believed Jesus was a prophet. Others thought that he was a great teacher (rabbi). Some even suggested that he was the Christ!

Nearly 2,000 years later, with hundreds of millions of people affirming themselves as Christians, it might be a little easier because *the way,* namely Christianity, has lasted for millennia. No, we did not see the miracles or hear his actual words like those early disciples did. We did not dine with Jesus or go about and assist in his ministry when he was alive. So we do not have that same sight or privilege of witnessing those events from salvation history, but we do have our faith. What must be emphasized is Christ is alive now and at work in the lives of his followers just as much as He was 2,000 years ago. Jesus continues to show up on the scene in a tremendously powerful way. You and I must keep our eyes open and fixed on Him. History proves not only Jesus' existence, but his premier significance. However, having reflected on all of that, including the Church's rich history, and knowing everything we do through the writings of the Word of God, the question remains...Who is Jesus? Who do you say that he is?

When you think about it and pray over it, there is something extraordinarily beautiful to uncover. It's not a specific name so much that matters or a title that should get the spotlight. The words "Christ" and "Messiah" carry great weight and importance, as they should. Yet, that deep question is more about a relationship. Like a child who relies on his or her parents for everything in the early stages of life, so must we fully rely on God. The years fly by and the child grows older, which means that independence settles in. Children seek the advice of their parents who continue to guide, love, and support them. However, experimentation, testing, and at times rebellion becomes the norm for them as teens. Into adulthood, the relationship changes again, but it has the potential to grow even further as there is more depth.

Wisdom comes to those with increased life experiences. The child has been shaped by their parents who love them and yet they are off on their own forever so to speak. Their mother and father never stop loving them and are there for their son or daughter no matter how old they might be. With more time passing, eventually their parents die and the child who has been loved for years by these people who brought them into the world is left empty inside. Death leaves them facing a tough separation. Although Mom and dad might not physically be there with them any longer, their spirit and soul connection remains forever. This holds true because love fuses us, melding our hearts in a way that cannot be broken.

The Lord desires the exact same for you and for me. He wants us to experience his overflowing love. Jesus wants to be your friend. Christ is asking you to come to him as his beloved child because he promises to provide everything you need. As children of God, know fully that you are the Lord's most prized possession. Take notice of small children around you. Little kids do many things really well. One of these includes enjoying being their parent's most prized possession. This allows the child to take great pride in who they belong to. This concept is a critical notion for us to not only accept, but to fully embrace on our road to Sainthood.

In a day and age where it seems like everything is centered upon the status of an individual and what he or she does, thinking differently is imperative. Moreover, doing things in a new manner with a reshaped mindset can lead to tremendous growth in faith. St. Paul says, "And do not be conformed to this world, but be transformed by the renewing of your mind, so that you may prove what the will of God is, that which is good and acceptable and perfect."[33] That perspective is counter cultural, but another element with regard to your roadmap to holiness as a Saint.

When you meet someone for the first time, a hello is uttered along with your name. Some kind of greeting occurs albeit a handshake or nod. Next, the person you've met often expects you to reveal what you do for a living. Although this is an important part of life, it should not define us as human beings. What you do does not matter at all in comparison to who you are; namely how you live and who Jesus is for you. Sure, I might do "X" for a job and you might feel that is a noble profession or maybe not. Regardless, what you do for money doesn't matter much in the grand scheme of your human experience and your road to Sainthood. However, what does matter is the thing that carries immense significance—who you are at the core.

Taking it even a step further, your search to discover who Jesus is

---

[33] Romans 12:2

will be an ongoing quest. Little kids don't care what people are known for. They mostly disregard statuses and don't tend to think too much about what a person does for a living. Children merely are concerned with connection. They desire to share loving experiences with people in their lives who they can trust and who care about them. Children want to be with people who bring them joy and provide an inviting atmosphere that stirs up excitement. Therefore, we must keep reframing our mindset from the "what" to the "who" when it comes to our identity. Not only is this important to apply when meeting others and encountering our friends, family, and people we engage with, but also with ourselves.

Your mentality and energy must be concentrated with asking and answering who Jesus is. Meanwhile, answering another sizable question is important..."Who am I?" or rather "Whose am I?" When we arrive at these questions and start to truthfully answer them, you and I can ultimately get to the point of thinking that holiness is possible as his sons and daughters. By flooding our minds and hearts with enough positivity and God's possibility for our lives it leads us to powerfully realize that by receiving God's grace, love, and blessings we are all Saints in the making. At that point you can allow God to build on the foundation of your faith and you will start to find out who Jesus truly is. Not to mention, you will discover who you are—a child of God. If this is your outlook, you will no longer misjudge others, fall short of your truest potential, or de-value your own life by diminishing how important the role you play is in building up the Kingdom.

Furthermore, you will not downplay God's presence in your life. You will come to understand how deeply loved and desired you are by the Lord. This change of heart and realization will allow your faith to blossom like flowers in spring. Jesus will allow you to grow in humility and holiness. Eventually you might even muster up the courage to take up your cross and be that mighty warrior in God's army. After all, you are a child of the light. Being a child of God means that you have the throne of Heaven awaiting, as you are sons and daughters of the most high. This might seem good to some or maybe far out there for others. It can be challenging to understand or tough to imagine while traversing through all the many things life throws our way. That is okay. Take it one step at a time. God is patient and he is willing to wait for you. The promise excites me. As his children, you and I have royal blood pumping through our veins. If that doesn't enthuse you to get after it when you start your day, I don't know what will.

St. Paul emphasized this in his letter to the Romans. During that time people around the city of Rome were on edge. Their uneasiness was due to the persecution and killings of Christians during the first couple hundred years after the death and resurrection of Jesus. We can't forget this same man called Paul who had been the key persecutor of the faith in the past, was now the biggest advocate for Christianity. Paul tells us, "The Spirit itself bears witness with our spirit that we are children of God, and if children, then heirs, heirs of God and joint heirs with Christ, if only we suffer with him so that we may also be glorified with him."[34] Don't forget that the road to Sainthood won't be easy. However, since we are all children of God we are benefactors of the glory that awaits us. So the "what we do," can be de-emphasized. Now, the "who we are," as well as *whose we are* must be brought to light.

Think of it in this way. When you use a telescope to bring into focus a far off object or distant planet, that magnanimous part of creation can be appreciated for all of its magnificence. What you view through that lens is grandiose on its own, but we so often don't see it for its truest self or in its purest form. From a distance the object can seem tiny or insignificant, yet it has been immense and noteworthy all along. As you and I come to embrace the fact that we are God's children and that he is seeking our hearts with an eternal pursuit, this helps us to wrap our minds around the epicenter of it all. Make no mistake, God needs no magnification. He is already big and present in our lives. What must occur is that we look through the lens of faith that focuses on and points us to Jesus. Christ brings the unclear into sight and he makes it comprehensible. The Son reveals the artistry of the Creator and highlights the amazing qualities of the created. In having this perspective, then you can get to the point on your road to becoming a real Saint because that holiness has been inside of you from the beginning.

This is where you embrace the biggest factor of being a child of

---

34 Romans 8:16-17

God, understanding *whose you are*. When you know with full certainty you are the Lord's and you feel his love fully, then everything changes. What you do in life or for a career will take care of itself. It is normal and consequently a frequent occurrence to hear of and see people caught up in titles, statuses, and the "what." Many fall into this pit and view what they do as having ultra importance. Unfortunately this leads them to being so tightly connected to the standards of the world, rather than God's desire for human life. This results in us at times missing the mark on our truest calling, the call to be Saints. As a human being you have a soul. There is great depth that exists within you and your spirit joins you to the Lord in a very special manner.

As St. John Berchmans put it, "Our true worth does not consist in what human beings think of us. What we really are consists in what God knows us to be." Therefore, *whose we are* connects us powerfully to *who we are*—Children of the Lord. In order for us to grasp how paramount this spiritual concept and reality is, it's worthwhile to share with you the words of arguably the greatest Saint and my personal hero of the past century, Mother Teresa. No one better realized God's great love for us and his desire to chase us down in order to be our best friend than Mary Teresa.

The example Mother lived out by serving the poor and being the hands and feet of Christ is something we can all hope to emulate in a small way throughout our lifetime. Teresa's explanation exists in the profound depth of the love of God as being more vast than the ocean and the most powerful force in the universe. She explains that God's love has always been and will forever be immeasurable. Yet, it's fully available for eternity. I invite you to rest in these words as Mother Teresa shares with us what the Holy Spirit put on her heart and what she wrote in her sacred diary during her days as a missionary sister:

> *Jesus wants me to tell you again how much love he has for each of you beyond all you can imagine. I worry some of you still have not really met Jesus—one to one—you and Jesus alone. We may spend time in chapel, but have you seen with the eyes of your soul how he looks at you with love? Do you really know the living Jesus—not from books, but from being with him in your heart? Have you heard the loving words he speaks to you? Ask for grace. He is*

longing to give it. Until you can hear Jesus in the silence of your own heart you will not be able to hear him saying, "I thirst," in the hearts of the poor...How can we last even one day without hearing Jesus say, "I love you"? Impossible. Our soul needs that as much as the body needs to breathe the air. If not, prayer is dead meditation, only thinking. Jesus wants you each to hear him— speaking in the sounds of your heart...He loves you, but even more he longs for you. He misses you when you don't come close. He thirsts for you. He loves you always, even when you don't feel worthy. We're not accepted by others, even by ourselves sometimes. He is the one who always accepts you for children; you don't have to be different for Jesus to love you. Only believe you are precious to him. Bring all you are suffering to his feet. Only open your heart to be loved by him as you are. He will do the rest...Jesus himself must be the one to say to you, "I thirst." Hear your own name. Not just once. Every day. If you listen with your heart, you will hear, you will understand... "I thirst" is something much deeper than Jesus saying, "I love you." Until you know deep inside that Jesus thirsts for you—you can't begin to know who he wants to be for you. Or who he wants you to be for him.[35]

Wow! What powerful words and imagery Mother paints onto the canvas of our hearts. My hope is that her words are branded onto your soul. Hopefully you and I never lose focus on being God's children and that we never cease to realize the Lord's infinite longing for us, even far greater than love for us. It is critical that we continue to remind ourselves and our brothers and sisters of faith—this profound truth. Especially during the days we fall or when times are tough and God feels distant, we must cling to this hope. His unparalleled love remains burning hot for us. Some of the Saints canonized by the Church and the *everyday Saints* we will meet later on in this book have had some unexplainable and exceptionally intense moments with the Lord. These can be likened to "burning bush moments" that transcend time and space.

Mother Teresa had a vision of Christ and he met her face to face. Jesus spoke to her plainly and his words struck her heart. As they both

---

[35] Diary of Mother Teresa

entered into the sacred mystery of the Cross, a powerful encounter took place and the Lord revealed his thirst to Mary Teresa. Mother recalls Jesus saying, " I have asked you. They have asked you, and she, my Mother, has asked you. Will you refuse to do this for me to take care of them, to bring them to me?" Knowing the thirst of Jesus and her coming to thirst for his little ones in India, instilled in Mother a relentless desire to quench the thirsty heart of Christ by sharing his salvific love with the thirsting souls of creation.

Called to be Great

Undoubtedly, we are the Lord's children. He is calling us and not just calling us, but challenging us to be great. Greatness does not necessarily mean having to do outrageous or miraculous works of charity. It's not found solely in taking care of lepers like Mother Mary Teresa did. However, what Jesus does need from us is our personal best and ceaseless pursuit of him in all things. He asks to get your personal commitment to prayer and that you spend time with him. The Lord desires your "yes" to follow him no matter what life throws your way. This is the essence of faith and the key to God unveiling the Saint within you.

A child trusts their parents. As we discussed earlier, a relationship is built over time and that cannot be replicated by anything else in life. This same rooted connection and irreplaceable bond holds true for us with our Lord. He wants us to invite him into our lives. Jesus desires to be your best friend and to grant you his Sacred Heart. He has the purest love for you and it will fill you with overwhelming joy! Your desire for Jesus and building your life on him alone is the only way to quench God's thirst. All in all, when you thirst for him it will lead you to do extreme things for him. Namely, the thirst will propel you to do the Lord's will even if it requires tremendous sacrifice and suffering because your heart becomes entwined with the heart of Jesus.

Oftentimes when people, like myself, think about the Saints, we have this correct notion that there is grand holiness intertwined within their lives. God certainly pours out abundant graces on those who answer his call. It pleases him when creation rises to the challenges of life, especially when it comes to loving service toward those in need. What must not get lost in translation is that this holiness is obtainable by all children of God. It is not just stowed away and saved for a select few. Instead, we receive holiness during our lifetime if we do two important things.

First, when we continue to mature in our faith and understand the great value that we have for just being ourselves, then we will come to realize that God wants us to be like him. As cliche as it is, "the apple doesn't fall far from the tree." In this case, being made in God's image and likeness, we are his chosen ones who he loves with an everlasting love. As a result, when we ask God to grant us this holiness as his children, he will provide it to us. So you might be thinking that is pretty easy. Really, all I have to do is simply ask? Yeah, that's right. Asking is the first step. There are so many powerful examples of the great Saints and extremely holy people from the Bible who made the big ask of God. One of my favorite scriptures about asking is found in chapter seven of Matthew's Gospel.

Now before we dive into a particular verse, let's recognize that Matthew was a tax collector. Paying taxes has never been favored by anyone since the beginning days when people started using currency, unless one was on the receiving end of the transaction. Personally, I dislike taxes and do not look forward to mid-September and mid-April when tax time rolls around. You probably feel the same, but it's a given part of life. As the saying goes, the only two guarantees in life are death and taxes. During the time of Jesus, tax collectors were some of the most despised of all citizens. The tax collector during the reign of the Roman Empire was critical as he was responsible for getting the money to Caesar. We all know that Jesus had an extraordinarily witty answer when the Pharisees and Sadducees were trying to trap Him. These religious elites posed the question, "Is it right to pay the imperial tax to Caesar, or not?"[36]

Jesus could have just simply said "yes." If he did then everyone would have gotten on his case about not being a Godly or Holy man. So what if he responded in the opposite manner? What if our Lord shouted with an emphatic, "NO!"? That would have sent shock waves across the Mediterannean being ammunition for the Jewish higher

---

[36] Matthew 22:17

ups to turn Jesus over to the Romans for discounting the law. Does it really surprise us that Christ says, "Then repay to Caesar what belongs to Caesar and to God what belongs to God"?[37]

So we too have to pay taxes. Yet, the tax collector, namely Matthew, was mostly hated because he would often inflate the tax and make people pay more than the required amount, pocketing the remainder. The IRS is a little bit more official these days and the information on how much we owe is more accessible to us. The major point of emphasis here is that Matthew was a hated man because of his profession and crookedness. All the while, the Lord still saw the beauty inside of Matthew and he used his life to make an impact. Not only was Matthew used by God, but he became a great leader in the Church being one of the four Gospel writers. Certainly, St. Matthew's legacy lives on.

My hope here is that you remember that holiness comes from God. It is a gift as Jesus put it, "I cannot do anything on my own...I do not seek my own will but the will of the one who sent me."[38] Matthew had to respond to the Lord's call to follow him, but he also had to ask Jesus to make him holy by inviting God in. Christ himself, who is one in being with the Father, was filled with the holiness of God. None of us, not even the so-called greatest of all Saints, arrives at holiness on his or her own. And that is why Matthew reminds us of the important nature of asking God for help and whatever we might need. The scripture powerfully articulates this from Matthew's perspective saying, "Ask and it will be given to you; seek and you will find; knock and the door will be opened to you."[39] Requirement number one is to ask our Lord to receive his holiness and to ask him with great faith so that it will change our hearts. If God can transform Matthew from the dishonest tax collector to a pillar of the Church, there is great hope for me and you.

---

[37] Matthew 22:21
[38] John 5:30
[39] Matthew 7:7

Active Work in Progress

Secondly, we must work with God toward holiness. No matter how many times we ask and no matter how great our conviction might be, the *ask* will produce no fruit if we sit around and wait for it to happen. Action is required. We are all probably well familiar with the phrase, "God helps those who help themselves." When we seek it out going after what we desire, when we pursue all that is placed on our heart, we stride toward holiness. Combining this personal quest with the power and grace of the Lord in our lives has unmatched potential. Watch out! The electric force of the spirit that is generated is unstoppable. That is why holiness is so important. We will discuss this more in later chapters.

It is pertinent to digest that in your life right now, as a child of God, you are called to something more. So what is it exactly? How will you get there? Where does the next step in the journey lead to? All of these questions are things that we have to uncover, figuring them out along the way. There is no "easy" button or straight path. Most likely we won't have some crazy epiphany. Chances are that a letter from God won't pop in our mailbox any time soon and there won't be an angel who knocks on the door to tell us what is next. Though, that is more than okay.

The Saints of the past figured it out and we will figure it out too. After all, we are Saints in the making. As long as you trust and keep taking daily steps toward the Lord, you will get one step closer to Sainthood. By asking for Jesus' guidance, you can do almost anything. As a kid I always loved superheroes. When I think about it now, there is still something pretty cool about a person like Batman or Superman who has these other worldly powers to do what normal people can't. What is even more impressive is realizing that the superheroes desire to save the day, help others, and use powers they have been provided to better the world. That is their ultimate aim.

As I grew up, I began to understand that being a child of God, you and I have special super powers. Whether we have a legitimate cape or not is besides the point. Our gifts and abilities that God has blessed us with are to be shared with the world. A common notion in the faith is that since we are children, we should desire to please our Heavenly

Father. This is all well and good, but life and the depth of our role here on earth goes far beyond that notion. I believe that God desires to know us intimately and for us to want to spend time with him because He needs us. How can the creator and most powerful entity in the universe need a small meager human being you ask? Well, our Lord needs us because we are needed by his children—the body of Christ on earth. Like a large family, we all play an important role and there is a web of connection that impacts everyone greatly.

As children of the Kingdom—*Hijos del Reino* or Niños de Dios—*Children of God*, we have so many brothers and sisters that walk this journey of life with us each day. Some we know really well and billions of others we will never meet on this planet. I do believe we will all be united in Heaven with the rest of the Saints someday. Until we get there, we have real work to do. That being said, we are needed. God's thirst for you and the rest of his children is deep and so vast. Only our faithfulness to him and our love of neighbor will quench his heart. When you go about loving others you bring Jesus to them. When you spread joy and bring hope to people who are hurting, this satisfies the Lord like nothing else.

It's the very soul of a person that radiates holiness and when you share this energy and the light of Christ, you have the power to illuminate the world. On our road to Sainthood paved with holiness, we—the children of God, have been blessed with life. Our duty as children of the light is to go and to tell our brothers and sisters the good news. This is best done by the example of our lives. Why else would Saint Francis of Assisi challenge us to, "Preach the Gospel at all times and if necessary, use words." Saints in the making are those who respond to this call. Being a child of God is free for us, but that freedom did come with a great cost. Our Lord paid the highest price on the Cross. His only ask is that we remain faithful. Continue to invite God into your life and love his children throughout the world. My hope is that you will consider the great opportunity and commission that is at hand.

Fishers of Men

Similar to Peter, James, Andrew, and John, we too are called to fish. The interesting thing about fishing is that there are days you go out on the boat and you wait patiently. You continue to cast out your line and nothing bites. The following day, the fishermen had slumped heads down fighting to remain awake as the break of dawn was near. Out in the early morning, just minutes after casting his nets, Peter lands a big catch. Jesus is asking us to go into the deep waters. If we do so and fully trust him, we will be able to do things for God that are powerful beyond all measure. We are called to be fishers of men. This topic will be uncovered more toward the end of our journey together. But for now, my question to you is the same query that our Lord put on my heart as I prayed in front of the Blessed Sacrament.

Since I now know that I am a child of God and you know this about yourself also, I invite you to think about this more. As I sat there gazing at our Lord hidden beautifully behind the host in the Holy Eucharist, I could only think how lucky I was to have been given this life. My prayer deepened and I began to listen more intently to what Jesus was putting on my heart. While sitting with the Lord in a small chapel in upstate New York I began to realize how small I was in comparison to the earth and within the scope of our universe. But then it hit me. The question that God spoke to my heart is a message that I desire to relay to you. Jesus is asking this of each person. He asks us to be his children and a light to the world...

Will you follow Me? Will you go for Me? Will you be My hands and My feet? Will you heed the call and live out the purpose I have created you for and had in mind since the beginning of time? Why are you worried, do you not know that I have equipped you with everything you need for the journey. Trust Me. Follow Me. Live for Me. Share my love with everyone you encounter. I will send you to do things far beyond selfish desire and what I ask of you just requires a sincere and generous heart. May each person young and old feel My loving presence after coming into contact with you. Don't worry, you need not have all the answers. After all, I am the way, the truth, and the life. I am the Alpha and the Omega, the beginning and the end. If I, who have numbered all the stars of the sky and the birds of the air can ensure that even the ants of the field have food to eat, won't I provide for your every need? I am yours and you are mine. Understand that you, like all My children, have a special mission. I am calling you because I need you to go and to live out your faith. It is not enough to float along through life. I have made you for greatness. You are called to be my Saint. Will you say "yes"? It will not be easy. I will lead you to the most abhorrent situations and the Cross you will carry will be heavy. You will not inaugurate these acts of compassion, but I the Lord your God will stir up the fire that burns within your soul to carry them out. Know with full confidence that I am with you always and will give you all the help you need along the way. I have already lined up the right people, places, connections, and situations to give you direction. Just take the next step of faith each time. Believe in me and believe in the power of love. You are a Saint, now it is time for you to change the world.

As I sat in that small chapel and allowed this prayer to sink into the core of my soul, tears began to stream down my face. It was at this moment that I began to think of the young man in scripture who asked the Lord what he must do to gain eternal life. Jesus tells him that he must not commit various grave sins like murder, adultery, or be a thief. The Lord says that he should honor his parents and love his neighbor. The young man gets excited because indeed he had lived faithfully, been a model citizen, and an obedient servant in all of these manners. Yet, the young man would soon grow sad after asking the Lord what he lacked. Jesus said to him, "If you wish to be perfect, go, sell what you have and give to the poor, and you will have treasure in Heaven. Then come, follow me."[40] Walking away with his many possessions, the young man was more empty than ever inside.

Despite having followed the commandments and living a pretty good life, the rich young man was unfulfilled. His heart was heavy

---

[40] Matthew 19:21

being clouded with the attachment to worldly things. True happiness had vanished. I thought to myself, if I too was going to be like the young man from the parable? Maybe you can relate to him also in one manner or another. If we are honest with ourselves, there are many things, attractions, and distractions from fully following Jesus.

Regardless of your age, Jesus is asking you to follow him. It is my hope that you will remain open to this as we continue to travel together down this road of holiness. Take a moment today or in the near future and spend some time with the Lord before the Blessed Sacrament. He is your Father and you are his child. God longs to spend time with you. Quiet yourself and allow Him to speak to your heart. You are Jesus' special and precious one. You are God's fierce soldier in his battalion. You and I have a battle to fight. We are called now and for the rest of our lives to build up the Kingdom by being God's faithful children and loving our brothers and sisters like Jesus would.

In a world filled with so much dissension, discord, and disbelief, we can look at this call to Sainthood in one of two ways. The first is to see it as impossible, unimaginable, and a task that is too tall or too heavy to carry. This mentality and approach will change nothing and will leave us feeling like the young man, empty inside. Or we can dig our heels in, muster up some courage, buckle up, and get after it one day at a time. Life is about progress. Each morning that we have the mindset and goal to get a little better, to love a little stronger, and to serve a little more we grow as Saints. In doing so we are committed to building up the Kingdom. This satisfies the thirst of our Lord. He provides us with lasting joy and we impact the world in profound proportions. None of this is going to happen overnight. This all takes place in time.

Before you and I know it, we are crushing life and taking large strides toward new heights. It is a beautiful thing when we take time to enjoy the journey and it is even more attractive to our Lord when we make the effort out of pure love for him and for his creation. We truly do love God by loving others. Jesus himself said, "Amen, I say to you that you who have followed me, in the new age, when the Son of Man is seated on his throne of glory, will yourselves sit on twelve thrones, judging the twelve tribes of Israel. And everyone who has given up houses or brothers or sisters or father or mother or children or lands for the sake of my name will receive a hundred times more, and will inherit eternal life. But many who are first will be last, and the last will be first."[41]

God has great rewards for his faithful ones. You never have to question if it will be worth it, as his retirement plan is out of this world. All jokes aside, serving God comes at a great cost. The *ask* is big and the challenges even bigger. However, we must never forget that the God we serve is in complete control. He will give us the grace and ability to do what we cannot do on our own. The words of Jesus remind us how uncommon the road toward holiness and the path to Sainthood truly is. It is not the way of the world, but then again we were not made for this world, we were made for so much more. I know that I cannot do this on my own and I am hopeful that you will take the challenge too. Undoubtedly, all of us are children of God. What still hangs in the balance is the key question.

A future filled with peace and joy remains in us by responding "yes" to the call to Sainthood. If you are at a point in your journey to follow the Lord in this manner and strive toward becoming a Saint, I commend you. For those out there who are still unsure, confused, or believe they aren't worthy, continue to listen to your heart. Be patient with yourself and allow God to reassure you. Doors can be closed and even locked, but we just can't throw away the key. It is never too late to give Jesus your "yes," but it will take great trust and tremendous faith. The corridors we traverse through in life are often dark and the unknown is out there standing tall before us.

Never forget that we are children of God and that means we are children of the light. Jesus wants to be your friend because you belong to Him. This means that you are one with Christ and the Father, being connected through love. The Most Reverend Bishop Edward Scharfenberger of the Albany Diocese helps us understand Jesus' longing to be our friend. He explains how this relationship as a child of God will be the gateway for us to reach a full life and greatly impact the lives of others along the way by saying:

Jesus is the one they can really call on that will never let them down. Jesus wants to be that "BFF" (Best Friend Forever) we

---

[41] Matthew 19:28-30

all need. He waits for us, comes to us, and meets us exactly
where we are. In some way the disciple—the true friend of
Jesus—wants to let his or her heart be the door through which
the heart of Jesus reaches the heart of the neighbor. Right now
our mission in the world has never been clearer: to bring that
love in the heart of Jesus for each and every one of us—that love
poured into our own hearts—to every person we encounter. To
fear less and to love more.[42]

As a Saint you must continue to walk faithfully. Step forward and
jump out of the boat into the deep waters. Understand that as a child
of the most high God, Jesus is your everything and he wants you to
share him with everyone you encounter. Be amor—love for Jesus and
quench his thirst by casting lines out there in the deep waters for
others. Allow courage to be your anthem and call on the Holy Spirit to
ignite the flame of faith within your heart. Soon enough, Christ will
stoke that fire and it will be burning even brighter inside of you than
ever before. With the Lord lighting your path, you will see clearly that
the best gift you have received is being a child of God. So, answer this
call to prayer that Jesus asks all of his children today and every day,
"Who do you say that I am?" and who will you allow Jesus to be for
you? You are Niños de Dios.

Challenge 5

Take some time this week to reflect on your childhood. What things
come to mind? Pay close attention to how you feel and the memories
that bring you the most happiness. Who did you trust the most and
why? Who loved you in the greatest manner as you grew older?
Meanwhile, what caused you, as a kid, to fear or doubt things and why
do some of those thoughts remain today? Now, go and take some time
to sit with the Lord. Allow him to work on your heart and speak to
your soul. Go and spend a few minutes with Jesus who is your friend.
Be with him in front of the Blessed Sacrament and allow Christ to
embrace you. Ask God to wrap you up in his love and receive the gift

---

[42] Reverend Bishop Scharfenberger (Evangelist Newspaper)

he promises. You are his beloved child. Think about who Jesus is for
you. The Lord desires your entire being and wants you to come to him
just the way you are.

BLINDLY FAITHFUL
CHAPTER 6

"You have to walk by faith and not by sight. Your faith is going to turn things around. Your faith is going to bring new opportunities. Your faith is going to bring unexpected favor." – Shehu Hamzaddeen

Believing Versus Seeing

The alarm clock sounds... It's 6 am and your groggy self pops out of bed unusually like a piece of toast ready to take on the day. There is no hitting the snooze button this morning. You muster up the strength to jump out of bed. Your eyes are now fully open and the piercing light is already filtering into the room through the cracks in the shades. Another bright sunny day awaits you. Stumbling into the bathroom to wash your face and brush your teeth you look into the mirror and take a long hard look. You smile. The Beyonce hit classic song *Flawless* is your anthem because you woke up like this. The Saint is the man, woman or child whose confidence soars because they eventually learn to see what God sees. The beauty staring back at them in the mirror is radiant, not to mention the most powerful soul that composes their eternal makeup, which God has given them, shines like a gem on the inside. You are looking good and ready to take on the world! Flaws and all you are flawless in the eyes of your creator. It's just a matter of seeing it for yourself.

Overall, sight is an amazing thing. The complexity of the human eye and its intricacies are mystical. The science behind the workings of the many facets that allow us humans to be able to access and utilize the sense of sight is mind boggling. Each morning our eyes open as we take in light and colors. We look at a world that has so many needs. For most people, myself included, being able to see is something we take for granted. It is very much like breathing, we don't think about it until we or someone we know is unable to use the eye in a functional manner. Without sight, the darkness is substantial and it becomes very challenging to live. Evidently, sight and light go hand in hand. Not only does this hold true when it comes to human anatomy and the metaphysics that are involved in the intricacies and dynamics of the eye, but it is relevant in our faith lives as well.

Like many small children, I recall being afraid of the dark. Not being able to see was something that made me anxious, especially at night time. This problem was resolved by my parents simply accessing a night light and plugging it in when I went to bed. My nerves were quickly eased and I could sleep calmly without fear. A lack of sight in our spiritual walk is something that makes us uneasy. Even the most unorganized people like to be in the know, having an idea of what's to come. There are hardly any guarantees in life, but one certainty is that most of the time we will not foresee what is coming in our future. A freight train can roar ferociously down the tracks and head straight toward you at any moment. Do you notice the light at the end of that tunnel or maybe hear the whistle the train lets off as the conductor goes full bore ahead? Perhaps this is the case from time to time.

There are some moments though in deep self-reflection that we do realize what is occurring in real time. Meanwhile, in other circumstances you and I are blindsided by life. The fact is that as nice as it may be to see and to know, you are not the captain of the ship. It is natural for people to desire to understand and to want to be in control. But there is darkness out there. Evil and a cold world with many problems come at you when you least expect it. We live in a scary society. We navigate through life and will only make it through if we have great trust. As much as not being able to see is terrifying to the toddler, especially in an unfamiliar place when his or her parents are not there, they must learn to cope with it.

Coping however is not good enough. Just getting by or surviving the events, circumstances, and challenges of life is not much of a life at all. What good is it to do life if you are not fully alive? We all have faced challenges and will continue to go head to head with obstacles throughout our lifetime. There will be moments that seem like you cannot go on and you may even want to throw in the towel and give up. However, you and I will be victorious in the mission of discipleship as long as we don't quit. And that is the reason why walking by faith and not by sight is the way of the Saint.

Learning how to Trust in the Dark

Not too long ago there was a wicked thunderstorm with powerful winds that rolled through the neighborhood. Trees were viciously crashing down on top of power lines and for a period of about 72 hours the community was without electricity. After the sun went down the only source of power was a flashlight, candle, or some other battery operated device to illuminate the room. Being hijacked by the lack of light poses a great challenge. Not seeing is dangerous and scary both physically and even more so spiritually. When the electricity is flowing, with the flip of a switch, we can see clearly in every room we walk into. Regardless of the time of day or night it is, sight provides people with comfort.

Well, life sure is good at throwing the uncomfortable our way. The darkness and curveballs tend to be unforecasted, just like that thunderstorm leaving the entire neighborhood in darkness. So what do you do when there are storms that hit you like a ton of bricks or your life is rocked by a raging sea? How do you respond to not being able to see where life is taking you?

It's interesting because all people come to a fork in the road when facing drastic life challenges, uncertainty, and the unknown. When we go head first into the darkness we can do one of two things. We can either pull the covers of life over our heads in fear or stand up to it. The former is like the toddler at night time left in the dark who hides from the adversity, pain, uncomfortable, and uncharted waters of life. The latter is the Saint who stands firm and tall, willing to get to work and do something to deal with the situation at hand. You and I have a choice and the opportunity to not hide in the dark, but instead to come into the light is crucial. We can leap through the darkness, taking it face on and allow our faith to light the path that ends in victory. That trek requires tremendous courage and immense trust. During the most deplorable situations and amidst the greatest suffering and pain our faith must remain steadfast. When life throws the trials and tests our way, this is where growth occurs when we have grit and fortitude. It is time for you and me to grow in holiness and take steps even closer toward Sainthood by walking by faith and not by sight.

How very sad it is to see people who walk away from the Lord. Spiritually checking out and turning your back on God is never the answer. It damages us internally and our situation only worsens. Oftentimes we stray like sheep, distancing from the Shepherd of our souls. This tends to happen due to some unforeseen and unfair circumstances that come about. After all, why would an all loving and all powerful God allow such terrible atrocities to happen? If God really loved you, he wouldn't allow you to be hurt. If God cared deeply about you, he wouldn't have you suffer.

Certainly bad things wouldn't be happening to a good person who believes and loves the Lord, right? Reality is that God does love you, but at the same time the messiness of life does not discriminate. A common misnomer is that people who have faith and those who pursue Jesus wholeheartedly will be free from suffering, hardship, and difficulty. This is absolutely false. However, the crosses you and I bear and the hardships we face is part of our journey. These difficult moments often become the most important and beautiful pieces to our story.

It's in the hard that our soul latches onto Christ and he humbles us enough to realize that we cannot do this on our own. We will discuss this notion in more depth later on. It is essential to realize that you and I have a choice. When times get tough and life sucks the wind out of us, we can blame God or we can remain faithful and stay the course. The road might be dark and dismal for a while, but certainly there will be pockets of light that shine forth. God will provide what you need so you can see enough, but it will take true faith to get through the darkness.

Perhaps you aren't facing anything gravely difficult right now in terms of suffering. Maybe illness, loss, or another damaging event hasn't entered your life, but you are struggling with the unknown.

Again, this is where having that rock solid foundation built on faith allows you to dig in deeply and Jesus helps us to carry on to the next day. Throughout most of my life I was afraid of the unknown. I disliked not having the answers or a set plan. It wasn't until more recently that I finally quieted myself enough to fully listen to God and believe that his plan is what is best for me.

Someone's personal will is one thing, but God's will is what matters most and it must be carried out. Life will teach you quickly that like it or not, you are not in control. Contrary to popular opinion, not being captain of the ship is actually a good thing. The steering wheel might feel good in our hands, but actually it will limit our lives. The God we serve is limitless and there is no ceiling for how high he can and will take us if we allow him. It just so happens that our Lord likes to use the uncomfortable moments, the times when things don't seem to quite fit or work out for us, as a way to expand us. These hard moments and the seasons of drought often lead to an oasis of prosperity. This happens when we faithfully remain close to our Lord, allowing him to work in our lives. Jesus enters in and makes a dwelling place in our hearts.

Shining Lights

Throughout the bible there are beautiful examples of Saints, holy leaders, and humble servants. The prophet Jeremiah is someone that I greatly admire. By examining their lives, you will come to see that these men and women faced struggle. Life was anything but easy for them, yet they remained faithful to God. Jeremiah didn't have it easy all the time and there was tremendous uncertainty in his life as well. But no matter what was taking place or what the life circumstances were that swirled about in Jeremiah's world, he stayed the course. Jeremiah is known to be the "weeping prophet." His cry and heartache came when God revealed to him that the city of Judah would suffer famine, foreign conquest, plunder, and captivity in a land of strangers.

This was a tough pill to swallow for a man who had much pride in his people and was someone of substantial faith. It had to be tough for him to go and relay this message to everyone in his community. Surely, he was not liked because of this truthful message he relayed to his fellow Jewish people. Nonetheless, in a true and Saintly manner, Jeremiah rose to the occasion. That is exactly what God is asking you to do. The prophet chose to lean on his faith and did all he could to encourage the people of his time to remain faithful and trust in God's sovereign plan through it all. Listen to these compelling words spoken by Jeremiah to the Hebrews in Judah, "For I know well the plans to prosper you, not to harm you, plans to give you hope and a future."[43] What a message to cling on to.

For the people of his age it gave them encouragement to remain hopeful in the Lord's promise. For us today, it keeps all possibilities alive thanks to the faith we cling to. You can certainly give up, but then it is over and the thing is you only get one shot at life. When you find a way amidst the darkness and reach deep within yourself, you can generate some light. Your spirit is resilient and God is on the search for you. The light of Christ will not only be a way for you to overcome the dark moments of life, but it will be the very thing that ignites your heart. The world and the enemy tries to put blinders on us continuously by way of doubt, deception, and fear. However, Jesus dispels all of this and will flood your life with light if you open your heart through relationship with him. Then through the perspective of faith and the lens of love, the Lord will work through us to spread his glorious light.

Saints are the beacons of light that illuminate a path for others. Saints are children of the light that help their brothers and sisters get through the darkness. Like a ship that is guided by the lighthouse far off at sea, so too are we asked to be that guide for God's people. Before this happens though, we must allow Jesus to come and show us the way in our own lives. Then and only then will you be able to light the way thanks to Jesus who is the way. Saints are the people who find the way, even when there seems to be no way. Their faith is ultimately what allows them to see. Although it is dark for them too, they choose to trust, to remain hopeful, and to ask God for his help.

Doing so causes a reaction in the soul that is likened to pouring gasoline on a fire. The match is lit and a gigantic explosion occurs. Consequently, the flames of faith inside the Saint are raging and they desire to spread this love and hope to all. As Shehu Hamzaddeen

---

[43] Jeremiah 29:11

emphatically explained, "You have to walk by faith and not by sight. Your faith is going to turn things around. Your faith is going to bring new opportunities. Your faith is going to bring unexpected favor." This eruption in the heart is the favor of God coming into your life and mine when we remain on board and don't abandon the ship. By choosing Jesus and to be faithful, especially during the hardest times, the Lord will increase your blessing. This inevitably will result in a future you could never have imagined. It is interesting how hindsight is always 20/20.

When we look back and take time to reflect on things, most often we end up seeing what we initially were blinded by. Jeremiah's message to the people of Judah speaks volumes to a faith filled life. Our very world must revolve around Jesus. He is the center of our lives. We fall out of orbit when we begin putting something or someone else on the top tier of the podium. This is when we are out of sorts and find ourselves lost. However, not being able to see is certainly different than blindness. Ask God to see. Keep searching for him and know that he never stops looking for you.

One of my favorite stories from the Bible is about a man who was born blind. It always intrigues me when I read this passage that people in Jesus' time believed that this particular fellow, who the story is about, must have done something horrible to deserve such a punishment. The blind man was well up there in age when he finally met Jesus and was healed. In the early stages of the faith, during Old Testament times, people believed bad things came to you when you sinned. The answer to any ill circumstance was that a person received a negative fate from God who cursed them for the wrong they had done. The fact that the man was born blind actually had nothing to do with sinfulness at all.

What it does involve is a powerful message regarding our faith. We all face spiritual blindness from time to time. You and I can choose to not see because we do not want to see. This happens when we know in our hearts what the will of God is, but we chose not to take the next step. We know in our heart where we must go, but we are not ready or willing due to fear, selfishness, or a lack of comfort presented in that future situation. It is even worse when we refuse blatantly and decide to go our own way regardless of the tug by Jesus. Consequently, we drift from the one who loves us most.

Be Light for Others

So often our spiritual blindness sets in by not being open minded or accepting. We create a chasm when we are no longer open to who and what God is putting into our lives. There is a reason why people come to us and often they show up with loads of baggage, pain, suffering, and a heavy cross. Did you ever consider that they come to us because the Lord knows that we need a spark, a ray of hope, and encouragement. We don't get to choose who crosses our path. The great Christian author Charles Dickens put it powerfully by stating, "A wonderful fact to reflect upon, that every human creature is constituted to be that profound secret and mystery to every other...Pause you who read this, and think for a moment of the long chain of iron or gold, or thorns or flowers, that would never have bound you, but for the formation of the first link on one memorable day...No one is useless in this world who lightens the burdens of another."

We live in a web of connectivity. The human experience is a great adventure. Many times in our lives by walking with faith it requires not only our trust in God, but in others who care about us deeply. The curious thing is that most people who the Lord brings to us were once strangers we didn't know. From time to time we lower our guard and invite a select few to fully enter. These people are the friends you share your deepest secrets with and rely on to be a light when you walk through the darkness. Hold onto these words and share yourself with others as God's word says, "Therefore, encourage one another and build one another up, as indeed you do."[44]

The human person, let alone the Saint, doesn't prefer struggle. Suffering and the way of the Cross is undesirable and it isn't even understood. However, it's part of the great mystery of life. So when we experience ache or sorrow, when we know how God can fill in the holes in our heart, then we desire to be like Christ for others. This is impossible without enduring the pain and persevering through the trials. Nobody is able to escape life, specifically the rough patches. Bearing the load that comes your way drains the vitality of life out of you. Jesus is asking that you endure it and embrace it. He then

---

[44] 1 Thessalonians 5:11

challenges us to take it a step further and lift the crosses of others. Why? Well, love is in the Cross.

The power of Jesus is found in running toward the sorrowful, sinful, broken, and hurting people in our world. Afterall, it is probably your hope and mine that those who love us will come to our aid when we are in the pits of life looking up and wondering how to climb out. The thing is that the Saint shows up and the Saint receives help gracefully. In addition, the Saint chooses to ask God for his grace to endure the Cross and to lift the scales of their own blindness. Fallen human nature can be a roadblock. Oftentimes our humanity or original sin becomes a scapegoat, something that we can cast blame on. This is a trap. The enemy who prowls around this world wants us to convince ourselves that we aren't good enough and we will never be worthy of God's love.

However, in order to responsibly respond to our own situation and to be the faithful holy Saint that God calls us to be, we must embrace life in all its messiness. This includes the person who is hurting, unattractive, and broken. Your call as God's Saint is to open that door of love and to see the hidden Christ because Jesus is coming your way. Think about your life right now. Who are the people who have helped you in your most difficult hours? Who was standing by your side and was willing to be with you in the bleakest situation? Now, think about those you have received with grace and for whom you have been "Christ" for. How did that make you feel and how did it make those people feel?

Finally, take a moment and try to recall some times that you can remember when you met someone by chance—out of the blue. Apparently, the people that you remember left an impression on you. They left some kind of mark or else you would not be thinking about them at this very moment. Perhaps one of them turned into a close friend or a spouse. Even if that has not been the case, you cannot look past the power of divine connection. Undoubtedly, there are moments of God's grace that only faith can explain. The dynamic nature that is found in the unexpected and hidden Jesus in our lives is tremendously powerful. The Lord is knocking through the stranger, the lonely, the broken hearted, and people craving love. Don't be blinded by the cynicism of this world. Have faith. Open your eyes and see. Open up the door to Jesus, He comes in a wide variety of shapes, colors, and sizes.

The encounters with each person, the circumstances and situations all add up to our chain of life and link us together. They make you who you are today, especially the hard moments. If you keep the faith, this can empower you and light a spark that ignites you in the best manner possible. Reflecting on these important people and experiences are part of the spiritual exercise for the soul. It is what walking by faith is all about. By living life in this manner you strive toward holiness. In doing so you get back up when you fall and dust yourself off because God's goodness awaits you. This faithful approach provides yourself and others the space and the freedom to keep on going because you know that it is always worthwhile.

As Dallas Willard, a respected American philosopher and Christian writer once said, "Discipleship is the process of becoming who Jesus would be if he were you." So who would Jesus be if he were you? That is a pretty tough question to try to digest and unpack. Maybe it isn't though. Maybe, just maybe, it is actually a lot more simple than we first might think. What I believe is that it boils down to you and I being the best faith filled version of ourselves that we can be. God knows your heart and he knows how he made you. Therefore, we can live out the answer to this question of holiness when we ask the Lord to come into our lives, to empower us with the advocate that he sent to us— the Holy Spirit. When we choose to give our all in humble service to the body of Christ on earth in a manner of great love, we will be fulfilled. Essentially, we become Jesus for others and we are made into "other Christs" by the power of God working in our lives. Saints become the light for others.

Look for Jesus

Jeremiah the prophet shared a powerful message with his people thousands of years ago. The great prophet did not stop after reminding us that God would give us a "hope and a future." Jeremiah continued by calling his people to action. Jeremiah challenged those in Judah who were facing great turmoil and distress. He pleaded for them to call on the Lord and to search for him wholeheartedly. That is yet another *ask* of us by God as we march toward Sainthood. My hope is that these words of Jeremiah fire you up and become a new song in your heart. He said, "When you call me, and come and pray to me, I will listen to you. When you look for me, you will find me. Yes, when you seek me with all your heart."[45]

As you trek through this life, are you searching diligently for the Lord or are you merely enduring what comes your way? Are we remaining in the dark and continuing to be blinded? St. Paul reminds us, "Faith is the substance of things hoped for and the evidence of things not yet seen."[46] Go now. Go and seek Jesus. Then when you seek him you will find him when you seek him with your complete heart. When you find him you will follow wherever the Lord leads you. Those who follow completely will never run out of God's grace. It doesn't matter how many times you fall off the horse or take a wrong turn. God is not bothered by that at all. His one concern is that you seek forgiveness and receive his loving mercy.

Jesus will provide another link to connect your chain so you can get to where you are meant to be. In fact, our Lord who loves us so dearly awaits us. He is there standing on the other side of that darkness. Christ is that glimmer of light that provides us with true hope. Where there is faith, there is hope. And where there is hope there is life. The unknown can be scary. There is no discounting that. It is okay to be afraid. Don't forget, Saints are forged in the fire. They are made in the darkness of life. Their courage to overcome fear by running full bore ahead for the Lord lights their path. The Saint continues on, especially when it is not easy and despite the difficulties that lie ahead.

That's why we call it faith and yet in my heart and in yours we know it is more than that. It is truth. It is real. The light that comes to us when we walk by faith is as real if not more real than the darkness we quell by traversing through it all. Know that you are not alone. There are many others across the earth who are journeying with you. They too are doing their best to heed the call and to walk by faith. Is it not our faith that gives us sight and the ability to continue on? Believe in God and his limitless power. That word is what faith is all

---

[45] Jeremiah 29:12-13
[46] Hebrews 11:1

about. It connects emphatically to the two most common words in scripture, "fear not."

Be Not Afraid

Over 365 times the prophets, apostles, disciples, and Saints who composed the sacred scripture remind us to not be afraid. God knows what it is like to fear. After all, Jesus' parents had to fear for his life from the start when Herod sent out a battalion of soldiers to find Christ and to kill him. Our Lord, who is divine and who once entered into the full humanness of the world, had all the reason to fear. Think about the brutal and tortuous road to Calvary and then horrific crucifixion Jesus endured. He could have feared dying and then descending to the depths of hell. Fear did not hold him down, nor did death. Jesus conquered the grave. Fear didn't settle in because he had the power of God in him. Saints have this power too! You don't have to be afraid, God has your back. You and I are called by name and we are called to defeat fear by stopping it in its tracks.

Always remember that the Lord is there for you. Call on Jesus and he will come to your aid. Like the Saints that went before us, we too walk by faith and not by sight. As they cheer for us from the Heavenly throne and as we pray for each other by encouraging our fellow brothers and sisters in faith, we keep going. Thomas, one of Jesus' best friends and truest apostles, doubted. He even went so far as telling his closest friends that he would not believe until he saw the Lord and touched his wounds. And that was right after spending a couple years following Jesus as an apostle. Needless to say, it is pretty unorthodox and an amazing miracle that a person would rise from the dead. However, didn't Thomas pay attention to anything Jesus said or did? Still, his human nature got the best of him and yet Jesus was merciful. Our Lord showered him with love and He does so for us as long as we believe...The scriptures say, "Blessed are they who have not seen, yet have believed."[47]

So what about you? Do you believe? Do you and will you commit your life to walking by faith and not by sight? If this captivates you

---

[47] John 20:29

even in the least bit, I hope you will read on. It's time to cultivate the next seed of faith God is planting in your heart as you journey toward Sainthood. The seed planted is to be watered and taken care of. It is something that will grow and blossom over time. It is a life force and energy that will challenge you to the "nth" degree and provide the greatest blessings with the utmost joy.

The seed that is being rooted in your soul will germinate and spread throughout the world. It is scattered and shared best when you manifest it in every fabric of your life through the way you live. The seed you are sowing as a Saint is a seed of discipleship. Not just any discipleship. It is iron tough. When you become iron men and women for the Lord, you grow in holiness. It is your faith that empowers you as Christ lives within. Together we can and will become iron disciples. Together we can and will be able to change the world with God who lives in us!

Throughout the centuries, the great Saints of the Church who gave themselves completely and followed the Lord by faith were not strangers to the Cross. Look no further than Job in the Bible who lost his children to death. He had all his possessions destroyed and was riddled with grave sickness. Job was not happy with this situation, but kept his faith through it all. He questioned the Lord, but did not turn away from him. Despite everything going wrong and while enduring great suffering, Job pushed on and believed saying, "Yet he knows my way; if he tested me, I should come forth like gold. My foot has always walked in his steps; I have kept his way and not turned aside."[48] And then later on he proclaimed, "I know that you can do all things, and that no purpose of yours can be hindered."[49]

Suffering was something that Job and many great Saints ultimately took on because they were sharing in Christ's journey as the ambassadors of our Lord. Namely, they chose to walk by faith and not by sight. When we look at the greatest Canonized Saints like Peter, Paul, John the Baptist, Isaac Jogues, Kateri Tekakwitha and many more, we can see that there is a price that is paid for following Jesus. Ultimately it is the price of love. *The Way* as it was called in the early years of the Church was not popular or well received. The Jewish

---

[48] Job 23:10-11
[49] Job 42:2

people at the time were still torn, especially the religious leaders. The Romans were also enraged about this man named Jesus who came onto the scene and was revolutionizing the world. They ruled by force, meanwhile Jesus won people over through love. The feeling of chastisement and the persecution endured by the faithful apostles manifested itself in the form of the heavy weight of the Cross.

This was the case for Peter (Simon, the fisherman), who was crucified upside down for his great vigor in sharing the Gospel message. But remember, this is the same Peter that Jesus gave the keys of the kingdom to and said, "Now I say to you that you are Peter [which means 'rock'], and upon this rock I will build my Church, and all the powers of hell will not conquer it."[50]

Saint Paul was the greatest persecutor of *The Way* for many years, but eventually he too came to the light of Christ. The miraculous conversion for Saul who was transformed into Paul happened on the road to Dimascus. Paul traveled thousands of miles around the Mediterranean writing the New Testament and preaching the good news. Eventually he was beheaded, a quicker and less gruesome death since Paul was a Roman citizen. Likewise, John the Baptist faced the guillotine after baptizing thousands with water in the Jordan River, as he was the messenger of the Lord. John famously issued Christ's entrance into salvation history as he prepared the way of the newborn King. The Baptist was literally served up on a silver platter to Herodias in the sight of Herod, who earlier on was the one seeking to find and kill the baby Jesus.

Then there were martyrs like St. Isaac Jogues who brought the message of Christ to the North American Natives only to be brutally murdered by the Mohawks. However, his works led to the conversion of Indians. Jogues' missionary efforts included reaching the mind and heart of the lovely Kateri Tekakawitha, who took the name Catherine upon her baptism and entrance into the Church. She spread the message of Jesus amongst her own people and ended up dying due to a horrible bout of smallpox. The woman known as the "Lily of the Mohawks," never would have come to faith if Jogues and the other Jesuit martyrs hadn't spread the gospel amongst her tribe just a couple decades earlier.

---

[50] Matthew 16:18

The list goes on and on. The examples of courage and walking by faith in the life of the Saints is profound. Is it comforting to know that many great Saints and disciples of Jesus including the majority of the apostles he chose suffered persecution for their belief? I suppose that is a question each one of us has to answer individually. Similarly, we know the Saints from long ago, as well as fellow believers, and the *everyday Saints* of today face the way of the Cross. Is suffering something you and I want to sign up for? No matter what it is that we endure, despite the hardships and mountains we climb, God is always with us.

The promise remains in the resurrection. The hope is found in the words of St. Paul to the Romans, "We were indeed buried with him through baptism into death, so that, just as Christ was raised from the dead by the glory of the Father, we too might live in the newness of life. For if we have grown into union with him through a death like his, we shall also be united with Him in the resurrection."[51] So is it worth it for you to be a disciple and tread the road of Sainthood? Is it worth it to plod through the darkness in search of the light? The answer to this is clear, yet the path and journey can be extraordinarily difficult. There is a great price to be paid for doing good and spreading love. It seems as if doing so in a world where sharing true joy and a message of hope is needed would be easier and met without such resistance.

Yet, here we are. It has been countercultural from the time of Jesus and remains so to this day. Have full confidence and trust in the promise that Jesus knows and the Father has a great reward waiting for you in Heaven. Saints endure the Cross. They overcome fear by tapping into their faith and they allow the Lord to show them the way as he provides a glorious light. Saints will receive the victorious prize for standing strong in the faith. Jesus said to them, "I am the light of the world. Whoever follows me will not walk in darkness, but will have the light of life." Although you might not see, trust God. Just believe!

---

[51] Romans 6:4-5

Challenge 6

Take some time today to find a quiet place. Ask God to help you to overcome the fear of the unknown and to quell the anxieties of your heart. Listen to what Jesus is saying to you right now. This week, how can you be light to others in your life? In what ways can you aid someone on their journey and share God's love that will undoubtedly impact them. Think about the ways you can embrace the unforeseen a little better. Reflect and pray on the crosses that you are facing in life and how these can be carried in a new way by trusting in God. Remember, he has it under control. Jesus is the Lord of your life and nothing is too heavy for him.

CROSS & RESURRECTION POWER

"Jesus Christ has taken the lead on the way of the Cross.
He has suffered first. He does not drive us toward suffering, but
shares it with us, wanting us to have life and have it
in abundance." – Pope John Paul II

Death & Darkness

The line was wrapped around the block. Inside there were throngs of people sobbing and paying their respects. Jeremy was a man of great stature in the community who had touched many lives. He would surely be missed. The casket would soon be closed and his family would pay their final respects before his dead body was buried six feet under. The cold engraved tombstone bore his name and a line that read, "Until we meet again."

Death is arguably the most difficult part of being human. It causes great pain and often comes with suffering for the person who passes. Not to mention the torment that exists for those who have to say goodbye. When a family member or friend we love is no longer with us here on this planet, we suffer from the loss. Separation and not being able to foster a relationship that mattered greatly is tremendously challenging. With death we can no longer receive love, however we still can give it. Our Lord knew from his early days that he would have to suffer and endure the way of the Cross. It was the price that he set out to pay to conquer death and the grave.

With death there comes darkness, despair, and a great angst of the unknown. But with life there comes light, joy, and great peace. Jesus came to fulfill the law and the prophets. He is the lamb of God who was slain, and he is the Messiah. The promise that is with Christ is powerful and the gift is something each person receives when they believe in the life that exists in him as the Gospel proclaims, "For God so loved the world that he gave his only begotten Son, that whoever believes in him might not perish, but have eternal life."[52] That specific scripture, John 3:16 has been around for the past 20 plus centuries and it's alive today because Jesus lives. It has been read and known by millions throughout history.

Whether people believe this life giving promise and truth or whether they have a relationship with the Lord is a matter of personal choice. However, there is a way to get from death to life. The Saint next door is the *everyday Saint* who remains faithful, relies on the Lord, and anticipates God's blessings. The person who never stops believing, trusts God's plan even in the messiness, and remains hopeful that a resurrection will occur won't close their heart to Jesus' love. In time the Lord heals them and brings them back to life both here in this world and prepares a seat at the table in the one to come. The words that fill the gospels and the teachings of Jesus give each Saint great hope and pace in the Lord. With it there is light. As the scriptures remind us, "But whoever lives by the truth comes into the light, so that it may be seen plainly that what they have done has been done in the sight of God."[53] This is real hope. When we come to the light and our lives and hearts are illuminated with Christ, everything changes. Even the darkest of nights cannot contain our hearts that burn with love for Jesus and with conviction that we were made for Heaven.

For many people out there, myself included, life has not always been filled with light or this reassuring promise of life forever wrapped in the arms of the Father. Darkness, tragedy, death, and

[52] John 3:16
[53] John 3:21

suffering are all part of the human experience. I recently heard an incredible testimony by a woman named Immaculee Ilibagiza. Growing up in Rwanda, located in east central Africa, life was not easy for her. She had parents who raised her family in the faith. There was tension that Immaculee and her tribe could feel from surrounding clans, but nothing out of the ordinary. However, in 1994 that all changed. The government in Rwanda decided to use propaganda, hatred, and the spread of dissension through the public radio system. This would eventually lead to the genocide in Rwanda where over one million people were brutally killed. Blood shed was everywhere. By the grace of God and as a result of her strong steadfast faith, Immaculee miraculously survived. She credits her faith, devotion to the Virgin Mary, and the power of God's love to be what saved her.

Having been locked in a bathroom for over three months, Immaculee lost nearly half her body weight and was a mere skeleton when she emerged from hiding. Looking like the walking dead is not attractive by any means, yet her spirit soared and her soul glowed. Through it all, Immaculee said she felt the Lord's presence and found her relationship with Jesus, as well as her devotion to the Blessed Mother. Saying 27 rosaries per day and countless Divine Mercy chaplets, as well as reading the bible constantly was where Immaculee found Christ. Or maybe it is fitting to say, Jesus found her and made his home in Immaculee's heart.[54]

It's truly miraculous and shocking to learn of the atrocities that Immaculee and her people faced. Yet, somehow and in some way, she was able to trust and not lose her faith. Actually, Imaculee suggests that this horrific situation is the very reason why she is who she is today. Her suffering led her to Jesus. The greatest agony of her life opened up her aching soul and thirst for the Lord. Maybe, just maybe, Jesus can do the same for you and me. When we are staring the cold hard darkness of life in the eyes, maybe we can start to see Jesus looking at us with tender love and outstretched arms. Like Immaculee, my hope and prayer is that you know that God is with you. He loves you and his almighty power can turn any situation you face around. I would even dare to say, God can take the ugly and the evil of this world and use the people who survived it, like he did with Immaculee, to use

---

[54]Left to Tell, Immaculee Iligabiza

it for the good.

After escaping that horrid situation and coming out of the tiny bathroom where she was stuffed in with countless others who feared for their life, Immaculee was free. The moment she saw the sunshine for the first time in months, she stepped foot into a world that was filled with catastrophic evil. Walking through the massive open graveyard with the sea of bodies scattered on the ground was brutal for her. The slaughtered masses were endless. Immaculee said that she cried for about five minutes and then an intense wave of peace and love filled her heart. Her external body was so frail and barely strong enough to walk. The once athletic and strong girl now looked horrid from the outside. However, deep down within, she was radiating light and beauty. Immaculee knew that God had saved her. She believed and is a witness that the Lord is capable of anything and everything, having spared her of the Holocaust in Rwanda. Her darkest days have been used for years now as a gift and blessing to others. This incredible story is now shared by Immaculee Iligabiza who is truly a living Saint. Listen to the power in her words that she shared at *Seek 21*, a Catholic Conference for young people in January of 2021:

> *What is in your power is how you choose to live your life. What is in your power is to love and give one moment after one moment. If you choose love and kindness, Jesus promises to be with you. He will be with you. Just ask God what is needed today. Take every day as a gift. The most important thing is that I have to be that loving person. I give credit for every blessing to God. No matter what you are going through, remember to reach out to God. Hold onto God. Do not fear. Focus on prayer. Dare to forgive. There is so much joy and so much freedom in Jesus. (Immaculee Ilibagiza, survivor of the Rwandan genocide)[55]*

---

[55] Seek 21, talk by Imaculee Ilibagiza about the Rwandan Genocide

Road to Calvary is a Road to Change

The way of the Cross is arduous to say the least. But what is even more is the power and love on the Cross, this being where true life is found. Jesus knows what we go through and alone understands what we face. Jesus looked the hard in his eyes and he embraced it. His love thirsts for you and he challenges you to take on what is hard. Jesus reminds us to do the hard. That is what the apostles, Saints, and disciples before us have done. Evidently, it is what we too are called to do. Immaculee's witness and my own life experiences remind me that we are tested by fire. Think about what happens when you place an iron rod in the fire. It quickly takes on the properties of the fire and is soon transformed. See, God wants to set your heart aflame with his love. You are transformed by the fire of your life and by the mystery and power of the Cross. When you allow God in, he shapes you into the beautiful creation that you were made for and intended to be. Even if it means making beauty from the ashes. The price that the Lord paid on the Cross was to win victory over death and to pour out his great love for souls.

Yet, we still face our own crosses daily. We endure patient suffering. Despite the heaviness and the challenge, amidst carrying such great weight for years, what I have learned is that through faith and by perseverance we can conquer the darkness. When you and I embrace the suffering and allow the Lord into our lives fully, Jesus will then walk with us. God is there to help us navigate the road that seems uncertain and to provide a way to carry the crosses that life throws our way. After experiencing my own setbacks, depression, doubt, and darkness, God helped me to rise above. By his amazing grace he made a way when there seemed to be no way in my life and Christ continues to do so for many others.

The road of life involves bumps, mountains, and great valleys. It has taught me that suffering has to come to us. It is part of discipleship and it is something that Saints on their road to holiness will endure. Take a moment and look at the Cross. Jesus has his head bending down and he wants to kiss you. Christ has both hands open wide and he wants to embrace you. Our Lord has his heart open, he's ready to receive you. The Lord says, "May they all be one, as you, Father, are in me and I am in you. May they also be one in us, so the world may believe you sent me."[56] We become one with the Lord through our suffering. He penetrates our hearts and enters our souls with great depth and compassion for us in these moments. Recall what Jesus told his followers, "Those who are well do not need a physician, but the sick do." It is when you feel miserable inside and you look at the Cross that you will know what is happening.

Throughout the Gospels there are endless examples of Jesus performing miracles. The interesting thing is that nearly all of them involve people who are sick, deaf, blind, and tormented by unclean spirits. Our Lord was attracted to those who were suffering. He fled to them and desired to be with them during their agony. Jesus did this so much to the point of using his great power to perform miracles. Healing was what Jesus wanted for his hurting people. Jesus was evidently a magnet to those who faced physical, mental, and spiritual pain. Each time we read scripture or hear a homily at mass we can gain at least a small take away from it. However, sometimes there are messages that strike us to the core and leave a lasting impression on our hearts. Recently I heard a homily by pastor Jim Walsh who explained the need for people to trust God in the midst of their pain and suffering even when they can't understand it. The way he unpacked this concept made a ton of sense because he outlined how God is likened to a parent who has a very sick child. Anyone who has a baby that is ill or knows a parent in this horrible situation can understand that there is nothing that will stop the parent from doing anything and everything possible to ensure that their child's health improves. Father Walsh went on to explain human suffering and trusting Jesus in their relationship with God who promises to never stop loving them by saying:

To understand God I think we need analogies. The one I find most useful in life is the analogy of the sick baby. When those babies are sick the parents themselves are hurting because their child is suffering. And they are all over that situation. Their love is infinite for that child. Now, the baby has absolutely no idea this is happening. It is beyond the comprehensive ability of the baby to understand that those parents are all over the situation. They have

---

[56] John 17:21

been giving maximum attention to that baby and its well-being. That is very much like God and us when we are hurting. You know we often ask that question when I am suffering or I am in pain, "Where is God?" Well, it's just like the baby, God is very present to us, but we have a hard time understanding what capacity he is present to us. But he is very much like that parent and is all over the situation and very, very present to us when we are hurting. If you take a look at the bible and take a look at what attracts Jesus, what is he like a magnet to? He is a magnet to those who are hurting. And for Jesus, the magnet goes right there and he heals them. He has moments when he goes to people who are hurting. Those times we are hurting and suffering and wondering where God is, it might be helpful to think about how we experience God in the closest way when we are hurting.

A transformation is going on within you and you are becoming more closely aligned to the Lord. There is great mystery in the Cross and great mystery in suffering, which is shaping your heart and inviting you to draw closer to Jesus. It is counter intuitive and unwanted, yet there is ultimate beauty in the reliance on God. His presence in your life and asking the Father to be by your side is marvelous. He wants to be there for us and desires us to be there for others, as they endure their own crosses in life. Suffering, pain, sorrow, humiliation, feelings of loneliness, are all the kisses of Jesus. They are a sign that you have to come so close that he can kiss you. This is because amidst the brokenness and the pain, the Lord is ready to heal you and to make you whole again. Sometimes this healing process happens in this world and lifetime. Perhaps people will fully recover. However, at other times it doesn't occur until after death. For all of us, when we pass from this world, as children of God, we are clothed in Christ. Our baptism makes us his heirs and as his children we too shall enjoy eternal redemption. St. Paul reminds us in his second letter to Timothy that our Lord promised, "If we suffer, we shall also reign with him...He remains faithful for He cannot deny himself."[57] Do you understand this?

Many times we can't fathom how our loving Father would allow

---

[57] 2 Timothy 2:12

us to go through such pain. When you are faced with the worst forecast in life and all odds are stacked against you, it's natural and fair to wonder why God is so far away? We live in an unforgiving world. Horrible things are happening to the nicest and most loving people. If God truly loved us, why would he allow such agony? Frustration, anger, and discontent are real. Life is not some video game where you can simply press the reset button and everything is back to level one again. The circumstances that you and I face in our lives is not fiction, it's the cold hard truth. The long suffering, confusion, and the heartache all feel like a knife being jabbed in your side. How could anyone blame you for walking out or losing faith amidst the chaos and the life draining factors that impact your heart. Life continues to drag you down, tossing you in the muck to and fro. Yet, your heart knows that it must stay connected to the vine. The vine is where life exists. Although everything is out of sorts, the hand dealt daunting, and nothing seems to be going your way, don't disconnect from the vine—Jesus Christ.

This vine of life that was discussed earlier in our journey together is coming up again because not only must we stay connected, but we are called to be the outstretching vine to others who face the Cross. Your brothers and sisters need you—the Saint next door, as their lifeline. Jesus said to his disciples, "Remain in me, as I remain in you. Just as a branch cannot bear fruit on its own unless it remains on the vine, so neither can you unless you remain in me."[58] Disconnection from the vine leads to our own loss of life. The spiritual energy that is within us dies out when we aren't receiving the life-giving nutrients of faith, most importantly a personal relationship with the Lord. Jesus then asks us to take it a step further by calling us to "go out and bear fruit that will remain."[59]

Forget doing the works of God if we are not fused to his heart and the vine of love. Instead of walking out on God during the hard moments, allow your faith to take a deeper root and stir up that mustard seed of faith because it will often be what gets you through. Tough times and defeat cannot turn to enjoyment and a purpose-driven life without keeping the reason at the forefront of all that you

---

[58] John 15:4-5
[59] John 15:16

do. Leading people to Christ has to be at the core. Jesus himself said, "I am the vine, you are the branches. Whoever remains in me and I in him will bear much fruit, because without me you can do nothing."[60] Without God we are dead and incapable. With the Lord in our lives we not only have a heartbeat, but we have hope and potential to be fully alive. When our hearts burn for Jesus and we are fully alive it is the most attractive thing possible for others who are drawn to us because of the spirit of God that lives in us.

Success is extremely attractive. Everyone desires to be on top. People define their lives by it, yet very few are truly willing to put in every ounce of effort and sacrifice to lay down their life to obtain it. Rising and grinding every day is what often sets successful people apart from those who merely wish or want things to happen. As a kid growing up, I had a number of heroes. One of them happened to be Superman with a basketball in his hand. Wearing that number 23 jersey, while cheering on the greatest player of all time in Michael Jordan, is something I will always remember. As a man of faith, it's certainly not about the stardom, the MVPs, or even the championship rings MJ won. It's all about his relentless approach. Greatness comes from within and it comes at a price.

Desire is born inside of the person who has a fiery spirit. It's found inside the heart that will not quit no matter what. There are many life lessons that Michael Jordan taught me through his magnificence on the hardwood, but I realize that this happened due to the maximum effort he exuded each game. The motto MJ lived by is something that each of us as disciples of Jesus must strive for especially when we are up against the world at times along our journey. MJ said, "Some people want it to happen, some wish it would happen, others make it happen." In life, you have to make it happen. Striving for holiness and working towards leading others to uncover their own Sainthood requires an unparalleled grit.

The journey to holiness and rising above the seas and storms of life involves the willingness to die to comfortability, familiarity, and easiness. Mental toughness, spiritual fortitude, and a desire to win can be stirred up in the hearts of the faithful and you can be that inspirer. The question is, are you willing to lay down your life for the sake of

---

[60] John 15:5

your relationship with Jesus? Do you desire to know him and serve your Lord by dying to yourself daily so you can become everything he created you to be? If you are willing to do this you will struggle and in that pain, beauty will be born. What is gorgeous about the champion and what attracts us to them is that they gave it all away so that they could have what they deeply desired.

Forget not that death—losing one's life by putting it completely in the hands of the Lord leads to the sure set resurrection. We will experience Friday moments that are unforeseen, some might even appear to be unbearable, but we are conquerors. This is the Friday that we actually choose to enter. In doing so, we forge through and blaze a victory trail that leads us one step closer to where we are meant to be—in love with the Lord and connected to his Sacred Heart. This example we can set as disciples and this lead is the way to usher our fellow brothers and sisters into God's loving arms. In order to do this and to be an instrument of salvation we must allow God to love us in our vulnerability and weakness. Through humbling ourselves and embracing the pain we then can rely fully on the Lord who makes us strong. Jesus promises us each day that he has our back.

There is a common phrase that carries great weight but is actually an uncommon way of living. When it comes to rising above the Friday moments and getting to Sunday we have to tap into the "I got you" mojo. Real growth happens within the struggle as long as we don't run away. So often we need our fellow *everyday Saints* to provide a shoulder to lean on for strength so we can keep going a little bit further. Life is about dying to yourself in the moment you are in, to rise above and get to where you desire to be. It's about dying to yourself and saying "yes" to Jesus when he appears to you in the face of your brother or sister who needs love even when you are too busy, unsure, and uncertain how you will help them with what they are facing. In time we make it and our strength is used as a blessing that is poured out onto others. It's only in surrendering fully and in your weakness, that the toughest battles you fight, especially those in the desert can be won. Never forget that the Lord tells us to take his hand because he promises to lighten the load and to guide us through the storms. God gets us past the rising tides as long as we keep carrying the cross with great faith. And then he asks us to do the same for others.

As Saints we are called to grow the vine and connect others by branching out to them to draw them into the heart of Christ and to our Father. It can be easy to unplug from Jesus during tumultuous times and to shut out God completely when facing turbulence when things are tough. The road of faith will include desert moments and potentially a feeling of abandonment or darkness that even great Saints like Mother Teresa faced. We even know that Jesus faced agony in the garden of which we will address together momentarily. But even when we are mad, angry, and disappointed in the Lord or with life, we must allow the flame of faith to at least flicker. So long as there is but a single ember remaining lit in your heart, the fire burning within you can carry you through the darkness and become fully ignited once again to blaze a renewed path with Jesus in your life. In the middle of it all—the weight of the Cross there is grace and love. My prayer is that the resurrection power of Christ will always keep us connected to the Lord because the vine nourishes our souls, feeds us with his love, and fills our spirit in time with restored hope for a full and abundant life! Hearts aflame then continue to stoke the fire inside of people like you and me with the wood of the cross. Suffering becomes the way we actually come closest to Jesus and are united with his wounded Sacred Heart as we traverse the road of Sainthood.

Brothers and sisters, the anguish, pain, humiliation, and the crosses you face all lead you one step closer to Jesus. If you allow grace to flow through, these unprecedented moments can be what draw us to him because in these times we need Christ even more. He thirsts for your heart and longs to take away all that is causing pain. When we draw near and lay it down at the foot of the Cross, this is when we feel the tender and merciful love of Jesus in a beneficent manner. Christ consoles us and wraps us in his warm arms just as we are. Father Michael Gaitley reminds us that, "At the times you come so close to Jesus on the Cross that he can kiss you, that suffering has to come that came in the life of Our Lady, that came in the life of Jesus. It has to come in our life also. Only never put on a long face. Suffering is a gift from God. It is between you and Jesus alone inside."[61]

When I think about these words and accept them in my heart, especially while enduring suffering and pain I know that I can make

---

[61] 33 Days To Morning Glory (Fr. Michael Gaitley)

it through. Carrying my own cross is one thing, but as Saints we are called to help carry the crosses of others as well. When shouldering the load with unwavering faith is hard, keep on going. Specifically when walking with those suffering in my inner circle, it might not always make sense. However, when I am in the turmoil of my own life or I enter into the hurt which is so deep with my brother or sister, it is in these moments that I get on my knees and pray harder than ever before. It is as if the human soul knows that only God can relieve that pain. As the scripture says in the book of Proverbs, "Hope deferred makes the heart sick, but a longing fulfilled is a tree of life."[62] Our Lord embraced the tree and in doing so he opened up the gates of resurrection. After all, is not Jesus the way, the truth and the life? Recently I was praying for a family member who was going through a lot. They were on my mind as I read about suffering and the Cross. I wasn't sure how they would make it through or if they would survive. However I could find continued rest in the hope of eternal life. That promise is there and will not go away. Meanwhile, I still can have trouble. But when I read this prayer by Father Gaitley it began to calm my restless heart...

Come Holy Spirit, living in Mary, bring me face to face
with the love in the heart of Jesus crucified.

Can there be a resurrection if one does not die? Contemplate the Lord's path from the journey, well before birth. He is inside Mary's womb awaiting to be born into the world in a manger. Birthed as a babe with the smelly animals and in an era with a king who wanted to murder the Christ child, Jesus arrived on the scene. He was the poor son of a carpenter and was discredited by all the Jewish Saducees and Pharisees. Our Lord faced agony in the garden before being betrayed by his followers and then was handed over to crucifixion and death. If the story ended there what a great loss that would have been. But we all know that is not how it ends. Jesus rose again and so will you and I. We will experience the power of resurrection in this life and in the one to come! You will inevitably face the Cross, but in Christ, through his power and grace you too will conquer the grave and be brought into the newness of life!

---

[62] Proverbs 13:12

Friday Moments Come Before the Rise

At times the mountain seems too tall that we are up against. You and I can face situations that are unimaginable to endure. Life is not fair and can be agonizing. How can an all powerful and all loving God allow for this to happen to you again? Why me, we ask. Why now? Why is my life crashing down on me? When will it stop? Will it ever? What did I do to deserve this? How can this be? What I have come to understand is that life contains *Friday moments.* Some of those *Friday moments* are manageable, while others seem like we will never be able to overcome them. Jesus faced Friday just like you and me. He even asked the Father to "allow this cup to pass, not my will but yours be done."[63]

Christ was whipped and scourged. They mocked him and put a crown of thorns on his head. Our Lord was forced to carry his Cross for miles and was exhausted. He fell to his knees, boom... and then Jesus fell again. He needed help from a poor man named Simon of Cyrene. After dragging that heavy wooden Cross for miles, Jesus was nailed to the tree. Spikes were driven into his hands and his feet. He hung there as the flesh was ripping out of his body and blood poured out of his limbs. Jesus endured mockery, buffets, and spitting. Finally, they struck him with a sword that pierced his side and life ceased. Friday was doomsday. Death knocked at the Lord's door and he felt its sting. The *Friday moment* in Jesus' life was a horrifying, excruciating, evil, and awful day. What *Friday moment* are you facing? What *Friday moments* have you faced? The pain is real, death is real. Darkness came to Christ and to the world at the three o'clock hour when our Lord passed and the veil of the temple was torn. The ground shook and the powers of Heaven seemed to be in the works. *Friday moments* are real. Those days and periods of life exist. But Friday leads to Sunday and for the faithful followers of Christ, we know Sunday means redemption!

See, in life we are going to face *Friday moments*, but remember that this is not the end. If the story ended with Friday for Jesus, all of that pain, suffering, agony, and sacrifice would have been for nothing. The good news of the Gospel and the good news for you and I is that

---

[63] Matthew 26:39

the story did not and does not end there. We are stretched and tested in life, as Jesus was tested. There are *Friday moments* and desert moments like the Lord experienced. He endured this way before his passion and crucifixion being in the desert for 40 days. At the end, the Devil tempted Jesus, but he did not give in as it says, "Then Jesus was led by the Spirit into the desert to be tempted by the devil. He fasted for forty days and forty nights, and afterwards he was hungry. The tempter approached and said to him, "If you are the Son of God, command that these stones become loaves of bread."

He said in reply, "It is written: 'One does not live by bread alone, but by every word that comes forth from the mouth of God.'"[64]

Friday moments are like a bow and arrow. The more torque, tension, or strain, the more power that exists. The more we are pulled back, the further we can and will be launched into a new direction. The potential energy that exists there is massive! Jesus had to endure the Cross so he could conquer the grave. He had to die and descend into hell to triumph over death and lead us to everlasting life! Whether your *Friday moments* come via a storm and a raging sea or maybe they are due to a poor choice, regardless of the circumstance or who is to blame, it's important to believe that redemption is possible.

Sometimes *Friday moments* are in the form of an unexpected diagnosis with your health, a horrific event that happens within your family or by means of temptation. You must be ready and be well equipped for the battle, putting on the Lord and calling on him for help. Life is full of trials and difficulties. However, God can and does make beauty from the ashes. This I believe. What say you? Do you believe the Lord is capable of turning your life around? Faith is the component you have to tap into. Turn it all over to the Lord and lay it down at the foot of his Cross. This is the very reason why he paid the ultimate price. The greatest sacrifice and holy moment was the victory won on that rugged Cross. God is calling the Saint in you to believe this and to receive his abundant grace and mercy. Saint Bonaventure who was a great spiritual writer and is the so-called second founder of the Franciscan order reflected on the sufferings of Jesus on the Cross splendidly. In Bonaventure's Soliloquy he wrote:

---

[64] Matthew 4:2-4

For Friday,
Christ on the cross bows his head,
Waiting for you,
That he may kiss you;
His arms are outstretched,
That he may embrace you;
His hands are open,
That he may enrich you;
His body spread out,
That he may give himself totally;
His feet are nailed,
That he may stay there;
His side is open for you,
That he may let you enter there.

Waiting in the Tomb

Friday moments, like those endured by our Lord, actually lead to death. Our lives can be totally upended in the blink of an eye. How often do you see other people being crushed by life? All that is good can be destroyed just like that and we are left to feel completely empty, both physically and spiritually. However, it's important to remember this is not the end—death does not win. We must have faith and cling to the hope that Sunday is coming. Yet, for now, we enter the tomb and we wait. After our Lord breathed his last, they laid Jesus' body in the Tomb and Mary wept. A moment before Jesus gave up his spirit He said, "It is finished." He finished it. The torment and suffering, the darkness and agony would no longer be able to hold victory over the Lord any longer. Death could not prevail and the gates of Heaven for all believers—the Saints, would soon be opened. Jesus did this so that we always could have another opportunity, another chance, and another way. Our Lord triumphed over the grave so that you and I could rise from the graves of life. He resurrected to bring hope and life into our lives. Christ is the living testimony as he said to his followers, "I am the resurrection and the life. He who believes in me, though he may die, he shall live."[65] This promise from the Lord was made so that we would not only have life to the fullest here on earth, but forever in the world to come.

Remember that you do not live for a Kingdom of this world. Day by day as you wait and call upon the Lord, he is refining you. The Lord is taking your setbacks and working on them in the Heavens. He is about to turn those trials you are facing into set-ups for a brighter tomorrow. As Saint Paul radically proclaimed, "But our citizenship* is in Heaven, and from it we also await a savior, the Lord Jesus Christ."[66] Paul was shipwrecked, abandoned, tortured, and put in prison. Yet all the while he stayed the course and understood that even death could not have victory over him. He believed and I ask you, do you believe that you can do all things through the Lord who provides strength? All you have to do is call on the name of the Lord. Jesus promised he would be there with you and not leave you or forsake you. He promised and did send us the Holy Spirit, our advocate, to help us. The spirit is here, teaching us, and guiding us through all things.

You are never alone and God's promise of life in Christ will overcome any *Friday moment* even when the wait in the tomb of life is a long one. Keep the faith, you must believe and continue to carry that cross. The resurrection is coming. I encourage you to rest and hold onto these words when times are uncertain and life gets tough. But don't merely read them, believe them. Pray over them and trust God because your faith in Jesus will save you from your darkest hour. The scripture says, "Trust in the LORD with all your heart, on your own intelligence do not rely. In all your ways be mindful of him, and he will make straight your paths."[67] The waiting that exists does something to our hearts. It provides a space for us to continue to hope. Actually, the promise of the resurrection—Easter morning, gives us the ability to cling onto new life and all of its potential and possibilities.

Pope Francis continues to emphasize that the human person is indeed born into a sinful world. Yet that sin, which leads to separation from God and eventually death, has no power over those who believe

---

[65] John 11:25

[66] Philippians 3:20

[67] Proverbs 3:5-6

in Christ. That's because through the glorious resurrection, hope remains as new life exists. Inevitably, the grave is a place where life is sealed off. This happens to all people and when we are alive we often have stones that block our hearts from receiving love. The power of Jesus is that he rolls away those stones so that we might run to him like the women did on Easter morning.

By running to the Lord our hearts are opened to his love. This allows Jesus to enter in. When we enter, we might have an experience at first, like Mary of Magdala and the disciples, who entered the tomb only to find it unoccupied. But the good news is that death no longer has occupancy, instead vacancy exists. Jesus lives in the person who believes, as they trust him and rest in the hope of the newness of life. Pope Francis emphasizes that hope is what each human person needs and that is what life and the resurrection of Jesus provides. The holy Father elected to the See of Saint Peter in 2013 said:

> *On Easter we acquire a fundamental right that can never be taken away from us: the right to hope...Jesus plants in our hearts the conviction that God is able to make everything work unto good, because even from the grave he brings life. The grave is the place where no one who enters ever leaves. But Jesus emerged for us; he rose for us, to bring life where there was death, to begin a new story in the very place where a stone had been placed. He who rolled away the stone that sealed the entrance of the tomb can also remove the stones in our hearts...God is faithful. He did not abandon us; he visited us and entered into our situations of pain, anguish, and death. His light dispelled the darkness of the tomb: today he wants that light to penetrate even the darkest corners of our lives...Even if in your heart you have buried hope, do not give up: God is greater. Darkness and death do not have the last word...And whatever sadness may dwell in us, we will be strengthened in hope, since with you the Cross leads to the resurrection, because you are with us in the darkness of our nights; you are certainty amid our uncertainties, the word that speaks in our silence, and nothing can ever rob us of the love you have for us.[68]*

---

[68] Pope Francis, The Right to Hope.

So let us have the patience to wait out the hard moments in life and cling onto the hope that remains ahead. I had a friend named Ady who used to say something so simple, yet so true. A few words he would share with me when I was going through some difficult times, "This too shall pass." There is great power in the "*Now.*" The present moment might be one that finds us in discomfort, but it will not last forever and in most cases will be over soon as long as we endure. Chances are we will learn something from it, even if nothing other than how to dig deeper and remain hopeful. Better days are coming and are just over the horizon. Surely, the power of the Cross would have no merit at all if what took place on Good Friday, namely with the passion and death of the Lord, ended there. We don't have to look far to experience this rebirth or resurrection power in our lives.

Nature speaks of this quite exquisitely. Every fall, the trees die, animals go into hibernation, and the darkness literally settles in over the land. However, we know that spring will be here in a matter of months. Flowers will blossom, buds will emerge on the trees, and the cheerful chirping of birds will fill the crisp morning air. The grasses of the fields turn from brown to green. The sun comes back out again, warming the earth and providing extended days as we enjoy the natural light. What was once dead and gone, dismal and dark, no longer occupies our physical realm. So it is true for us because we receive this gift of life that comes naturally on this planet amidst God's creation. And far more powerfully, this promise exists in the hearts of those who believe. Hope exists where there is life. A life found in Christ is the greatest gift because in him we no longer are dead, but are fully alive!

Sunday: A Time for Resurrection & Redemption

Friday came and the Lord died. Saturday was another day to wait in the tomb. Sunday morning the twelve and all of Jesus' disciples, including our Lord's mother, woke up saddened. However, little did they know that their sorrow would soon turn to the purest joy! Mary of Magdala went to the tomb early that morning and it was empty. She did not know that Jesus had won victory, but soon after arriving the angels told Mary that the Lord was not there. Christ had risen! Without the Cross and death there could have been no resurrection and newness of life would be impossible. This reminds us that without the pain and the suffering, there would be no glory or eternal reward. Your resurrection is soon at hand and your day of redemption is around the corner. I encourage you to embrace the hardship and *Friday Moments* when they come. Saints are the faithful followers that despite the Cross and its great weight know that it's part of the journey. Most importantly, Saints believe the Cross is not the end, in actuality it is only the beginning! You don't carry your cross alone. Jesus himself cried out, "Eloi Eloi lama sabachthani," translated to mean, "My God my God, why have you abandoned me?" We must believe that God will never leave us or forsake us.

Jesus conquered the grave once and for all. Our Lord lived out the truth and is the resurrection and the life. Never forget his words that are seared into the human heart, "I came so that they might have life and have it more abundantly."[69] Your God knows how your story ends. Jesus not only wants you to be victorious, he wants you to triumph. The Lord desires that you are filled with life here on earth. You are an overcomer and the same power that rose Jesus from the grave is within you. After all, numerous times he said, "Behold I make all things new."[70] You always have another chance with Christ in your life. It is never over until your final hour and even then that is when I believe you and I will experience his love to the fullest magnitude forever. Understand that they went to the tomb and it was empty because the suffering and death was done. How could this be? As the great Psalmist wrote, "Weeping may endure for a night, but joy comes in the morning."[71] Only the Lord can do this in our lives. When you allow him in and unlock the door of your heart, his mercy will flood you with everything you need. God's power will upend any *Friday moment* you face as his love and grace can override any situation.

It saddens me to think that the toughest *Friday moment* and Cross I personally endured almost ended my life. However, I overcame it because the Lord's power has no limit. As a man who is striving to be

---

[69] John 10:10
[70] Revelation 21:5
[71] Psalm 30:5

a Saint for the Kingdom, I understand that you and I are called to holiness. I am inspired by people like you for all you endure. I pray that you too will be able to brag on the Lord someday soon for all his goodness and mercy. I hope you will come to a point when you can share the miraculous power of Jesus in your life and the ways in which you overcame the *Friday moments* as a witness to others. Why we face the Cross in our lives is hard to understand, but God can cause a 180 turn on any hardship or difficulty you are up against. I encourage you when the opportunity comes and God speaks to your heart that you are able to share your story. There is great power in sharing our crosses. Being vulnerable and willing to open up to others is life-giving to those who ache. What God has done in your life is sometimes exactly what others need during their time of challenge. Your witness is immense and you are the "light of the world" and "the salt of the earth."[72]

As we continue on in this journey toward Sainthood together, let's shine our light before others and always know we do not walk this road alone. Our answer is one prayer away. Be moved by God's love in your life. Remember that nothing great comes easy and that when we grow in our faith we often do so by enduring struggle. We may fall and even fall often, but we can always rise again with God's help. Be determined and be relentless. When Friday knocks, keep your eyes on Sunday and the resurrection.

You and I are constantly in perpetual bloom. Like a perennial flower, once the seed of faith has been planted in our hearts, we grow, we blossom, and then we die. Again, we come back to life through renewed cultivation, another beautiful blossom opening as we have "spring moments" throughout the journey of life. We then radiate a new elegance before the cycle occurs all over again. This process is ongoing and it's good because we remain a blooming flower. We might even retain the same outward appearance in size, color and shape, but we become more firmly planted, as our roots submerge deeper into the earth. Like a photograph where the picture doesn't change, but the people inside of them do, our outward selves transmit increased vibrance and allure. That's because beauty radiates from within us and attracts more people to us who desire to be pollinated

[72] Matthew 5:13-14

with the life force and positive energy that we emit.

Love and redemption courses through our being, giving off a pungent fragrance, our lives becoming a most pleasing aroma that leaves people wanting to remain there just like we do when we smell something so glorious being stimulated in mind, body, and soul. The fact is that you are loved and God's grace will supply your every need. Stay the course, finish the race and "do not grow tired of doing good, for in due time you shall reap the harvest if you do not give up."[73] You might die and these deaths will always lead to renewed life so long as you keep hope and faith alive. God bless you and may the resurrection of our Lord Jesus Christ empower you to conquer the Cross and walk humbly with your God. It's not about how you start, but all about how you finish!

Challenge 7

Take some time to think about the struggles of life. What crosses are you facing or what hardship exists for people you love dearly? Now, pray that God will be with you and that he is present to those you care about so deeply. Go and be with the Lord in the chapel before the Blessed Sacrament. Realize that you are a flower ready to be re-rooted and blossom again. Give God the burdens and troubles of your life that have led you feeling dead inside. Sit in his presence and allow his healing love and outstretched arms from the Cross comfort you. Allow Jesus to embrace you. Recall the power of his resurrection and his promise, that you too will rise. We can do hard things and God will help us to be victorious no matter how challenging our road might be. Resurrection power is coming your way!

---

[73] Galatians 6:9

PERFECTLY IMPERFECT
CHAPTER 8

*"If everything is imperfect in this imperfect world,
love is most perfect in its perfect imperfection."*
– Gunar Bjornstrand

New Mentality

God is pleased by our progress, not our perfection. We need a new mentality. When we dare to let down our guard and invite the Lord in, we grow in holiness. If we can keep fighting our battles and learn to forgive then we are really on an accelerated path to Sainthood. Like many people, I am my toughest critic. This is not a bad thing because when a person cares about life and the direction in which they are going it motivates them to be better. When a downfall bothers us it is a good thing since the outcome matters. It isn't easy to make mistake after mistake or have certain things in life that are out of our control, unable to be changed. What is even more difficult is to come to terms with the fact that the hurts we have imposed on ourselves or others, the sins we have committed, and the errors we have done throughout our life cannot be erased.

Wounds can heal, but scars remain. Pain and negativity can flood our minds like fierce rapids that tear up a river. At a moment's notice we are left overwhelmed and angry. If we are not careful, we can find ourselves in a polarizing vortex spiraling downward and caught up in the mire of depression. It is beneficial to be a critic when we use it as a catalyst to motivate ourselves to grow and improve. It serves as a positive asset when we reflect truthfully and stay humble. As Saint Augustine said, "This is the very perfection of a man, to find out his own imperfections." Humility is key, yet simultaneously, we must remain hungry to foster faithfulness to our Lord.

Forgiveness is the X-factor element in the equation when it comes to realizing that perfection is not a standard nor should it ever be. Greatness is something we all can strive for and being our personal best must be what our aim is. However, no one will ever be perfect no matter how hard they try. God's grace though and his forgiveness allows you to go beyond the wounds, the scars, the mistakes, and the hurts of life and to be human. Part of the road to holiness is embracing your own human nature and understanding that flaws, insufficiencies, and limitations make us, they don't break us. In the beginning we touched on St. Thérèse of Lisieux and her "little way" because the lower we become and the tinier we realize as a human being in this great cosmos that we are, the more dependent on God we must be. Humility stems from dependence. St. Thérèse of Lisieux embraced her littleness in order to enter into God's greatness. She understood that when we are able to lower ourselves to the point of full dependence on the Lord then God's limitless power will elevate us up the staircase of holiness. When reflecting on her life and becoming totally reliant on God, Father Michael Gaitley explained that during our own quest to Sainthood we must take notice of God's merciful love. The great priest and author said, "Like water, it [merciful love] rushes to the lowest place—and Thérèse knew this. Therefore, she saw her humility, that is, her awareness of her littleness that attracted God's merciful love." This great Saint of the church believed that God would fill her little soul with his great love and would make it overflow with tremendous abundance.

This actually makes us far better and helps us grow in holiness because in our weakness we are filled with God's almighty strength. What ends up happening is we no longer rely on ourselves, but we have no other choice than to fully let go and let God. Our imperfections and humanity is taken by the Father and he transforms us. The Lord shapes our hearts and draws out the Saint within us as we become in a sense spiritual beings living in a human realm. Being patient, losing control, and most importantly forgiving yourself and others is imperative.

God Looks for Imperfect Saints

The Saints of the Church were perfectly imperfect as well. There is no better way to describe them than that. This is great news! Well, I will speak for myself. I don't know about you, but I feel fortunate that I don't have to be perfect to make an impact on the world and to become a Saint. God does not care about perfection. It is all about perseverance and forgiveness. When we learn to be truthful, admit our wrong doings and then forgive ourselves it does something monumental. Inside of us, we grow. Our faith explodes and our love meter goes off the charts. What I mean is that people who learn to forgive themselves, who are humble enough to realize their sinfulness, and then ask God for a new start, will excel in discipleship. Think about it for a moment. When was the last time you asked for forgiveness? When in the past did you forgive yourself and accept God's forgiveness? Now, when was the occasion where you last asked someone else for their forgiveness? We must stop thinking of the sacrament of reconciliation (confession) as the penalty box. Jesus doesn't want you to hold onto your sins nor does he want us to hold onto the wrongdoings of others. Forgiveness sets us free and takes a great weight off your back. The Lord never intended for anyone to travel with a fifty pound sack on their back, constantly being weighed down during the journey. Sometimes we have to take that thing off daily, but over the course of time as our merciful Lord works on our imperfect hearts, the excess layers are chipped away and discarded. Out of the block the divine sculptor carves us, shaping you and me into the beautiful masterpiece he saw all along.

As a result of being forgiven and accepting the grace that flows from it, we have hearts that can expand and are able to bring forgiveness to others. This type of love is radical because it goes against the norm. Uncommon love changes lives. Hearts turn from broken to healed and in time Christ is revealed. I am willing to bet since you know how powerful forgiveness can be in the human experience, you then can start to perceive how perfection is not a characteristic or requirement for holiness. Perfection is not a must for Sainthood. Instead, your daily effort, mixed with accepting God's grace is. Effort and grace is where progress exists. Just imagine how things would radically change if we focused on being simply 1% better every day. God's beauty evidently shines best through the process.

I would go so far to argue that forgiveness is absolutely one beautiful way we grow in holiness. In scripture there are many parables and events recorded where Jesus taught forgiveness. Many of us are familiar with the story of the woman caught in adultery and how Jesus said, "He who is without sin, let him cast the first stone..."[74]

She was surrounded by a crowd of people. They were like sharks ready to tear her to pieces, everyone staring her down. The woman's face was flushed red and her guilt was oozing out of her pours. The eyes of the crowd that wanted to pummel her for breaking the law were vengeful. Their stare pierced her soul like a razor blade. The woman who seemed to wear the scarlet letter on her chest, understood the weight of her sin and felt great shame. There was nowhere to go, although she wished she could hide. So what was she to do? It didn't matter that she was truly sorry and desired forgiveness. Mercy was not an option amongst the stirred up crowd. The woman's life flashed before her eyes as she waited for the rocks to be hurled at her. Complete strangers and those who knew her grew angrier by the second. Each person picked up large rocks to do her in. Consequently, she deserved it. Death by stoning was normal for the grave sin of adultery.

All of a sudden, there were murmurings among the crowd. From a distance they could see someone approaching the circle. It was a man. He walked up to the crowd calmly meandering his way through. Maneuvering around the bystanders, this bearded figure pushed people aside and entered the circle. What was he doing? The man saw all those gathered with the stones in their hands gripped with intensity. They certainly were ready to fire them at her. Picture this scene now. Just imagine, Jesus is there and he is witnessing the young

---

[74] John 8:7

girl paralyzed by fear. She is clenching her teeth and covering her face being mere seconds away from a death sentence. Jesus utters a one sentence sermon that rocks their world and one by one stones are dropped. The massive crowd that had gathered out of hate was taught a profound message of love. Hearts began to be changed that day as the seed of forgiveness and its prolific force set in. Every single one of the accusers and those joining in on the condemnation who were circled around the adulteress realized they were also in need of forgiveness. At the end of the day, who isn't?

The next words Jesus speaks is one on one with the woman. Everyone else is gone. The girl must be thankful to have her life spared. Who is this man? How did this all happen? She was in sheer disbelief. A minute prior she had been preparing to die. Now, by the grace of the Son of God himself, she was not only physically alive but her spirit was restored. Jesus scribbled some words in the dirt and then asked the girl, "Woman, where are they? Has no one condemned you?"

She replied, "No one, sir."

So Jesus calmly said to her, "Neither do I condemn you. Go, [and] from now on do not sin anymore."[75] This is a prime example of how forgiveness is applicable to every person and in every situation. No matter how grave the sin might be or how dark the path that was taken, God always is able to bring us back into the light. Merciful love and Jesus go hand in hand. That's exactly why our perfect Lord hangs out with us, the imperfect.

Watering Your Soul

Another story that comes to mind that is extremely powerful is the event that happened between our Lord and the woman at the well. During the time of Jesus, Jews and Samaritans did not even walk on the same side of the street. It was unheard of for there to be an interaction between the men of these clans, let alone for a Jewish man to have an encounter with a woman from Samaria and speak openly to her. So why did Jesus do this? Why did he decide to break the

---

[75] John 8:10-11

cultural norms of his day at that well in Sychar? It's intriguing to ponder why our Lord took such a large risk and why he decided to continue to break the barriers of life so often throughout his time on earth? Rebel and revolutionary they would deem him on Good Friday and in the greatest sense I suppose he was. Pejorative terms made into holy outcomes. It reminds me of this powerful phrase, "Won't he do it!" Still we question God's actions and capabilities.

Maybe Jesus bucks the systems of life and crosses the grain of culture because he was always searching to show people a better way. Without a doubt, that better way was filled with love and he showed primarily that love often comes in the form of forgiveness. After all he is *the way*. There she was going to gather water in her cistern for her family to drink. The Lord approaches the woman after a long journey and asks if she would draw some water for him. She is shocked that this Jew asks her, a Samaritan, this. Her bewilderment continues when she notices that Jesus doesn't even have a bucket to put water in. However, Jesus knew what he was doing all along. It was not about physical water.

For those familiar with this part of the Gospel, you know that the Lord goes on to tell her that he has spiritual water that she can drink. This being the water that the woman and anyone who drinks of it will thirst no longer. Listen to his words, "Jesus answered and said to her, 'Everyone who drinks this water will be thirsty again; but whoever drinks the water I shall give will never thirst; the water I shall give will become in him a spring of water welling up to eternal life.'"[76] What needs to be mentioned here is that Jesus then goes on to ask the woman to call her husband and to return there to the well. The woman doesn't have a husband and tells our Lord this. He then tells her that he knew that she has had many husbands, five actually, and she is amazed thinking that Jesus is a prophet.

Instead of judging the woman, instead of condemning her and writing her off, Jesus does the opposite. He met the Samaritan woman where she was at that place in her life and Christ embraced her pain. Jesus then showers her with his love and invites her into a relationship with him. It is amazing that by the end of this encounter that the woman goes to tell others her experience and that she believes she has

---

[76] John 4:13-14

met the Messiah. Her guilt, shame, sorrow, and distress turns immediately to radical joy! The scripture states, "The woman left her water jar and went into the town and said to the people, 'Come see a man who told me everything I have done. Could he possibly be the Messiah?' They went out of town and came to him."[77]

How could this happen? It shows us that the power of forgiveness and the transformative grace that God alone can provide is what we all need in our lives. It's the Lord's grace and his willingness to continue to meet you where you are that draws you in like the woman at the well. Christ forgiving you and me over and over has to remind us to do the same for our fellow brothers and sisters. I suppose Jesus knew what he was doing when he taught us how to pray by giving us the Lord's prayer. The words "Forgive us our trespasses as we forgive those who trespass against us..."[78] are much more than words; they are the highest act of love. The Samaritan woman went to the well thirsting, however God knew in her heart that she was thirsting for something far more important than physical water. She and Jesus left that day without taking a sip, yet they were fulfilled completely. This demonstrates that grace is able to heal and to bring wholeness to our lives.[79]

Some might be thinking that they are not a Samaritan woman and are probably not going to a well for a drink. Most of us cannot relate to having five spouses in one lifetime either. And yet, even the greatest of all Saints were in need of the power of grace and forgiveness in their lives. God did not ask his apostles, the disciples, or anyone throughout history to be perfect. He certainly is not asking this of you either. All the Lord simply asks is that you follow him, open up your heart to his love, and allow his grace and mercy to flow through you to others. Certainly, no one around the city of Rome was expecting Saul to transform into Paul; to go from the terror of Christians to writing two thirds of the New Testament. St. Matthew was a lying and cheating tax collector who cared only about getting wealthy at the expense of the average Jew in Jerusalem. He went as far as exploiting the poor. His heart was turned from focusing on material wealth to

---

[77] John 4:28-30
[78] Matthew 6:12
[79] John 4

investing in the kingdom. Matthew came into the light because Jesus saw straight through his sinfulness into the hidden treasure buried in the apostle's heart.

There were extraordinary followers of Jesus like Mary Magdalene who was there at the foot of the Cross to witness the Lord's Crucifixion. Then she was the first to experience the resurrection of the Lord on Easter Sunday. Mary became the messenger responsible for going out and spreading the most significant event in salvation history—Jesus had indeed risen.[80] Yet, we tend to forget that most scripture scholars and historians believe that Mary Magdalene had been a prostitute. We know for sure that she was demon possessed, before Christ healed her. Mary of Magdala not only was converted and transformed by the Lord, she followed him closest along with the twelve for his three years of public ministry. She and many others are prime examples of Jesus' powerful words in the Gospel, "For human beings it is impossible, but not for God. All things are possible for God."[81]

Saints Win the Day

God knows your heart and he also understands that no person is too sinful or evil to repair. The only one that cannot be healed is the person who does not want forgiveness. Time after time we see that Jesus can and will do the miraculous. There is a comeback or underdog story for each of us as his Saints. The power of the Lord and his grace working in our lives can radically change the human heart. Through the great healing medicine that we call forgiveness, you can be born anew. Forgiveness is often the first step, but then what? When life is overwhelming Saints keep one thing in mind, win the day. The leg of the race you are running today is what our time and energy go to for each day is sufficient in and of itself.

Winners in life, namely the greatest champions of the faith all have one thing in common, eyes fixed on the prize. Each of them, as well as you and I will stumble and fall throughout our lives. The

---

[80] Matthew 28
[81] Mark 10:27

question is, will we have the wherewithal and the resolve to get back up. If the fighting spirit exists in us and we dust ourselves off, how will we respond? Perseverance is something that the great Saints of long ago and the living ones of today exemplify. The no quit, nothing can stop me attitude is essential. Having the mentality that I will find a way or make a way approach is what it takes. I truly believe that perseverance is the next piece of the puzzle when it comes to holiness as we journey on the road toward Sainthood.

Failure in life is inevitable. Falling down, bumps, and bruises will occur. After all, it happened to Christ. Lest we not forget that he fell on the road to Calvary numerous times. Having courage and ultimately the will to win is something that people like you and me either have or not. In the words of my late Uncle Jim Anderson who now looks down from above, "Deal with it." This phrase packs a serious punch when fostering the grit to take on what life throws our way and reminds us to dig deep. It is more than a motto, it is a lifestyle of Saints because they know no quit and are resilient to keep fighting the good fight of faith.

It really comes down to your *WHY*. When your *why* is big enough you will be able to do hard things and you will make it happen regardless of the cost. So maybe it is time right now to think some more about your *why*. For me there is only one reason that we are on this earth and that comes down to love. Our mission in life no matter who we are, where we are from, and regardless of any differences we have, is to love. This is my why because he (Jesus) is my reason! You and I were created to love others and to be loved. Love is a choice. Love also requires perseverance. On this journey we must never discount or ignore loving ourselves. To fully love others, you have to love yourself first and come to grips with who you truly are.

Our faith points us to the shining star—the gold standard of the Church which is love. Therefore, as children of God, we are ultimately called to share the love of Christ with others by allowing it to flow abundantly from our hearts to everyone we encounter. Not just our friends or family. Not simply those people who are desirable, but everyone, especially the undesirable. Being called to love our Lord and accepting his love allows us the ability to love fully. This quantum jump and growth in faith becomes most noticeable in the situations where our human nature would rather not love, but we do anyway because that is what Jesus would do. Sometimes it isn't about those around us at all and this happens most powerfully when we look at ourselves in the mirror.

Believing that we do play an important role in building up the kingdom is important, but our hearts must be right first. We will discuss the fact that we do not belong to a kingdom of this world later on in the journey together, but for now it is important to stay focused on the *why*. Continue to persevere. Those who do not bail or jump ship are the champions in this life. These are audacious human beings who honestly just keep going. You must stay hungry in this life and be willing to get back up and get through the tough times. It is well worth it. Better days are ahead and we can learn from these difficult experiences. However, there are some things that seem almost impossible to overcome and this is where our faith has to kick into another gear. Earlier on in our journey together we began to discuss the story of the man known as the paralytic in the Gospel. Now we will see how God is speaking to us in another profound way through the events that occurred:

> One day as Jesus was teaching, Pharisees and teachers of the law were sitting there who had come from every village of Galilee and Judea and Jerusalem, and the power of the Lord was with him for healing. And some men brought on a stretcher a man who was paralyzed; they were trying to bring him in and set [him] in his presence. But not finding a way to bring him in because of the crowd, they went up on the roof and lowered him on the stretcher through the tiles* into the middle in front of Jesus. When he saw their faith, He said, "As for you, your sins are forgiven." Then the scribes* and Pharisees began to ask themselves, "Who is this who speaks blasphemies? Who but God alone can forgive sins?" Jesus knew their thoughts and said to them in reply, "What are you thinking in your hearts? Which is easier, to say, 'Your sins are forgiven,' or to say, 'Rise and walk.' But that you may know that the Son of Man has authority on earth to forgive sins"—he said to the man who was paralyzed, "I say to you, rise, pick up your stretcher, and go home." He stood up immediately before

them, picked up what he had been lying on, and went home,
glorifying God. Then astonishment seized them all and they
glorified God, and, struck with awe, they said, "We have seen
incredible things today."[82]

The story of the paralyzed man is one of my favorite stories in the
Gospels for a number of reasons. At first we discussed the importance
of seeking out the Lord. This is a central theme of Sainthood and
discipleship that is extremely important. In hearing the full extent of
the Gospel, a few more things come to mind. First, it is a prime
example of the power of forgiveness. Jesus shows his mercy on the
man, emphasizing that forgiving sins is far more important than even
the healing of a physical ailment. This story also demonstrates to us
that we must show up in life. God could care less about what you are
wearing, your appearance, if you have it together, or any baggage you
carry. What our Lord desires is that you are there and are present. At
times we or someone else in our family or group of friends might be
unable to do something or need that encouragement along the way.
This was on full display with the man's friends who carried the
paralytic not only to where Jesus was, but they then lowered him in
through the roof!

Collaborating with God

When you go out of your own way and put in some significant effort
to seek Christ or help someone in their life, look out because God's
grace will be flowing like you have never seen it flow before.
Something beautiful and profound takes place when we aid others in
life, especially with their journey to come closer to the Lord. A twofold
blessing reigns down from Heaven. God uses us to be a vessel of hope
for the other and he will greatly bless us and turn our situation around
as well. It involves love. It requires forgiveness. Grace is accepted and
shared with people when we are present. Additionally, Jesus saw the
deep faith of the people which moved the Lord to heal the paralytic.
This reinforces the power of our faith and relationship with God.

---

[82] Luke 5:17-26

Perfection is not what he asks of us or expects. He asks that we have faith. When you demonstrate great faith, faith that is so trusting it has the power to move mountains in life and in the lives of others, big things happen. Jesus said, "If you have faith the size of a mustard seed tell this..." and then he went on many times to say, "Whatever you ask for in prayer with faith, you will receive."[83]

Perfectly imperfect is the recipe for discipleship. Unwavering faith and trust in the Lord and his power in our lives is what it takes. Even when you don't see how there could be a way, cling to the fact that Jesus is the way. He is the truth and Christ is the life. The faith we have is built upon the Lord and becomes the bedrock of our lives. It's a firm foundation and we cannot be shaken. So why does Jesus say, "Be perfect just as my Heavenly Father is perfect," to his apostles and his many followers? Is this not contradictory to the imperfect Saint on the road to holiness? I believe that Christ means when we allow God in and have great faith, the Lord's grace does wonders and turns our imperfection into perfect love for him and his people. Love and forgiveness, perseverance and faith are the recipe. As long as you try your best and put forth all you can, God will take care of the rest! Reflect on these words from the book of James, "Blessed is the one who perseveres under trial, for having withstood the test he will receive the crown of life which God has promised to those who love him."[84] Keep going and spread love. In doing so you will never be the same. Love and allow the love of Christ to flow from within you. This is the anthem of the Saint and this is the road to holiness which will change the world!

Perfection is not in the Lord's vocabulary nor will it ever be. When it comes to his expectations of us, God doesn't call us to be perfect. The Lord simply asks that we remain open to him. To be his faithful followers and to come just as we are is true discipleship. He desires your heart. Christ wants all of you including all of your brokenness. Jesus promises to take the fragments of your life, gluing them together as only the great artist can do. God asks that we receive his abundant love and the Lord asks us to try our best. He takes care of the rest. In the words of Ralph Waldo Emerson, "Though we travel the world over

---

[83] Matthew 21:22
[84] James 1:12

to find the beautiful, we must carry it with us, or we find it not." Despite imperfections, there is beauty inside of you that is to be shared with all.

Nearly everyone knows that Mother Teresa had the most beautiful heart to serve and love God's people. What many people don't know is that Mother Teresa battled her own doubt of God's presence in her life. She questioned her inner beauty and Christ's presence in her life. Mother disagreed with the Lord, was upset, and even wondered at times if God existed at all. These things she wrote about in her journal and they articulate her humanity. But no matter what phase of life Mother Teresa was in and no matter how difficult the situation was that God led her into when serving the poor, she brought love. As a result of that love, beauty and joy followed her and was the gift of God to others. We can all learn from this example. The key question is not about where or how you started. It isn't even that important where you are right now. It's truly all about where you are going and how you are going to finish! Where do you want to go and who do you want to be? All of these are important things to ponder and then live out. However, when you can answer this question without hesitation your life will become fulfilled and limitless. Mother Teresa lived this concept out. She asked something profound and when you answer it, your life and the lives of others will change forever: "Will you collaborate with God so he can use you to do his work here on earth?" Just say "yes" to Sainthood. Don't worry, perfection is not required. Show up, Jesus is waiting for you.

Challenge 8

Write down all the things that you dislike about yourself. In what ways are you imperfect? What things have you done in the past that you are still hanging on to? What areas of your life do you want to change? Now, crumple up that piece of paper and throw it into a fire. God is with you right now and he loves your imperfection. You are more than good enough just the way you are. After all, you were made in his image and likeness. Contemplate these words of Dr. Steve Maraboli, "There is nothing more rare, nor more beautiful than being unapologetically yourself, comfortable in perfect imperfection. To me, that is the true essence of beauty." Allow the Lord to work on your heart. Receive God's grace, and be confident that you are beautiful in the eyes of Jesus. Love yourself perfectly so that in an imperfect world, you can love others the way God intended you to.

UNIVERSAL CALL
CHAPTER 9

*"To be Saints is not a privilege for the few,
but a vocation for everyone." – Pope Francis*

Don't Overthink it, Just Follow & Love

The boat rocked back and forth. With each wave that passed, the bow would rise and fall. It was just another ordinary day at sea for the fisherman and his crew. The blazing sun beat down on them like a drum. Mouths began to get salty and hunger was settling in as the day began before sunrise and would conclude just prior to sunset. They hadn't caught too much, but enough to go to market and have a decent dinner feast with choice wine to celebrate Shabbat. What would separate this holy celebration from the others? Did they realize that soon they would cast their nets and be fishing for something far greater than what they were used to? The very next day on that same shore they would follow Jesus. See, following the Lord isn't really that complicated at all. As we read earlier in our journey, Peter, Andrew, James and John did see a miracle when their nets were overspilling with tons of fish, however the biggest point to not overlook is the simplicity of saying "yes" and following.

The stained glass iconography, fantastic relics, and marble statues are not what Sainthood is about. Over the centuries there has been this grave misunderstanding of who a Saint is and what personifies holiness. One will never find an actual Saint inside the walls or next to the pews in an array of beautiful hues that fill the walls of so many churches. The juxtaposition is that the Saints so many people idolize would want nothing to do with the pedestal, fanfare, and idealism. Instead, they, like the first apostles, would want everything to do with being devoted, faith-filled followers. Through their humility, servant nature, and willingness to listen to God they would draw closer to him. We too are asked to give Jesus a daily "yes." *Everyday Saints* love him by loving others, follow even when the path isn't seen, and trust in him.

There are many events, encounters, opportunities, roadblocks, and decisions that must be made during the course of your lifetime. Doors open and others close. This is all part of life. So much is uncertain and oftentimes you are left at the fork in the road wondering what you should do, how you ought to respond, and which path to take. The next move, choice, and action is important. Not only does every decision we make impact ourselves and our future, but it carries great weight and causes a chain of events to unfold for those in our circles. It is evident that the cosmos is connected. There is a deep and profound link, namely a web of connection that runs throughout the universe. If we focus too much on this, we can become overwhelmed with anxiety and can be stuck in our tracks. Calling this all to mind is not to scare you or make you worry. We are not reflecting on such an important part of life in order to be stymied.

Fear certainly can be paralyzing. However, know that your faith and having God by your side provides you with everything that it takes to make crucial life changing decisions in a responsible manner. In this moment, think back about some of the best times that have brought about the most excitement to your life. What were the occasions that come to mind that have given you the greatest joy? Now, take a minute to recall the biggest life happenings that have led you to where you are today. Jot them down and connect all of the dots. If you are like me, there are probably innumerable small decisions that led to larger choices. Mixed with them were people who entered your journey. A door opened and good favor came your way. Another door shut when we least expected it. Then, boom! All of a sudden we can find ourselves in a deep valley that is unexpected. We weave and we turn. We go up and down. We zig and we zag. Two steps forward, one step back. Now you are here. Tomorrow you can be way over there. Whatever your *now* looks like, you have the possibility for change. Despite the forecast of your future due to the present situation, you have new opportunities that await you.

No matter how hard we try, we cannot change the past. I do not say this to upset you, but for you to recognize that both positive and negative events occur. Life experiences are traveled through to get to where you are today. Although this cannot be avoided, amidst all of this, you do have a beautiful chance daily to shape and work collaboratively with God. When you do so, you help pave the path for your own future. The road ahead is full of possibility based on your outlook, attitude, and willingness to remain flexible. The future is unknown, but that is okay as long as you know who holds your future. Life is inevitably a summation of the choices we make over the course of time. I also believe that after reflecting and replaying the joys, sorrows, and major events of our lives, we probably can see how life is similar to a colander. It is important to allow things to flow through us, especially to let go of the negativity and junk that can stick around and disturb our inner peace. Sometimes by looking back we must take the time to strain out what is unnecessary and to collect and then utilize all the good we have been blessed with. Through this meditative recollection of events, we can see that life is quite often more about how we choose to respond to what comes our way. How are we seeing the world and how are we reacting to the people we encounter and events we participate in?

As you and I travel along on this pilgrimage to Sainthood, each of us has a specific mission. We were created for a unique purpose to be carried out because we are God's *everyday Saints*. There is a great call on your life. Sometimes, people search and search, but don't seem to find what it is that God desires them to do. The road to Sainthood and the path to answering God's call really comes down to one word, *love*. *Everyday Saints* live love to their highest capacity regardless of who they are with or what task is at hand. St. Augustine summed it up nicely by saying, "Love and do what you will." After all, Jesus continued to share with the disciples the importance of the two-fold commandment; to love God and love our neighbor. At this point you know fully that love is a powerful word. It is actually a noun and a verb. Jesus is love and when we love or are the recipients of love, we experience God. The Lord's presence is revealed to us in this beautiful love exchange. We come to know him more even though we don't see him fully yet. As it says, "Beloved, if God so loved us, we also must love one another. No one has ever seen God. Yet, if we love one another, God remains in us, and his love is brought to perfection in us."[85]

You know what it feels like. You recognize it when you see it. You enjoy sharing love with others and your soul is satisfied when you encounter Jesus by way of love. Our hearts and our souls need love. Love is a choice. Whether you are thinking about the people that you love, the things that you love, or your love for the Lord, it all comes down to choices. Sometimes it can be really hard to love, as it requires great effort, self-sacrifice, and putting the needs of others before your own. So why all this talk about love and what does it have to do with answering the call of God on the road to Sainthood?

All human beings were made for relationship. Clearly, the God of the universe did not need us, but still chose to give us life. He loves you beyond all measure and wants you to know his love and the love of Christ. In addition, we were made for relationships with one another. But it isn't always easy to love others. The world is filled with evil, terrible situations, and life sucking moments. There are people who commit such grave acts that are hateful. When you love and it is embedded in your DNA you become attractive to others. Then you go and spread love to people, which changes the world. By sharing your love amidst the human community, you essentially love God and share him with all. The answer to the purpose of our lives and the call that God has placed on us as humans comes down to that one simple word, love. And yet, when we love deeply and we enter into a personal relationship with Christ it isn't easy. When you seek to do the Lord's will and to go where he needs you most, it can be the most difficult, arduous, and challenging path.

What you and I must understand is that our "yes," like the yesses uttered by the first apostles and the Saints that came before us, as well

---

[85] 1 John 4:12

as our Blessed Mother, pack such a powerful punch. It fires me up and excites my spirit to no end knowing what God's love can do when fully shared with others. Saint Francis knew this very well. He lived out love throughout his life. Francis was dedicated to being in the presence of God and through his shining example showed how attractive it is to be fully alive. Fullness of life flows from within a person when they allow the wood of the cross of their life to stoke the fire inside of them, as the spirit burns and is ignited with great force. When Jesus lives in you and you allow the Lord's will to flow through you, it is then that you actually become the living will of the Father.

Being the Beautiful Creation You Are

The crazy thing is that we don't have to do much at all, nothing actually. What is required is that we "just be." After all, God himself said, "I am who am."[86] This was the Lord's response to Moses who questioned who Yaweh was. St. Francis shows us that when we are present to God and when we abide in God's love, we are fully who we were created to be. Like the Beatles song goes, "All you need is love." You and I have the ability through God's power and love in our lives to change the world! But it first starts with us accepting who we are and whose image and likeness we were created in. I am a firm believer that nobody is more drawn to people than those that are fully alive. And that comes with being grafted to the vine of life and to God's love that fills our hearts, flowing through us to others.

Some people, maybe many for that matter, might call me crazy. They have the mentality that the world is far too big and has so many problems that we cannot impact everyone. There is no way that we can possibly do enough in the course of our lifetime to impact the eight billion people who span nearly 200 countries across the globe. My challenge to you is to think about how you can impact one person and one life at a time. My challenge to you is instead of thinking about what you can't do, let's get to work on what you can do with what you have. As Hunter S. Thompson put it, "Life should not be a journey to the grave with the intention of arriving safely in a pretty and well

---

[86] Exodus 3:14

preserved body, but rather to skid in broadside in a cloud of smoke, thoroughly used up; totally worn out, and loudly proclaiming, 'Wow! What a ride.'"

If it is not hard and if it doesn't challenge you to some degree, in most cases it is not worth it. Remember, you and I are called to be Saints. We certainly were not put here just to float along and be comfortable. I am not saying we cannot enjoy life. Actually, quite the opposite. There is nothing wrong with eating great food, traveling the globe, taking part in hobbies that bring us happiness, and spending quality time with family and friends. All of this is good. In fact it is very good and we must receive these blessings. What I am saying is that God did not design us or bless us to just exist and be apathetic. No! We are a chosen people and we are set apart. Your destiny is out there and you have a great call to answer. That call is to love and to be a Saint. How you get there and what you do along the way is left to be unlocked. However, it is up to each of us to answer the call by taking the first step. As you know, the first step is often the hardest one. Listen to these compelling words of prayer that articulate why love and giving of ourselves to the Lord is so essential:

> *...a delicate gift of God to me, unworthy. I do not know why he picked me up. I suppose like the people we pick up because they are the most unwanted...this my new vocation has been one prolonged "yes" to God without even a look at the cost...Today his work has grown because it is he, not I, that does this through me. Of this I am convinced that I would give my life gladly to prove it.*[87]

After receiving this message by Mother Teresa, what would you gladly give your life for? What is it that brings you the greatest fulfilment and joy? What or who makes you feel truly whole? Joy is found where love is and God is present in every moment that involves love. Mother Teresa's prayer and her treasured words remind us of this. So if you are truthful with yourself and you go out and love with all you have to offer, your life becomes a living sermon. You are the good news for the world. Sainthood is not about having all the

---

[87] Teresa, Mother. *Come be My Light*, p.6-7

answers. It is not about a perfect life or making no mistakes. Instead, it is all about getting up each day and sharing your love with the world. When you have this mindset and when your heart is focused on loving no matter what the cost, then you and I can and we will change the world.

As you read this you might have some things racing through your mind. Perhaps you begin to think about your career, the time you commit to various activities, and the things you do on a regular basis. You might be reflecting on different relationships from the past and important people in your life. All of this is good and healthy. Remember, what we do is not as important as how we do it. Our attitude, the way we carry ourselves, how we conduct our lives, and the manner in which we treat others speaks volumes to who we are.

When I was in college, I was discerning the priesthood. I did not know what God was calling me to. Back then I thought that the "what" was the most important part of the puzzle. Now, all of these years later I recognize that God's call and answering him is more about *the how*. Love is found in *the how*. Consequently, what we do does make a splash and a difference. The greatest situation is when what we do becomes what we are most passionate about. When this occurs, the "doing" is able to be lived out fully through the *how*—the way in which love is manifested in and through our lives. For me, *the how* is at the heart of Sainthood. When your life is over and you breathe your last, will it matter what you did if you didn't do it with love? Paul writes in his letter to the Corinthians, "If I have all faith so as to move mountains but do not have love, I am nothing...So faith, hope, love remain, these three; but the greatest of these is love."[88]

No matter what you do in your profession, *the how* applies to each of us because that matters most! As Maya Angelou so beautifully put it, "People will never forget how you made them feel." Love lasts and it is irreplaceable. It gives great hope to everyone we encounter. It provides comfort. Love warms the human heart and connects two people in a profound manner, even strangers. Love tears down the walls of hatred and flips animosity on its head. Love puts out fires of evil and brings enemies together. Love wins and love is *the how*. When Jesus told his disciples, "Come follow me and I will make you fishers

---

[88] 1 Corinthians 13: 2 &13

of men," this was *the how*. The way that people would know the Lord, the way that trust is built, and how a human comes to know Christ is through love. There is no other way.

The greatest act of love ever done, the purest and most holy choice was Jesus' sacrifice on the Cross. How we conduct our lives and the way that we love others, especially those who no one else wants to love is our call to Sainthood. Love takes risks and it can hurt. But only love can conquer and love is the gateway to life. Love provides the greatest joy and no one can take that joy away. My hope is that by reflecting on love you will realize that *the how* is something that God is asking of you and me. He is calling each of us in our own unique and special way. You have your own race to run and your own fight to fight. There is so much that can be done and the mission field is vast. No matter what you feel called to, you and I can make a radical difference by the way in which we share love with the world. Each moment you answer "yes" to this, whether it is a big encounter or something small, you spread hope, love, and joy. Doing so makes the world a little bit brighter and illuminates the hearts of those around you.

The influential Martin Luther King Jr. understood love and the power of light as people transfer this life invigorating force to others when he said, "Darkness cannot drive out darkness, only light can do that. Hatred cannot drive out hate, only love can do that." Love is the essence of *the how*. When we come to understand this completely and accept that we have complete control over the way we conduct our lives and how we treat others, many things will change. Your heart will no longer beat the same. You will see the world in a new and different manner. This is because why you are here on earth will make full sense, as it is to share in the joys of life. Love will provide clarity and you will desire to spread the love of Jesus. Then it becomes a little bit easier to bear the weight of the Cross and to be with people walking with them in their ache that exists. Essentially this is when we arrive at the heart of Christ, to love without counting the cost.

Jesus was clear when he went around and asked people to follow him. He was bold and he did not merely suggest it was a "good idea." No, Jesus said, "I am the way, the truth and the life, no one comes to the Father except through me."[89] The way and *the how* are closely connected. There is a great alignment because what Christ desired 2,000 years ago for his first apostles and the disciples was to have a full and complete life, namely a whole—holy heart. No matter what takes place, transpires, or comes your way, no one and nothing can separate you from the love of God. St. Paul writes about this emphatically in his letters and he discusses what love is as he describes it to be patient, kind, knowing no record of wrongs, and being all about self-giving. In order to fully answer the call on our lives, we must lose complete control and surrender. When you surrender that opens up the floodgates and potential that God has for you. Abundant blessings and opportunities will start chasing you down. *The how* eventually will become ingrained in your soul and it is the anthem to be lived by. What is important for you to know is that while you and I are on this road to Sainthood, the more we grow closer to the Lord by living a life of service and loving those we encounter, the more challenging it will be.

Many of us often think that people who have come to holiness, especially Saints, do not face challenges or difficulty since they are fully in the army of God. That's the farthest from reality. When you take a look at those over the centuries who followed the Lord closely and were willing to answer his call, it is quite evident that suffering was part of the recipe of discipleship. After all, love was won on the Cross. So what would you do right now if the Lord were to knock at your door and say, "Come follow me and I will make you fishers of men"? How would you respond? If you are not sure, it is time to deeply reflect on and ponder the things in your life that make you fulfilled internally.

A deep faith and trust in God will bring peace to your life and lead you to be complete. The beauty is that God continues to meet people where they are. He did this thousands of years ago and Christ continues to do so today. This is your year to come into *the how*. Now is the time to take that "yes" to the next level and lose control so that the Lord can elevate you to levels that will blow you away. Listen to these powerful words of Jesus... "Amen, amen, I say to you, whoever believes in me will do the works that I do, and will do greater ones

---

[89] John 14:6

than these, because I am going to the Father."[90] The reason that our Lord spoke these words to his disciples and the reason why they hold true for us today is because we are called to greatness. With God alive and working in us, there is truly nothing that we are incapable of doing for him.

Bewildered, perhaps. Feeling a bit perplexed or overwhelmed, that's okay. Be patient. Greatness is not found in grandiose things we say or do. It is never going to be discovered in life achievements or accolades. Where it's found is in the one who declared, "I am." It's uncovered in the truth of the Father's love brought to full perfection through his Son, Jesus Christ, on that rugged cross. We are called to love greatly. How could we possibly do greater works than the Lord? I think it's important to understand that the powerful message existing here is in *the how*. Jesus living in us and working through us can make anything happen. It especially makes love real and people come alive. We all have been blessed with incredible abilities. Your potential must continue to be tapped into. When you and I invite Christ in, we allow him to shine through us, and then we have unlimited potential. That is what the Lord wants you to understand about the call. His call on your life is for you. Together, we remain on a love mission. We continuously exist in the mission field of life. Show up and love. God will be there and your heart will never be the same.

Let's always strive to be our personal best each day. The famous basketball coach and legend of the hardwood, John Wooden, got this right. The hall of famer won 10 national championships at UCLA, achieving unprecedented feats in the world of sports. He was arguably the greatest basketball coach of all time and an even better mentor of men. Coach Wooden said, "Success comes from knowing that you did your best to become the best that you are capable of becoming...*Make each day your masterpiece.*" If we make each day our masterpiece and we strive to be great not for ourselves but for others by spreading Christ's love, the world will be changed. Dr. Joseph Dutkowsky, a friend of Bishop Scharfenberger, shared an experience he had visiting Rick Guidotti's Museum in New York City. Dr. Joe's reflection puts into perspective the magnificent picture that God sees all of his creation

---

[90] John 14:12

through. Evidently, this is the lens which the Lord desires us to view life through, especially when encountering our fellow brothers and sisters. God's holy view is a complete lens, a vantage point through which the beholder sees others with great compassion and selfless love...

> *While sitting alone in the (museum) gallery surrounded by gorgeous three foot high pictures of persons with disabilities and genetic conditions, twice I had what I called at the time a sensory overload experience. Maybe it took a long ride home to realize it was a mystical experience. You know I see the image and likeness of God in every face. I realize now I had the mystical sense of being in an Eastern Rite Church surrounded by contemporary icons.*[91]

So the great challenge is to allow God to open up our eyes to see more clearly and to change our hearts to be more like his. In receiving Jesus' love for us, we then can love one another more deeply. Then, we can and inevitably will view the world in a different manner. We will respond faithfully as love becomes the pattern for our lives. God makes space in our hearts so we no longer view people we encounter through judgment and condemnation, but his grace allows us to see through the eyes of Christ—eyes of love. Bishop Scharfenberger reflected on Dr. Joe's experience at the museum as he articulated the meaning behind the tender loving eyes of Jesus who gazes into the souls of each person as if they were the only one to exist in all the world. Bishop Ed says that the challenge and ask of the Lord is for people to allow God in. Then, God can transform our hardened hearts and allow us to truly see the beauty that was there all along. He suggests that holy experiences happen all the time and it is in them that we come to see more clearly. Bishop Scharfenberger stated, "Icons, like masks, like the corporal component of our nature as incarnate spirits can only hint to perfectly human senses what God sees. Your realization was a flash, like a lightning bolt at night that, but for a second, illuminates the dark landscape with a stunning revelation of reality, a transfiguration."

---

[91] Dr. Joseph Dutkowsky

Uncovering the Call & Embracing Suffering

God sees us for who we truly are. Jesus knows us best and brings out the best in us. After receiving his love, we then can more fully respond to the call God places on our lives. But this all comes by remaining open. I encourage you to be willing to go to do what he asks and needs from you. Hear him. Listen to him. Answer him by practicing Heaven. This happens by living love. When you live out *the how*—actions with great love, understand that your life will impact society because your mark cannot be erased from the human heart. What could be better than being filled with lasting joy and spreading that joy constantly? Be the best friend, daughter, son, father, mother, brother, sister, or grandparent that you can be. Bloom where you are planted. Never stop loving and never count the cost. By living life fully in this way you will not only be filled up with peace and have abundant joy, but in sharing that joy, your love will reshape the face of the earth.

The call and *the how* is hard. Jesus said to them, "Whoever wants to be my disciple must deny himself, take up his cross daily and follow me. Whoever finds his life will lose it and whoever loses his life for my sake will save it."[92] Sometimes people might think to themselves if it's worth it. What's the cost and what's the price I'm willing to pay? The road to Sainthood and holiness is paved with great sacrifice. There are many things we will have to deny, give up, and just flat out say "No" to. But what are mere things worth in comparison to the love and joy we will receive, let alone that which we bring to the lives of others. The souls we can bring to Christ and the people we can impact for God's glory are all worthwhile. Intense, yes. Hard, yes. Worth it, always! As we gallivant through life, let's remember that there is no straight line. God helps us to connect all the dots and he will always lead us to where we need to be next. You have a destiny to fulfill and it is up to you to decide whether or not you are brave enough to chase it down or watch it drift away.

Think about John the Baptist. From before he was born into this world, he had a special call placed on his life. When Mary went to visit John's mom, Elizabeth, the little baby leaped in her womb as soon as he came to be in the presence of the Christ child. John was the

---

[92] John 9:23-24

messenger that prepared the way of the Lord. He walked differently. John talked differently. Clothed in camel's hair and eating locusts and wild honey out in the desert, he was on a unique mission. Nothing would stop John from carrying that plan out which the Lord had designed for him because God knew what he was capable of. Why? One word, love. John lived with conviction and his faith was the purest guide for his life. *The how* was realized and was his way of responding. And yet, John the Baptist would ultimately suffer by laying down his life for Jesus.

To be a disciple and a Saint for God's Church requires that we accept all that comes our way. Glory is for God and his kingdom. The price we pay sometimes will be the gravest cost—persecution, rejection, and even death. John baptized thousands, his life and ministry dedicated to leading souls to Christ. He was a great messenger. Rightly so, John's work was known through the centuries and his impact lives on. Yet, he was handed over and beheaded. John's faith, his devotion, and his love for Jesus won. Most chances are that you will not have your head chopped off and displayed on a silver platter for answering the call to discipleship. The point here is that the journey on the road to Sainthood is hard, yet the beauty that comes when the call is answered has no end.

Suffering, the Cross, and experiencing difficulty should come as no surprise. Jesus was pretty clear when he said that he came and was bringing the sword and division. Entire households are separated because of Jesus. Why? Maybe an even deeper question to ponder is how is this God's will? Certainly, the Lord doesn't want you and me to suffer. Our loving Father doesn't take pleasure by inflicting pain on our lives. What God does however is that he's able to use it to lead us closer to him. When we lean into the suffering, the hard, and the aches of life we cannot depend solely on ourselves and we must receive help from the Father. In doing so, we come out of ourselves and are shaped into the authentic people God created us to be. It is in the messy and dirtiness of life, the times of hardship and challenge where life gets real and we cling to Jesus who loves us through it all. We grow through what we go through.

Furthermore, if you are walking with the Lord and you answer the call he places on your life, you cannot please everyone. At times, the road to holiness can be one where nobody agrees with you and that's okay. Doing what is popular doesn't mean that what we are doing is right. This is where prayerful reflection and discernment comes in. Asking the Lord to continue to guide us, show us the way, and open wide the path is important. No matter what, you are never alone. Do not be afraid if your call and *the how* leads you away from some people in your life, even family. Chances are that the love you share and the road you walk will become clearer in time. Not to mention, as the desires of your heart are lived out in their greatest capacity, this will most often lead others closer to the Lord. And even if those in your inner circle do not understand, God does. Jesus is with you walking the road and he promises to accompany us on the way to Heaven.

Where are you right now? Are you living out life for the approval of God or for others? This is a crucial question. When you live for an audience of one and your life is a song in the concert of love, the call becomes a little bit easier to answer. It creates a space for God to tune our heart, allowing us to play in sync with his will for our lives. Remember, as members of the human community, we are parts of his orchestra. Each of us is the Lord's instrument, playing different notes based on the call we have received. While working in harmony by learning to collaborate, God leads us to produce the greatest of sounds in this fantastic concerto of love called life. Keep in mind the reward will be great in Heaven. That is the final destination of the Saint!

Undoubtedly, by living for the approval of God alone, you will lose some people and friends along the way. Can this be really hard, definitely. But what is more important than living out your truth? If your heart is not full and you are not living out your truest self, you are selling yourself short. Be who you were made by God to be. Your life and ultimate calling will fill you. Otherwise, you will be empty inside. You will be like the young man who was rich, but never reached his fullest potential because he was unwilling to give up the things that blocked him from arriving at his personal destiny. The scripture articulates this well by saying, "What good is it for one to gain the whole world and yet forfeit his own soul?"[93] This question is deep and the call and *the how* fold into it strongly.

You and only you alone, with God, know what it is that you need

---

[93] Mark 8:36

to do for him. No one else has the right or can tell you what your mission is. Your calling is unique and special. Your race is to be run wildly and completed thoroughly during your lifetime. The most important thing is that you listen, you love boldly, and you run fiercely. If you and I are willing to do this, we will grow in holiness thanks to the grace and power of the Lord in our lives. Love is where the Saint's journey begins and love is ultimately where it ends. Although, there is no real end because the fullness of that love is entering into God's eternal presence in Heaven. Before arriving home, we practice Heaven on earth.

St. Paul reminded the early Church of this centuries ago and the encouragement remains for us today, as we have full confidence in God's great ability to raise us up through the power of prayer and by his mighty strength. In Paul's letter to the Thessalonians he powerfully proclaimed, "So we keep on praying for you, asking our God to enable you to live a life worthy of his call. May he give you the power to accomplish all the good things your faith prompts you to do."[94] Love surely has no limits! So open up your mind and heart because Jesus is waiting to take you on the greatest and most wild ride. Your Saintly holiness emerges from within you. Love also is unselfish and does not do anything to seek out what is good and pleasing to yourself, but that which builds up the communal Church. By looking out for the interests of others we can be the frontline men and women who battle for Jesus daily.

Father Pedro Arrupe understood this well and lived it out to the fullest capacity in his ministry as a priest. Throughout his lifetime he dedicated himself to the service of the poor. Pedro's love for being with and for people in their suffering allowed God's love to shine through him. Arrupe was named the Superior General of the Jesuits (Society of Jesus) in 1965, as he held that position for nearly twenty years until 1983. Prior to his election as head of the Jesuits, Father Arrupe had experienced great resistance and turmoil. Nonetheless, he used every challenge and bleak situation as an opportunity to share God's love and experience Christ with those he encountered.

Arrupe and his fellow Jesuits were expelled from Spain in 1932. He traveled and studied in Belgium, Holland, and the U.S. over the

---

94 2 Thessalonians 1:11

next few years before being sent to Japan in 1938. After the bombing of Pearl Harbor, the Japanese government seized and arrested him on suspicion of espionage. Solitary confinement in a Japanese prison was where Pedro Arrupe spent the next 33 days. It must have been a spiritual desert for him, as Father Arrupe was unable to celebrate or receive the Eucharist at all during that month-long period of incarceration. Being deprived of the presence of the physical Jesus in the Blessed Sacrament was troubling. The body and blood of Christ— holy Communion, which he had celebrated daily prior to being locked up was not an option. Arrupe had great reverence for the Blessed Sacrament, having loved to give to his fellow brothers and sisters this spiritual food and drink as a priest. The absence of Jesus in the Eucharist tormented him. It caused intense pain and great distress in Pedro's soul. Arrupe considered Holy Communion to be a way to Practice Heaven. His love and devotion for Jesus in the Eucharist was gorgeous to witness, as he showed that the hidden Christ was the greatest spiritual and physical connection between God and man.

Pedro's love and strong devotion to the Lord, as well as commitment to serving God's people, helps us call to mind the unconditional love of the Father. It challenges us to stop asking the question, *Why would God allow us to be in this horrible situation?* Instead, we can embrace it and ask the Lord how he can use each of us to *"be love"* for others. During unprecedented times, it is in the moments when we are in the garden of Gethsemane, that we cry out to the Lord for help and he answers. And sometimes, he calls us to be his answer for others by living out holiness in the most unselfish and uncommon ways. As we embrace the cross, we put on the full valor of love and in doing so Christ becomes alive in us. In these times when we question where he is, Jesus shows up. The Lord arrives on the scene in and through us, the *everyday Saints* because we love. Being open to Christ working in our lives, especially during the detestable parts, allows God through the working of the Holy Spirit to manifest himself to those we encounter and walk with. We then have our eyes opened as we see the hidden Christ in the person we are with. This holy encounter changes our heart and the person we are with, all thanks to the merciful love of Jesus who is present.

As Father Arrupe sat in his jail cell his spiritual suffering continued, yet he was the recipient of a special moment of grace. In 1941 on Christmas night, Arrupe heard a group of people coming toward him and thought that his time of execution had arrived. Much to his surprise, Arrupe's ears were blessed with the most stunning sweetness of a melody he knew well, a Christmas carol. Bellowing out of the mouths of numerous prisoners he had taught the song to, emerged the voice of God. It was as if Christ himself was now singing to him. The light of Jesus had been issued to Arrupe by his fellow inmates that holy night bringing him great hope and joy through the song they shared with great love.[95] In a book that commemorates Father Pedro Arrupe's life, his reflection beautifully states:

"Suddenly, above the murmur that was reaching me, there arose a soft, sweet, consoling Christmas carol, one of the songs which I had myself taught to my Christians. I was unable to contain myself. I burst into tears. They were my Christians who, heedless of the danger of being themselves imprisoned, had come to console me."

He surely had experienced Jesus face to face in the prisoners who came to his cell as Arrupe recalls, "I felt that he also descended into my heart, and that night I made the best spiritual communion of all my life." Arrupe was eventually released and he made his way to Japan to spread the faith by serving the poor and sharing God's love with those he came across.[96]

Free at last from an unjust imprisonment, surely the road ahead would be easier for Arrupe. Not so fast. The difficulty continued in the mid 1940s. World War Two grew even worse with the atomic bomb being dropped on Pearl Harbor and then Hiroshima being decimated in retaliation. The city and area where Arrupe and his Jesuits lived and worked was the recipient of horror. The bombing in Japan caused the initial massacre of 200,000 innocent Japanese people. Moved with great compassion, Father Pedro Arrupe and his Jesuit community searched frantically for survivors. Eventually, they took in over 150 people, many of them children. Father Arrupe and his friends

---

[95] 20th Century Ignatian Voices: Pedro Arrupe, SJ (1907-1991)

[96] *Pedro Arrupe: Essential Writings*, Kevin Burke, p. 57

provided life-saving medical aid, nourishment, and spiritual counseling for the people's shattered hearts. This led him to fundamentally unlock his highest calling, discovering an intense and beautiful heart for the poor. The spirit moved Arrupe to go to the most detestable places. He quickly found himself with those who were in dire need, just like Jesus had done for him during his agony in jail.

Father Arrupe brought the heartfelt love of Jesus to the suffering, lonely, and materially deprived in Latin America. His tireless efforts led to the decree from the 32nd General Congregation, *Our Mission Today: The Service of Faith and the Promotion of Justice.* This transformative decree and movement was passed in 1975. It led the Jesuits, in places like El Salvador and many other countries throughout Latin America, to work in practical ways with the poor including education and spreading the faith.[97]

Living Mission with Conviction

What can be learned from this holy man who was a living Saint is that love finds a way when there seems to be no way. Pedro Arrupe dedicated his entire being to living out the mission of bringing Christ's love to whoever and wherever God called him. Shortly after the 1989 tragic martyrdom of six of his priestly companions in El Salvador, Arrupe spoke out emphasizing the Jesuits most important justice work—missions with the poor. He explained, " Today our prime educational objective must be to form men and women for others; men and women who will live not for themselves but for God and his Christ—for the God—human who lived and died for all the world; men and women who cannot even conceive of love of God which does not include love for the least of their neighbors; men and women completely convinced that love of God which does not issue in justice for others is a farce."[98] Assuredly, Arrupe is a prime example of God's love and the invitation remains for you and me.

As instruments of Christ's love in the world, together we can compose a great symphony of love in our lives by allowing Jesus to

---

[97] 20th Century Ignatian Voices: Pedro Arrupe, SJ (1907-1991)
[98] *Pedro Arrupe: Essential Writings*, Kevin Burke, p. 173

live through us. Father Arrupe's heart was transformed by love. It was love that led him around the world, as he gave himself in full service to those who thirsted for the love and mercy of Jesus. What he did serves as a beautiful testament to the power of God. Presence is required of the Saint. Be there and be fully accessible to the "other." Share your heart, give yourself away, and be the love of Jesus. Equally as important to our spiritual growth and well-being is to receive the love of Jesus that is found inside of those people you encounter. So often, Christ shows up in our lives through others. He appears to us as the hidden Jesus. He is revealed to us by looking us in the eyes when we meet a stranger. This openness to God's love and bringing Jesus to the world creates an avenue where we enter into a place that is not of this world, being connected mystically with the person we share this divine love exchange with.

As one heart in love is given to another, the very heart of Jesus himself is shared and he is fully present. Christ there with you and your fellow brother and sister. He heals the brokenness and fills the human soul with his lasting joy! This encounter with the Lord, which is found through love is handsomely professed by Father Pedro Arrupe in his poem and prayer entitled *Fall in Love*. The words beautifully illustrate the power of God's love and how our souls crave it. Through his poem, Arrupe explains in a succinct manner how our Lord made us—the human race for him—to be loved. Essentially, love dictates every decision you and I make. Either we as people do things with love and therefore God is present as the driving force or we resist love and Jesus is absent. There is no in-between. When we find love we find God.

Fall in Love

Nothing is more practical than finding God,
Than falling in Love
in a quite absolute, final way.
What you are in love with,
what seizes your imagination, will affect everything.
It will decide what will get you out of bed in the morning,

what you do with your evenings,
how you spend your weekends,
what you read, whom you know,
what breaks your heart,
and what amazes you with joy and gratitude.
Fall in Love, stay in love,
and it will decide everything.

Thy will be done. Saying "yes" to God's call and his invitation to love is crucial. These four words first uttered by Jesus himself in the garden before he chose to enter into his passion are spelled out through love and commitment. These mere letters strung together as a formation of consonants and vowels are so pure to the ears, so profound to the heart, yet the hardest to live by. In scripture they carry tremendous weight. The most well-known and recited prayer throughout world history—the Our Father—highlights them to the max. How do these few words fused as a branding for the soul pack such a prodigious punch? Four, not four hundred words contain the greatest complexity, searching, and questioning for us as human beings. They involve listening, quieting ourselves and being open to the direction of God in our lives.

As we discussed previously, the Blessed Mother understood the weight and the promise of these words the best. For many of us, we might want a sign or some kind of clear indication. Imagine if it was as easy as a knock on the door and God showed up at your home and told you, "I want you to do this..." Would that be nice and give you ultra clarity, perhaps? However, that would not make the great commission and what the Lord asks of you any easier. Discernment is a vital process in our faith development and our growth. An on-going relationship with Jesus and the Father is where the heartfelt courage to pray like Jesus in the garden comes to full light.

By contemplating, praying, thinking, and searching, we come to know who we are at the core and what God created us for. Even if we still have questions and might even doubt who we are, we find rest in knowing *whose* we are. The Holy Spirit is that still small voice that we hear whispering to us when we give God some of our time and space. The Lord's grace is needed and his love is at work in our busy lives, helping us to discern the call of Christ who continuously says, "Come, follow me."

So what does that mean for you? How do you truly know what God created you for? What is it that he desires above all else that you do? If it were that simple or easy maybe we would already be doing it. Perhaps we do know and the answer is closer than we might think. Recall the *how*. Throughout life, God's call in terms of a vocation or the "what" and purpose might look different. People change jobs as frequently as underwear and careers are altered from one moment to the next. However, the way you go about your work on a daily basis must remain the key and focal point. As Saints, our ultimate calling is to discipleship. Holiness and wholeness exist in sharing the love of Christ with others in all that we do and in whatever arena we are in.

As time marches on, one door closes and another opens. This all happens for a reason. I believe that God is leading you to the "next right thing" for your life so that you can continue on your path to Sainthood. The purpose of life truly is Heaven. We were made for ultimate communion and relationship with God. That promise has been made and will be fulfilled in eternity. God wants you to be happy and more than that, he desires that you are joy-filled here on this earth and forever with him in paradise. So how can you get to this place and state of joy? We get there through the course of our lives. We get there through a continuous relationship with Jesus, our best friend. We reach it with God our Father who wants the best for us. It is obtained as a gift by listening to the Holy Spirit which comes in many forms.

Be open and receive the signs, wonders, and messages, as answers arrive in the stillness of prayer. I encourage you to take some time to prayerfully reflect upon your life. Happiness is fleeting and eventually it will fade. We cannot deny the ebb and flow of life. However, deep-seeded joy comes through knowing your purpose and reason you are on this earth—love. Discipleship and becoming a loving Saint for God's Kingdom is your ultimate call. How we reach that comes in a variety of ways, jobs, careers, places, encounters, and experiences. Think about what fills you up with that inner peace and leaves you with a lasting feeling of deep joy. No matter what it is that God calls us to next, as long as we are open and ready to say "yes" to that call we will be filled with his joy.

When we die to self and align our will to God's will, we can reach this state of grace and peace that leaves us with the joy that only Jesus can fill. For the Lord said, "I came so that they might have life and have it to the full...I have told you these things so that my joy might be in you and your joy complete."[99] It is evident we must make heartfelt and smart decisions. Life keeps us on our toes and we have great responsibilities to take care of, our family needs us, and we have to provide a solid future. But I encourage you to listen to the Lord and seek what he is calling you to. As it says in Matthew's Gospel, "Seek first the Kingdom of God and his righteousness, then all these things will be added onto you."[100]

Imagine Jesus sitting there with you now as he was with his apostles. Listen to the sound of his voice when he says, "Come follow me." Perhaps we are afraid that if we go, we will never be the same. Why is that a bad thing? Our lives might not be easy and it might not always be comfortable. However, don't lose heart. Remember, as John A. Shedd once said, "A ship in harbor is safe, but that is not what ships are built for." Ships were made for sailing. Take a step out into the open water and set sail. Even dare to go where it is rocky because that is especially where the Lord will help you and guide you since you place your trust in him. Your heart will be filled so much that no one will be able to take the joy you will receive—the joy found in Jesus living within you. The Lord is there to direct your steps and guide your path. Continue to have that childlike trust in him, the God who wants what is best for each of us. We are the Lord's children and we are his Saints that are called to build up the Kingdom one day and one person at a time.

The love of Christ is something that we desire and what people in our broken world need. We are called by God in some way to serve. Lately, I have been thinking a lot about missions. By responding with a "yes" to Christ, the first apostles became the first missionaries. Jesus called them to follow him because he knew what they were truly capable of doing. And follow they did. They set out to catch not just fish, but men! Like those first followers of Christ did 2,000 years ago, so are we called to do the same today. In our own way, in our own time, you and I are called to serve. So what does that mean? How do

---

[99] John 10:10, John 15:11
[100] Matthew 6:33

I go out and share Christ's love with others?

For many of us we have an opportunity every day to brighten someone's life with a simple listening ear, a compliment, a random act of kindness. As author Matthew Kelly suggests, when we respond positively to what he calls the *holy moments* that come our way, we grow closer to God. A *holy moment* is any encounter where we give or receive Jesus. It can be as simple as holding the door for someone and offering a smile. On the other hand, it can be as profound as traveling across the globe to serve the poor in a third world country. Saint Mother Teresa lived in perpetual holy moments. Her life motto of doing the smallest tasks with great love embraces this. She said, "If you can't feed a hundred people, then feed just one." Love doesn't cost us anything, except our time and energy. We all have love to share. It begins one person at a time. After all, this is what loving and serving God is about.

When I came back from Mexico City in April of 2019 my life was forever changed. After spending just five days with the poorest of the poor, I realized my life was a gift that I needed to share with others. I also realized that the hidden Jesus was in everyone, especially the poor. As I played in the dirt with kids at the city dump, I had an encounter with Christ that I had never experienced before. It was then in this moment that God's love showered me with graces that opened my eyes in a new way to love. There is a reason why Jesus says, "Unless you become like one of these little ones, you shall not inherit the Kingdom of Heaven."[101] When we serve we become children of God. Love allows us to give from the heart and share all that God has blessed us with.

The gifts we receive from above are the gifts we are to share with the world. When we serve others and shine Jesus' light in the broken world, we share Christ; and when we share him, hearts and the world itself changes. Joy is something that is given and it is something that is received. Serving allows this spiritual and fruitful explosion of God's love to come to completeness. It lightens your heart and moves your soul. So the next time you are with someone, be open to those opportunities to serve. Stay open to the grace of Jesus and to *the how*. Even more importantly, live out *the how*.

---

[101] Matthew 18:3

Service comes in the form of being a good friend, a loving spouse, a helpful neighbor, and a willing listener. Service comes in the shape of praying for others, writing an encouraging note, sending an uplifting text message, or making a call on a lonely night. Service is all about love, as it comes in the form of being the hands and feet of Christ. The love of Jesus is unlocked through our action. By visiting the sick, spending time with those in prison, and heeding the cry of the poor, we live love. As it says in Matthew's Gospel, "...whatever you did for one of these least brothers of mine, you did for me."[102] Whatever you do, know that when you give, you shall receive. Blessed are you because you loved as Jesus called you to do.

Never was there a day or a time when I gave myself and served others that I wasn't changed. It is not easy and you might not want to all the time, but know that love is your gift to this planet. So this week go out and find your mission field. Serve others with love and sprinkle the Lord's joy amongst his people. Allow the love of Christ to flow through you to the world so that "your light might shine before others, so that they might see your good works and glorify your Father in Heaven."[103] Go out and serve by being a light. We will discuss leading a life of service more in depth a little bit later on in this book, but understand that your call, namely living *the how* and service goes hand in hand. Together we continue to journey on toward Sainthood. Together we give and receive God's love through encounters with the hidden Christ.

Challenge 9

When the phone rings, what do you do? Most people look at the caller ID and then answer. Some wait for it to ring or send it straight to voicemail. If a person calls who you were eagerly waiting to hear from and their number pops up on your screen, you greet them on the line with excitement. There is energy and joy in your voice. Your challenge this week is to reflect on life and spend some time with the Lord. Assess your current situation and your heart. I encourage you to use the

---

[102] Matthew 25:40
[103] Matthew 5:16

"caller ID" to filter your time, uncovering who you spend it with, and what you are doing with your life. Most importantly, reflect and pray on the "how." Answer when Jesus calls or puts something or someone on your heart. Maybe you have been letting the phone of life go to voicemail a lot lately, but he keeps calling. Answer, just listen, and trust in him. There is great excitement and joy that awaits you, but you have to first listen. The call to Sainthood is a universal call to be all God created us to be—creatures of love. See God in others and be changed.

STRIVING FOR HOLINESS

CHAPTER 10

*"Holiness is the aim of the Saints on Earth and it is
the reward of the Saints in Heaven." – Joseph Caryl*

Uncovering the Holy One Inside

What is it that you most desire or long for in this lifetime? Many
people out there want to feel they belong. Above all else, most of us
crave community. Still, we often hear others suggesting that they will
be happy when "X" happens. Then the event they had been waiting
for or the experience occurs and nothing drastically changes. True
happiness comes in the form of joy. It's found in receiving peace
internally when the human heart is made complete. Beyond this warm
feeling exists something that has greater worth that no one can place
a value upon. What I am talking about is holiness. A sense of belonging
is essential to your happiness because we need this communion with
God and our fellow brothers and sisters. What is holiness and how do
we achieve it? One translation for the word holiness is derived from a
Hebrew word qadowsh, literally meaning, "to cut."

Essentially, the act or state of being holy actually means to be
removed—cut off from anything and everything else besides what
makes us whole, namely God. Holiness comes with significant clout

because those who are deemed holy, albeit the canonized Saints or *everyday Saints,* have been folded into God's loving grace. By distinguishing our purpose and aligning it to what our Heavenly Father desires from us as members of his Church, we then strive to remove ourselves from anything contrary to love, truth, and pace. In addition, *Qadowsh*—to be holy means to be morally pure, and to live in a state of sanctity in every way possible!

We reach holiness when we have the Lord at the center of our lives and we are in tune with the world around us. Holiness is not something that we can get to on our own, rather it takes place little by little throughout the course of life. Holiness grows based on our merits, but it is most often thanks to the grace of God working in our lives. When we sit back and think about some deeper things including life's great meaning and the concept of holiness, we can probably call to mind a few people who we would call holy. Whether it be an iconic figure of the Church like our favorite Saint or a humble servant such as Mother Teresa, there are people from history who have been examples of holiness. Each of us also has met or maybe even known people in our inner circles who exude holiness by the manner in which they live and how they love.

It is important for us to recognize on our journey toward Sainthood that we are all called to holiness. My hope is that you understand that being holy—whole and filled with the grace and spirit of Christ does not mean in any way shape or form that you are expected to be perfect. When asked who he was after taking the position of Pontificate and Bishop of Rome, Pope Francis so humbly responded, "I am a sinner." We are all sinners and each of us falls short throughout our lives. This occurs every day for that matter. We are all human and we will continue to make mistakes and sin. God understands this and knows that this is part of our fallen human nature. Even the most holy of all Saints in the Kingdom do not walk a road of perfection. So let's stop limiting ourselves and thinking that we cannot obtain holiness. Remember, his mercy abounds.

The truth is that God calls everyone to holiness. Whether you or I accept that is our own decision. Like a mountaineer who is traversing great facades of sheer granite to summit the top of a peak, your journey and road to holiness is systematic in nature as it is a process. As much as you might want to go quickly from point "A" to point "B" and hit the top without much effort, that is not the case. Then again what merit would there be if holiness were simply given away like candy on Halloween? The great fruits of your labor, especially regarding faith, are well worth the effort. After all, this road to holiness is not only to be kept for ourselves. It's really about building up the Kingdom and bringing others closer to the Lord, while we find the holiness within ourselves that only God can pull out of us.

Imagine setting off on a climb. Your bag is packed, you have a map in hand, and the weather forecast is looking favorable. No, the climb does not start with Mount Everest, maybe it is a short hike through some smaller mountains. No matter what the elevation is that we are climbing, it is important to follow the guide or set of directions provided. During the ascent, the climber must use the appropriate gear to ensure safe travel and keep a steady pace. While hiking upward, there will be many obstacles along the way including some that have not been accounted for ahead of time. Such is life for us as we navigate through the roadblocks and challenges that come our way. As any experienced climber knows, it is crucial to think about the route, make appropriate adjustments, and to guide the inexperienced climbers so they can achieve success on the climb. Well, as it pertains to holiness, who are you and what are you climbing for?

Recognizing Holiness in each Saint

In his apostolic exhortation entitled *Gaudete et Exultate,* Pope Francis reminds us and explains that holiness is all around us and comes down to seven specific aspects:

1. *Holiness is next door*
2. *Holiness is attractive*
3. *Holiness is possible and unique*
4. *Holiness is for you and for me*
5. *Holiness makes us more human*
6. *Holiness has enemies*
7. *Holiness means going against the grain*

Holiness is next door

The Holy Father said, "The Church has repeatedly taught that we are justified not by our own works or efforts, but by the grace of the Lord, who always takes the initiative."[104] So how do these seven facets of holiness apply to your life? I encourage you to take some time and to reflect upon them. We will be filled with the spirit in different ways when journeying toward completeness in the Lord. The first aspect of holiness is important to contemplate because holiness is truly in our midst. We don't have to go far at all to witness the love and grace of God flowing from human to human. When you are in your neighborhood, on the street corner, in your workplace, or in your own home, holiness is happening. The holy moments that we witness and those that we initiate change our lives and our hearts.

Carrying them out and by being on the receiving end of these sacred times, transmits God's love to and from during these encounters. The challenge is to be the "holiness next door" for your neighbors, the people in your family, and those you know. This is a gift. Many times people wonder how this can be done and yet it is quite simple. To live out holiness means to live out love in the greatest manner that you can, while leaving space for Christ to move within your life to fill those you encounter with joy. There is no limit! This aspect of our spiritual journey is the X-Factor of growing closer to the Lord and becoming whole. Holiness is arguably the most impactful force. Each of us can take part in it in our own way by living out our faith with pure love.

Holiness is attractive

Pope Francis suggests that holiness is also attractive. When people are able to remove themselves from worrying about what others think or wondering if they can still be "cool" while having faith and striving for holiness, they will be astounded by it. People who are open to God's will, are committed to following him faithfully, and are striving for greatness are those that I am drawn to. Why? Well, for starters

---

[104] *Gaudete et Exultate* by Pope Francis

they are much different than the norm. Second, there is something that makes them physically glow. Perhaps it is their smile or calm aura. A holy person's presence is evident due to the great peace and joy that radiates from within their heart. Holiness is the "it-factor." When we see it or experience these beautiful human beings living a life that is Christ centered, we too are attracted to God who lives in them.

Oh and did I mention, it is actually really cool to be holy. When was the last time one of your friends walked on water, cured someone who was sick, turned water into wine, or was able to feed 5,000 people with five loaves and two fish? Just saying, that is nothing to scoff at! No, holiness doesn't mean we will be miracle makers every day like Jesus was during his few years of public ministry. However, it does guarantee that the Lord will live in you and will give his faithful followers the power of the Holy Spirit so an exciting life worthy of your calling can be led.

We have all heard the saying, "Bees are more attracted to honey than vinegar." This is true in the natural world and it is the case with human relationships. When we see someone loving and giving of themselves so beautifully, we desire to be around them. When we notice those who go out of their way to lift the spirits of the suffering and who share their time, treasure, and talents to better others, we are drawn in. Holiness is attractive because we all desire to be loved and to give in love. It is attractive because each of us desires to be whole, at peace, and to experience extreme joy. Amidst the great storms and the chaos of life, holiness is the calm which quells all storms. It comes from our faith. It is uncovered by our merits of love in action. Holiness that remains within is unlocked by God's profound grace. Nothing can or will ever be able to fill us the way that holiness does because it is a pure gift from Heaven. The best part is that we then share this with others, use the gracious bestowed upon us to make the world better, and pour out the love we have received to those we meet. The wholeness of God—holiness, is shared in a transcendental manner going far beyond the limits of time and space.

Holiness is possible and unique

Sainthood is possible and it is an individual calling by God to everyone. As the Gospel states, "Many are invited, but few are chosen."[105] This is a very important aspect of holiness—it being possible. The many here refers to everyone. Jesus came for all and desires every human heart to receive his love which leads to holiness. Yet, few are chosen not because the Lord doesn't select them, but because they decide to remain distant from God, not seek him out and at times walk right away. Therefore, holiness and God are two peas in a pod. You cannot have one and not have the other. If Christ is truly the Lord of your life, you are made holy by the blood he shed and the love he shares!

Similar to what we discussed earlier on, this ever so important notion articulated by Pope Francis reminds us that holiness is possible and unique. It calls out the incorrect ideology that holiness and Sainthood is only for the elite. Holiness is not "untouchable." It is meant for everyone in their own particular manner and that is the very essence of what makes holiness one of a kind. The unique quality of each human being who enters the breath of life is a blessing by God to the world. It is time for each of us to think of ourselves as a blessing to others and then to take the next step forward, actually being that blessing. When you are able to overcome your own doubts and shortcomings, you then can be elevated by the grace of God and be all that he created you to be. The best part is that since everyone is so different, the uniqueness adds such great flavor to the world we live in. Remember, if the greatest sinners were made into Saints, we too have a very big part to play in order to impact others and make our mark on history.

Holiness is for you and it's for me

The Holy Father is most likely held in highest regard by the majority of society, not just Catholics. Pope Francis' stature is something that holds such great clout around the world between all religious people and spiritual leaders. It is critical that you and I understand and

---

[105] Matthew 22:14

believe that holiness is not just for those that are in Rome at the Vatican or the one in a billion Mother Teresas that come along every century at best. In actuality, we are all called to holiness just the way we are. You don't have to be a priest, a nun, the Pope or perform great miracles to be a Saint. By being your authentic self and by living out your faith to the best of your ability, you can love others in every circumstance you emulate holiness. We hear this over and over in God's word, "But, as he who called you is holy, be holy yourselves in every aspect of your conduct for it is written, 'Be holy because I [am] holy.'"[106] God asks you to strive for holiness, just like he asks you to be the best person you can be. Don't worry, he will give you everything you need and will fill in any gaps that might exist.

Holiness makes us more human

Pope Francis suggests that holiness actually makes us more human. Some people might not understand how this is the case. Think about it for a moment though. Holiness—the state of being complete or whole is what being human is about is it not? We were made to be who God created us to be. So who did the Lord create us to be anyway? Well, you were created to be with him in a relationship. We know that all relationships need love to thrive. So therefore it makes sense that you were made for holiness because when you love in this world and receive it, you are giving and partaking in the very presence of God. At the end of the age when we breathe our last breath and pass on from this world, we will enter eternal glory with Christ. Since our citizenship is not of this world, but it is in Heaven as St. Paul reminds us, we are basically in a Saint bootcamp here on earth and journeying on the road to complete holiness, which will be fulfilled in Heaven!

Holiness has enemies

There is nothing that the enemy despises more than holiness and heeding God's call to Sainthood. There is no doubt that when you are

---

[106] 1 Peter 1:15-16

living to your greatest capacity and striving to be the best disciple possible, you will have enemies. These will come in the human and spiritual forms. There will be many people who dislike you because you decide to go against the grain and do what is unpopular. Not only that, but you will even be hated because of your faith. Your conviction to live out what is just and your desire to walk humble with God will be looked down upon by many. Mark Twain put it in a light hearted manner, "Always do right. This will gratify some people and astonish the rest." Human beings have a tendency to attack anything that is not mainstream, let alone something that they envy. Yes, I said envy. People will envy those who live out holiness. Why, you might ask? Unfortunately, we live in a world where instead of joining forces that are good and building people up, we have a society that thrives on tearing others down. So you become the enemy since you stand for what is good, holy, and true. Love pays a price and so does holiness.

In addition, we will have to be ready for battle to fight against the spiritual realm, which is even more powerful and influential than the voices that resound amongst even our own kin. Most people do not think about this part of the equation. However, it must be recognized. If you are not prepared to battle the enemy of holiness which is ultimately the evil one—Satan then you will be exposed. We must stay on guard so that the lies, negativity, doubt, fears, and other wicked devices of the evil force used to draw people away from God will not win. Be ready and be armed because the more holy you become and the closer your walk is with the Lord, the more you will be attacked. There is nothing that the evil one hates more than holiness.

Holiness means going against the grain

Lastly, the seventh emphatic point that Pope Francis makes is that holiness involves living and going against what is popular. It is very uncommon to desire to become holy and to strive to be a Saint. Most people who are authentically living out their call of true discipleship with pure hearts are uncommon. The conviction in building up the Kingdom comes from the heart, not doing it for a title or pat on the back. After all, we don't do the Lord's work so that we gain a label or some kind of recognition. If that is our motive, people will smell the BS from a mile away. Not only will that hurt us, it will have a negative impact on spreading the love and message of Christ to the world. Not many people like to be unpopular or disliked. However, if we are pleasing everyone, we are definitely doing something wrong.

Jesus himself was deemed a radical and a revolutionary. Do you recall when he turned over the tables in the synagogue? Sometimes tables need to be flipped in life and we must walk to the beat of our own drum even if we are left playing a drum solo. That is okay because when your why is big enough, it is all worth it. There are plenty of average people in the world and so many common folks who blend in. What a damn shame. It is such a disservice to the world to simply have a limited mentality. Being okay with the status quo and just blending in with mainstream society is sad. Every person has something special and different to offer. But if you want to strive for holiness you will have to go against many people and take an unpopular approach.

Even your own family and best friends will most likely disagree with you from time to time, perhaps often. So you must ask yourself, what is my why? How is my life and living out the truth that God has placed in my heart something worthwhile? Remember these words from Matthew's Gospel, "Enter through the narrow gate; for the gate is wide and the road broad that leads to destruction, and those who enter through it are many. How narrow the gate and constricted the road that leads to life. And those who find it are few."[107] So it boils down to choice as do all things in life. Would you rather take the road less traveled that is paved with everlasting joy and peace or do you prefer to have what you don't truly desire and get it now? The former will last forever, meanwhile the latter will be gone in the blink of an eye. The narrow gate is the way for me and my hope is that you will continue to journey with your eyes locked on the prize. There is a road that we all walk on. It seems silly to think that many people choose not to walk the road that leads to life. Then again, it's not easy. Don't forget that the banquet awaits us, but for now we must simply keep going and we cannot look back.

---

[107] Matthew 7:13-14

Be Holiness by Living Authentically

One of the greatest disciples and officially canonized Saints (formally recognized by the Church) is Saint John the Baptist. Most would argue that he was on the road to holiness and was destined for greatness since the beginning of time. Yet, John the Baptist still had to answer the call and walk through the narrow gate. Holiness was not a given and he had to choose to say "yes" to the Lord in order to live out his mission in this world. Every Christmas season I thoroughly enjoy Advent which leads up to the Lord's birth. The readings at mass are so powerful and rich. One of my favorite parts of scripture, which strikes a new chord and fires me up every time I read it, is where John the Baptist prepares the way of the Lord...

> As it is written in Isaiah the prophet: "Behold, I am sending my messenger ahead of you; he will prepare your way. A voice of one crying out in the desert: 'Prepare the way of the Lord, make straight his paths.' John [the] Baptist appeared in the desert proclaiming a baptism of repentance for the forgiveness of sins. People of the whole Judean countryside and all the inhabitants of Jerusalem were going out to him and were being baptized by him in the Jordan River as they acknowledged their sins. John was clothed in camel's hair, with a leather belt around his waist. He fed on locusts and wild honey. And this is what he proclaimed: "One mightier than I is coming after me. I am not worthy to stoop and loosen the thongs of his sandals. I have baptized you with water; He will baptize you with the Holy Spirit."[108]

Certainly John the Baptist lived out his call and completed his journey to holiness. The road was one that was taxing for him, as we discussed previously. However, he finished his race by fighting the good fight of faith. I believe that there is a John the Baptist in each of us. No, we are not all called to literally baptize the masses, preach every Sunday from a pulpit, or proclaim the Gospel until we are beheaded. Although most of us are not likely staring down the

---

[108] Mark 1:2-8

guillotine because of our faith, Jesus still desires you and I to be like John by living out the good news boldly. Crazy John, as he can sometimes be referred to, tends to emerge in each of us. During our personal voyage to Sainthood the John inside comes alive because in our own time and space, God does ask us to prepare the way. John is Hebrew for "Graced by God." Being the light in the darkness and hope in a world that needs something to cling to is a great responsibility for us as believers. It is so important as well. My mentality is and always will be, why not me? And if I can say why not me after considering all of my sins, failures, and downfalls, why not you?

Be a trailblazer. Be willing to listen to the Spirit and go where God needs you. Be true to who you are as a disciple and live without abandon. In doing so you will be full, complete, whole, and holy. Your radiance will brighten your community, send shockwaves of grace and goodness throughout your circles, and ultimately change the world. Holiness is indeed a journey and the road will not be smooth. Rough patches exist. Growing pains are inevitable and pot holes will transpire along the way. That is all okay.

Our map to arrive at holiness is the star. It's the same star that guided the holy family and the three wisemen to find the baby Jesus. The Lord is providing the way for us and will continue to do so as long as we trust, give our best effort, and ask for his help. Pope Francis summed up the human person's road to holiness by saying, "The Solemnity of All Saints reminds us that we are all called to holiness...the fruit of God's grace and our free response to it." What is important here is that holiness is both a gift and a call. It is up to us to respond to the call and to accept the gift. When we do, it will change everything. Now, will you dare to try it? Don't worry, perfection is not required.

Challenge 10

Get out a piece of paper and split it into three sections. In section one, write down the people who come to mind when you think of holiness. These can be people you know personally or they can be humans past or present that you admire. In section two, jot down the qualities that make each of those people from section one attractive to you. Why do you look up to them? Finally, in section three, jot down your favorite qualities or gifts that you have been blessed with. Continue to use these great abilities and the passions you have to become that Saint for our world which needs your holiness!

IRON DISCIPLES
CHAPTER 11

"Being a disciple means being constantly ready to bring the love of Jesus to others, and this can happen unexpectedly and in any place: on the street, in a city square, during work, on a journey." – Pope Francis

Defining Who You Are

While laying on her bed, Miranda scrolled through her phone checking the latest posts her friends made. The pictures that filtered into that small screen and the innumerable videos she watched had become her reality. The teenage girl read the comments, noticed the "views," and numbered the "likes." Her self-worth was tightly aligned to those metrics. Today, Miranda was satisfied. A little smile appeared on her face. Next, she went into the bathroom to brush her teeth and wash her face before bedtime. While lying in her bed, Miranda thought about the popular girls at school. She was becoming one of them, but still hadn't gotten the approval of a few who called her a jock because she was a terrific athlete. Meanwhile, to others, she was known as a bookworm, having taken her studies ultra seriously. Maybe someday soon Miranda would win them over and fit in with the trendy crowd. It was really hard because she didn't fully know how to be herself around them.

Titles carry considerable weight and prescribe certain expecta-tions. Based on the name that comes before someone's actual name, various preconceived notions are made and stereotypes can be placed. An array of assumptions fall upon those who bear them. Like we discussed earlier on, the name you have and the label that is bestowed on you does not determine who God says you are. Since you and I fully know that we are children of God, there is only one title, label, or name that should matter to those who believe—disciple. By definition, a disciple is a person who follows another, namely the student of someone like a teacher, philosopher or leader. It is amazing that people are vastly concerned with how many followers they have on social media. This notion of gaining "likes" by ultimately receiving the approval of others runs rampant in society and is mind boggling.

Popularity is extraordinarily important to this generation, as it is an ongoing competition to see who can gain the most followers online. In a similar breath, think about how many do you follow? What type of accounts, things of interest, and overall number of people do you like and follow on the social media scene? If you have not reached 10,000 followers or don't have "X" amount of digital friends you are not successful by the world's standards. Why are people so enthralled with ensuring they have their own personal fan club? Value is never found in this. Not to mention, if you really think about it, how sad it is that such energy is expended on winning over the endorsement of others.

Human beings need connection and we crave relationships, but we don't get true fulfillment from people we will never even meet inside our black boxes. Endorsing others who we will never know or attempting to gain their attention and following for popularity's sake is silly. At times, this leads people to aimlessly getting sucked into meaningless entertainment. It distracts society from the truth and the reason we are here to begin with. What is worse than that though is falling down the hole of conformity to thoughts, beliefs, and ways that pull us in the opposite direction of God. Doing what everyone else is doing is an easy scapegoat or mentality to have. Not being compliant to blindingly follow the way of this world is challenging. Each day our lives unfold and our hearts are shaped by the choices we make.

Consequently, who we are at the core is created by who we hang out with, what we do, and the way we go about life. If you are not careful, these seemingly meaningless moments or the decisions that don't appear to be that crucial on the surface can cause our values to get all twisted up. Over time we can even lose sight of what really matters—who really matters. What if you and I were equally concerned with another kind of following? What if the discipleship we were concerned about involved only one person to follow and one "like" so to speak?

The definition of discipleship that Saints focus on and live out is being a personal follower of Jesus Christ. The only place you will find that is in your heart. As Saints, we are called to be strong and faithful followers of his way. Specifically, you are asked to be iron tough for the Lord. When it comes to iron discipleship I really love the story of Jesus and the paralytic. In the gospel, Jesus is teaching and sharing the Pharisees and teachers of the law. Along comes a group of men. They can hear Jesus, but cannot see him or get to him because of the great crowd that was gathered around the Lord. Their faith drove them to that place because they believed that if somehow they could get their paralyzed friend to the Lord, he would be healed. The door and all entrances were blocked. There was no room inside.

They could have left saddened and discouraged. They could have given up and lost hope. No, they found a way. Instead, the men took their friend and climbed up on the roof. Then, they pulled off the straw and other pieces of the ceiling and lowered the paralyzed man down on his stretcher right to the feet of Jesus. Now imagine being in the crowd that day. You see some men carrying a guy on a stretcher and they climb onto a roof. That is wild enough. Or what if you are inside listening to Jesus' teaching and all of sudden you hear a noise coming from the ceiling. Out of nowhere a person emerges and descends, being lowered down through the roof. Bewilderment, curiosity, and a sense of "wow" must have set in. Finally, picture yourself being the Lord. Did Jesus know they would show up that day and how the events would transpire? Of course he did. After all, he is God.

How moved our Lord must have been to see the great faith and discipleship of these friends. I believe that is why Jesus decided to perform a miracle that day. It spoke volumes to all those gathered and in the surrounding region of Galilee, Judea, and Jerusalem. If you saw this story pop up on your social media feed, would you give it a "like" and would you follow this guy named Jesus? See, the point here is that if you have your heart in the right place and you are a disciple of Christ, none of the things of this world whether good, bad, or indifferent will truly matter. Your priorities will be aligned and your heart will be right. Jesus honors people's great faith and he loves our willingness to be his disciples by loving others like the group of friends did for the paralytic that day. The Lord wants us to be concerned with and use our time on things that matter. True discipleship is about following Christ candidly, using our time and talents to build up the Kingdom, and sharing God's love with everyone we meet. Looking back at the story of the paralytic, it's pivotal to recognize that before the miraculous happened, Jesus forgave the man of his sins.[109] Everyone must have once again been astonished. Jesus knew what the people he was teaching were thinking about. They could not have actually believed that Jesus was blaspheming, could they? Like he so often did, Jesus next asks a question. He inquires their opinion by asking those gathered what would be harder to do—forgive someone's sins or to heal the man so he could walk again.

The crowd then is left silenced. They are waiting with eager anticipation to see what would happen next. Luke's gospel reminds us what Jesus said and did afterward, "But that you may know that the Son of Man has authority on earth to forgive sins"—he said to the man who was paralyzed, 'I say to you, rise, pick up your stretcher, and go home.' He stood up immediately before them, picked up what he had been lying on, and went home, glorifying God. Then astonishment seized them all and they glorified God, and, struck with awe, they said, 'We have seen incredible things today.'"[110]

There are many incredible things about this story and a lot to be drawn upon here. In a little while, you will see how God has something else to reveal in this spectacular story—a historical event centered around Jesus with the healing of the paralyzed man. Right now however, the piece for us to think about most on our journey to Sainthood as iron disciples is not in the healing. It is found more so in the seeking. It is revealed in the power of faith and the willingness of the group of friends to get to the Lord despite the obstacles. They did not take no for an answer. They followed Him. You and I can too. To

---

[109] Luke 5:17-26
[110] Luke 5:24-26

actually follow Jesus is as easy as a click of a button. The only expectation in being God's disciple is to remain faithful and to be receptive to Christ's love. Jesus is the best friend you could ever gain. Saints follow the one—the Lord God almighty. Saints live for an audience of one as well. Jesus is always following you. As long as you follow him, you will have a joy filled life and be on the road to holiness –Heaven.

Saints Play More than Sundays

The ball has been kicked off and the monstrous crowd filling the Superdome in Louisiana goes wild. It is Sunday and that means time for football. For Drew Brees and his team rocking the gold and black in New Orleans it is game day. But see, Saints play seven days a week, not just on Sundays. Drew Brees is one of the all-time leaders in passing yards in NFL history. Throughout his 19 year career he racked up over 80,000 yards and threw for nearly 600 touchdowns. During his illustrious time in the pros, this legend of the gridiron accomplished a ton. However, Drew didn't arrive at the pinnacle of the NFL world overnight. Instant success was not in the recipe for him. Early on he faced adversity. After being selected in the second round, 32nd overall pick in the 2001 draft from Purdue University, things were not so easy for Brees. It was fitting that Drew had been a Boilermaker in college. The mascot his NCAA team was known for and the grit Purdue University stood for would soon have to be lived out in grand proportion for this new kid on the block as a professional in football. The thing is, there was no easy road ahead.

Sweat, blood, and tears were coming for Drew. Not to mention there would be linebackers every Sunday, like Ray Lewis, who wanted to take his head off because he was the quarterback! Although he was the new guy, like many outstanding players that came before him, Brees had a positive outlook. His fiery spirit set him apart. Constant effort and belief in himself and in the Lord changed everything for Drew and it can for you as well. Drew Brees struggled in his early playing days for San Diego. In his first three seasons he went just 12-20 (.375%) as a starter and threw for 29 touchdowns as opposed to 31 interceptions. Having no quit and a relentless work ethic, Brees began to turn it around by fine tuning his game. In 2004 & 2005 he flipped the script going 20-11 (.645%) for the Saints, including a Division title along with Pro Bowl numbers, tossing 51 touchdowns. But then at the tail end of 2005 in the very last game of the season, Brees tore his labrum. He suffered the worst injury possible for a player in his position. Many doctors and teams doubted his ability to come back fully from the gruesome injury.

Drew's time in Southern California came to a close. It was anything but a "Brees" for the young signal caller. He was knocked down, but he wasn't knocked out. In true Saint fashion, Drew believed in his heart that he was not finished. This man was not going to settle and his story was far from over. Actually, it was just getting started. Brees was not satisfied. He understood far too well that immediate success and stardom was never handed to any of the all-time greats, let alone some young gun who had just arrived on football's biggest stage. The players who received their gold jackets in Canton, being elected into the Hall of Fame, certainly had some exceptional talent.

However, hard work can trump talent, especially when a fire is ignited. See, Brees was doubted. Even after having a solid collegiate career, people discredited his abilities and future. He was well under the gold standard of 6' for a top prospect and to have success as a quarterback in the league, that said he was "just too small." In addition, the scouts felt his arm strength was not good enough. He certainly did not possess the rocket cannon arm of the greats like Staubach, Bradshaw, Montana, Elway, and Favre had. Without a missile for an arm and not being the most fleet of feet, doubt continued to sink in. Now that Brees was riddled with a magnanimous injury, this ultimately meant his fate was decided. His time in a Chargers uniform was over.

The Miami Dolphins and many other teams did not want him. Imagine being unwanted even after bringing your franchise from one of the worst teams in football to the playoffs, while putting up the best numbers of your career. That has to hurt. At last, the New Orleans Saints took a gamble and called Brees to sign him to be their guy. What they didn't know, along with the rest of the NFL world, was that Drew Brees was just arriving. He was more concerned with the constant preparation outside the lines of the football field. That happened six days a week because the greats don't just play on Sundays. This became Drew's prime focus so that on game day everything would take care of itself.

Sunday in New Orleans is game day and this holds true in every major city in the U.S. that hosts a pro football team. Fans care about one thing and one thing only, winning! Jesus and football go hand and hand in the Bayou. The Big Easy has had its fair share of tragic events, including multiple hurricanes over the past two decades that have decimated the city. Brees not only brought hope on the gridiron, but he became a spark in the community. His willingness to go far beyond the football field and impact the lives of the people of New Orleans has been special. In fact it is uncommon. This Saint was dedicated to working with underserved children and aiding those in the city who were in grave need during times of devastation.

Drew continued to show up. His commitment to excellence turned him into a hero. The consistent efforts he dispersed in order to bring hope to people who were struggling came by way of his charitable acts. This led Brees to be named the NFL man of the year in 2006, as he received the Walter Payton Award. This distinguished honor is given annually to the player who demonstrates the most community service. Drew's forthrightness to walk as a great example for youth and to help rebuild the city of New Orleans by walking by faith has been legendary. Southeast Louisiana needed Superman on and off the football field. That is exactly who they got! Drew delivered in superior fashion on Sundays tossing touchdown after touchdown and by pouring out his love to others in the community. This guy was a winner. After a Super Bowl LXIV victory in 2010, his career comeback was solidified, yet a decade plus remained for Brees to lead the charge for the black and gold as he continued to win.

Saintly Discipleship

So what does all this discussion about a football player, besides for the fact that he played for a team with the name Saints, have to do with holiness? How can we learn about iron discipleship from an NFL star? Well, the answer lies in the important aspect of the details. The everyday moments and the ability to bounce back, dust ourselves off, and keep going makes someone a Saint. The no quit attitude, tapping into the fire that burns within, and the drive to be great is uncommon. The will to win, the work ethic to beat the odds, and the hunger for more are aspects of Sainthood.

This is what living a life that impacts others and the world is about. The humility and desire to serve others is what you are called to. You may never put on shoulder pads on Sundays, but you are called to put on the helmet of life and become Saints. As the famous preacher Billy Graham once said, with regard to working in God's vineyard, "Salvation is free, but discipleship costs everything we have." Work ethic is huge. The gift of God's grace has the power to change our lives. When we combine that with an effort to be his laborers, there is no task too tall. Like Brees, you must stay ready, keep after it, and crush life because every day is game day! Before leading the New Orleans Saints onto the field, Brees pumped his team up to get them ready for action. Like all good leaders do to rally their troops, Brees gave his pep talk. After the huddle with the squad, they gathered around and started jumping up and down. What he shouted out to his teammates and their response is something for us all to learn from and live by. The resounding sound that echoed through the stadium was, "Who are we?" and the emphatic reply of his teammates was, "Saints!"

There is a lot to be learned about discipleship and faithfulness to your call here that transcends far beyond the world of sports. Each person has their own story to tell. It is up to you to join forces with God to carry out your destiny. Iron disciples go out there and take it. As Neil L. Anderson put it, "Wherever you now find yourself on the road of discipleship, you are on the right road, the road of eternal life." Saints don't sit around on the sidelines and wait for things to happen. Like the great athletes of your generation you can learn to attack life and grab it by the horns. This is necessary because it's not about you or me at all. See, football is such an awesome sport and metaphor for life. It's a team effort that lands the big "W" on Sundays.

Victories don't simply come on auto pilot. Each team needs great leadership to win. Saints are the iron disciples and the leaders of the Church. They go out and find ways to impact the world and bring people to God. Certainly there are leaders in the institutional Church. However, there is great importance and a need for the laity to take charge and rally the troops. The main thing to keep in front of us is that we work on this together. Jesus had his team of twelve apostles along with some other very close disciples. Each member of Christ's team knew their specific role and carried it out. Along the way there were many bumps and bruises, mistakes, and even outright discord. However, they endured it all. The reason is because champions are all about the *WHY*.

The *WHY* might be the single handed most important aspect of this commitment to rise to the occasion and become a Saint—an iron disciple for Christ. Clearly the damaged and troubled world we live in needs you. Humanity is craving those people who spread positivity and live with conviction. Society needs Saints like you to go above and beyond to bring love and hope to the world. So if your *WHY* is big enough, if the reason for following the Lord wholeheartedly is at the epicenter of your life, dynamic things will happen. After all, "The cost of non-discipleship is the irrelevance of the church," proclaimed Ray Altman. I couldn't agree more! The future of our faith is at stake and there are souls on the line with eternity in the balance. Nothing could possibly be more important than this. Perhaps there are many people who would feel overwhelmed and think this is far too important of a responsibility for them to carry out. Taking that a step further, some might even argue that it's not up to them at all. However, the approach of the Saint is that God blesses his people with life. He calls each by name and gifts us a measure of faith.

On Fire with Love

Therefore, you and I have a decision to make. It comes down to love. Love is something we can choose to do. Love will bring Jesus to the world and that is what Christian discipleship calls for. On the other hand, we can choose to go in the opposite direction. One will leave us feeling full and the other empty. So why is there hesitation? Well, life is complex and when you go all in on becoming an iron disciple, you are saying "yes" with no limitations. This answer manifests itself in loving every person, going to a variety of places, and carrying forth a mission that God will call you to. Yes, that is a huge deal, but what is even cooler is to know that you can and will do things beyond your wildest imagination that will forever change the world. At the forefront of the *WHY* and answering the call to iron discipleship is having a heart for others and building up the Kingdom for our Lord. As long as we keep our focus on Christ and bring his good news to the world by living out his great love for his children, we cannot go wrong.

There is no such thing as a person who makes a difference in this world by being lukewarm. The scripture speaks about this in Revelation that we should be either hot or cold, not on the fence. Let's keep that fire stoked and blazing because it will make a large difference to those we encounter. As St. Ignatius of Loyola powerfully expressed, "Go out and set this world on fire." Not allowing our own fires to simmer is challenging, but that is why having the backs of our fellow disciples and the Saints we journey with is so important.

One of my favorite scriptures can be found in the book of Proverbs. This compilation of wisdom outlines values and discusses moral behavior. Reading powerful messages that talk about the meaning of life is influential. Proverbs is a strong assortment that should be included in the disciples playbook. The verse that sums up your role and significance as disciples and leaders of the body of Christ is, "As iron sharpens iron, so does one man sharpen another."[111] Iron discipleship is about pouring into the lives of other people. The iron disciple is the man or woman who is committed 100% to giving. By blessing, sharing, inspiring, encouraging, and challenging those around them, the Saint is bound to make a difference. When the disciple has the truest goal of impacting other people for the good both of them in the encounter grow in holiness. When we do so we give and receive Jesus.

For our fellow brothers and sisters, this makes them even stronger. It allows them to grow closer to the Lord. For the disciple, it stirs up their faith and produces good fruit for the glory of God. The fruit of our lives happens in a two-fold manner. First our hearts ripen and our souls become deeply engaged in a blossoming relationship with our Lord. We are drawn to him, we turn to Jesus in prayer, and we focus on the things that are above as God increases and we decrease. Through our humility and bearing the fruit that Christ provides to us when we love him we are filled with hope, increased measure of faith, and resounding joy.

---

[111] Proverbs 27:17

The second aspect of bearing good fruit that will remain occurs because our hearts which have been imbued with God's love then desire to share that love with the world. The heartfelt acts of service, spiritual deeds of charity, and corporal works of mercy that we do, plant the seed of faith that is deeply rooted by way of our apostleship in the hearts of those we encounter. Our Lord waters those seeds in these people we have shared his love with and those seeds within their souls eventually flower into lasting fruits of faith. This happens amongst members of our families and communities, which eventually leads to growing the garden of God as more of his children become grafted to the vine. Through sharpening, we all grow in holiness. That is another purpose of discipleship. It is a tremendous blessing to sharpen our brothers and sisters because that makes the Church—the body of Christ—stronger. It leads us to be more equipped to build up God's Kingdom here on earth.

Subsequently, the dividends have an eternal payout in Heaven. The Lord promises to take extra care of those who carry out this call. Dietrich Bonhoeffer said, "Christianity without discipleship is always Christianity without Christ." In other words, it is impossible to be a follower of the Lord if we don't commit our lives to loving our neighbor and seeking out opportunities to lead others closer to Jesus. This is why Jesus himself tells us that we will bear much fruit that will remain when we act upon our faith through love. In a society that values material possessions so much and in a culture that is saturated with gifts and having stuff, the greatest present we can provide to others is love. Iron discipleship provides love by carrying out faith in action.

Jackie Robinson is another sports hero of mine who changed the world forever. Not only was he one of the greatest ball players to ever step foot on the diamond, what is more is that in 1947 he broke Major League Baseball's color barrier. His efforts to desegregate the sport became the catalyst that started a transformation of the world as we know it. What most people don't realize is that Robinson refused to move his seat on a bus years before Rosa Parks came around. Back in 1944, while he was riding on a city bus during his service in the Army, the second lieutenant was approached by a white man. This fellow requested Jackie to move his seat. Robinson, already a man of God and someone who understood his greater purpose, courageously stood his ground and refused to budge. Knowing his rights and most importantly standing up for what he believed in, Jackie ended up being court martialed. The thing is that he would go on to win the court case. This led blacks to one of the very early and ever so important civil rights victories.

The legend who wore number 42 on his jersey would have that number retired from baseball forever. After all, Robinson became the first African American to play a game in the major leagues. However, what is more important to recognize is that his love for people and his desire to create a change in society did not end on the ball field. Jackie would go on to team up with historic leaders like Dr. Martin Luther King Jr. Robinson played a pivotal role as an example on and off the field during the civil rights movement. Jackie suffered extreme humiliation. He faced grave racism and was physically and mentally battered. Nearly every time he took the field or spoke in public he was ridiculed. Yet, being the true Saint and a holy man of God that he was, Robinson stood tall and walked by faith. His will to win victory over racism became his sole purpose for life. The punishments he faced were turned into fuel for his fire. The life Jackie Robinson lived is the gospel message. The way he approached every day in service toward making the world better is what we should all strive for.

Before the Brooklyn Dodger great died, he continued to go to bat for a multitude of organizations, groups, and people. Robinson's work for the rights of minorities, women, and the working class is noteworthy. Certainly, Jackie Robinson's clout on a ball field will forever be remembered. He slugged 197 home runs and led his baseball team to their first ever world championship. As Robinson now smiles down from Heaven on us, those great stats ultimately mean nothing and pale in comparison with his ability to change America. The hope is that each person can learn something from this great man, who was a Saint. You most likely will not do the exact things Robinson did throughout his lifetime. That's okay. Those are some big shoes to fill with regard to the caliber of heroic measure he infused on society. However, what we can do is we can all heed the call to be iron disciples. God is asking you and he is asking me to get up each morning and to make a difference in our own unique way.

Robinson explained iron discipleship and our call to universal holiness as servants in a beautiful manner by stating, "A life is not important except in the impact it has on other lives."[112]

Who are You Living for?

How will you play the game? How will you go out every day and impact your community and the world? These are crucial questions for all of us to think about. What is more important than the thought is ensuring that bold action is taken. We must answer this call because the world needs us. Iron discipleship is about being tough. Bearing down and grinding so that others can be lifted up. The great missionary priest, Father Gregory Boyle, dedicated his life to working with gangsters in Los Angeles. He believed in the power of mercy, love, and forgiveness. Building people up, especially the marginalized and outcasts of society, was his greatest aim. Father Boyle said, "It is not enough to take a stance on an issue. We must walk with people and stand with them in their issues. That is what Jesus did."

After reading his book *Tattoos on the Heart*, I quickly realized that it was time to wake up and step up to the plate. My positions and how I felt about things didn't matter. What was important was figuring out what I was going to do about the issues. What was even more imperative to comprehend was deciphering who I was standing with in their issue. It was time for me and it is time for you to get out there and find our mission field. There is a Calcutta waiting to be found by us, as Mother Teresa would say. To be honest, a number of years ago when I looked at myself in the mirror I wasn't willing to stand with anyone in their issue. I simply took a bunch of bandaids and put them on situations. The mentality of service was a "fix it" mentality. People do not need fixing, they need love and Jesus. Thankfully, my eyes are now open thanks to God's mercy and grace. In the past, who I was willing to stand with in their issue was sadly no one. I disliked this quality because I had previously always taken the safe route of discipleship.

Honesty and listening to the Lord can be sobering. Humility is

---

[112] Promises to Keep by Sharon Robinson

often what we need in order to listen to God and see clearly. When Jesus enters your heart fully it is a very transformative recipe. God has a special way of translating a message that we need to hear and he reveals to us how to get there. Christ can strike us in the center of our souls in such a powerful manner that we are never the same. Intense moments of prayer happen in chapels and they take place in the mission fields of life. You just have to remain open. Jesus is there and he is waiting. Showing up and giving the gift of your presence is the Saint's call to iron discipleship.

Each person has probably done a thing or another during the course of their lifetime that has surprised them. What I have realized is that doing things outside of the norm tends to grow our seeds of faith. During the unique moments and uncomfortable times, people seem to grow in faith in an exponential manner. For me, a prime example of this was getting involved in prison ministry. Occasionally, it takes a gut punch or as a prisoner named Drey told me once when I was helping lead a REC (Residents Encounter Christ) retreat weekend for the inmates, "Sometimes God uses a hammer, sometimes he uses a sledge hammer, but for me he brought out the jackhammer." We must be woken up. Prison ministry shook me to the core, but as I look back, should I be surprised at this? The corporal works of mercy, which we will discuss later on, are a prime way to grow in holiness. These acts of benevolent love during our quest to Heaven helps us to recognize the Saint within us and to be the Saint for those next door. 2,000 years later, Saint Paul still reminds us of this through this message to the early Church when he stated, "Awake, Oh sleeper, rise up from the dead, and Christ will give you light."[113]

Unquestionably, iron discipleship requires great toughness and takes substantial courage. To be a Saintly follower of the Lord takes humility and honesty. It involves rising from the dead. Further along on our journey we will designate some time to unpack what resurrection means for us on our path to Sainthood. Being an ironman or ironwoman with regard to discipleship is a constant challenge. It is certainly not for the faint of heart. The hurdles you will face in your life will in most cases not be easily conquered. And the *ask* of the Lord, as discussed earlier, is quite extensive. However, it's all worth it. The

---

113 Ephesians 5:14

Saints have decided to approach life one day at a time. Through the embracing of holy encounters with others and being the hands and feet of Jesus in the world, they have answered the summons to discipleship. This faithfulness and decision to live out the most powerful words in the Lord's prayer, "Not my will, but yours be done," has inexplicable positive consequences in store. Iron discipleship is key and for the world; it changes everything. Leadership in the faith is crucial with regard to discipleship.

To bring others to the faith, you and I must show by our example. When we are the instruments of God's grace and have the willingness to walk with others constantly, lives are changed. Twelve were originally called and they were the first leaders who radically spread the faith. They made disciples of all nations and you and I are asked to do the same. What an honor and privilege it truly is to work for the Lord. To catch souls in the net of love as Mother Teresa referred to is a tremendously beautiful thing. When we cast out the line for Christ, he will keep working in our lives to bring his children closer to the Father. Leadership is huge, it is time for you and me to step up to the plate and be Jesus for others. Our Church and world needs us. In the words of Pope Francis, "Be leaders wherever it behooves you to be. Leaders of thought, leaders of action, leaders of joy, leaders of hope, leaders of construction of a better world."

Challenge 11

Your next challenge is one that will require some more thought and prayer. I encourage you to try to get to mass one extra time this week. Free up your schedule to spend a few minutes in front of the Blessed Sacrament. When you are with Jesus, listen to what he is putting on your heart. What have you been resisting or in what manner have you held back from taking the next step of faith? How can you embrace the Lord more and allow him to flow through your life as you walk as his disciple? Allow Jesus to work on your spirit and ask the Lord to reveal to you where he is calling you to be. Jesus will give you clarity. He will open wide new opportunities and grant you ways to lead. Christ will bring you to people with whom you will share special encounters. In these experiences you can share your heart. It will be there that you give and receive God's great love.

QUEEN OF HEARTS
CHAPTER 12

"Am I not here, who am your Mother?"
– Our Lady of Guadalupe

An Average Girl with an Uncommon Heart

Think back to when you were fourteen years old. What do you remember about that time in your life? What things mattered to you and how did you tend to spend your time? Imagine shortly after your birthday that year, you were told the heaviest news of your life. No, it wasn't that the kid who sits next to you in math class who you had the biggest crush on likes you also. Sorry, that's not the case. And it's not that your parents bought you front row tickets to your favorite music artist's concert and you would be able to invite your best friend. Envision yourself sitting there and hearing not only the most important news of your life, but receiving a message that would turn into the most significant mission ever. You are told that you would help to carry out something which would have the greatest impact on humanity forever. Are you overwhelmed yet? You would be asked, actually told, that in year two of your teens, you would help to change the history of the world. You and only you would be needed to carry out a task that has never been done before and that people have been waiting on for centuries. The fate of your generation and the future of humankind is hanging on your decision.

Do you have the courage to utter one simple word? The weight and unfolding of eternity comes down to a single "yes." Would you come up with the cure for cancer or a way to resolve poverty? No, far more impactful. Perhaps you were able to somehow stop the violence that has plagued our world since the beginning of time. No, even more powerful than that! What if the magnanimous decision taking place was planned for you to help carry out forever? What if I told you that the one person who would help change the world and humanity even until the end of time would be a young teenage girl. Would you believe that this girl would be uneducated and from a poor family? You might think to yourself, who could this person be and what would they be responsible for? How could she be someone so influential? What if you personally knew her? What if you allowed her to change your life and the life of those you loved?

The answers to each of these profound questions are simple, yet not easy. It comes down to a three letter word that you have said countless times before. Yet, when it matters most, chances are, like me, you too have a tough time saying that word. It carries tremendous weight to utter it, let alone act on it. You have to say the same word that she did. You must give a mere, "Yes." So who is this mysterious figure? You might have been able to piece the puzzle together and understand that this beautiful, pure, holy, and immaculate one is none other than the Mother of God. Mary, our Lady, is not only the Mother of Christ, but your Mother also. How much comfort and peace comes to the one who not only recognizes this wonderful truth, but allows her to enter into their life and permeate the very depths of the human heart. When we invite Mary into our lives, she comes to us. Her desire is to aid us, love us beyond what is fathomable, and bring us to the very Heart of her Son. You will grow closer to the Lord Jesus Christ by understanding his Mother and inviting Mary into your life as Queen of your heart.

Every December we have the opportunity to be immersed in the great narrative known as the Christmas story. It unveils to believers and the world how the beginning of salvation history and Jesus—Emmanuel—"God With us" came to be. It's truly remarkable when we connect the dots as the prophets foretold what was to come thousands of years earlier. Isaiah the prophet was writing about the Savior being born of a virgin centuries prior to the actual event taking place. To see the way that God came into human history through Mary in the most humble of all ways is majestic. In believing and receiving this holy experience and taking part in this special time annually within our faith journey, you and I are left in awe.

The babe in the manger fills our hearts with wonder and excitement. And yet it should not surprise us that the plan of the creator came in an unexplainable and unorthodox fashion. However, what is important to wrap our minds around is that the Lord used an ordinary girl to do and rather to be his extraordinary instrument of love. This is an example of how God takes the familiar and infuses his power and grace to bring about the unfamiliar—the spectacular, as he himself became flesh through the birth of Jesus by way of Mary and the Holy Spirit.

God called Mary, a young girl who had exceptional potential because of her greatest capacity to carry out his will for the sake of the world. Was Mary different, unique, and set apart? Absolutely. Besides Jesus, who was both human and divine, Mary is the only person to walk this earth without being tainted by original sin. She was conceived perfectly. She is after all the Immaculata—which comes from the Immaculate conception. Most people think about this holy event being when Christ was conceived in Mary's womb, but in actuality it is referring to Mary's own conception and coming into being. She lived her entire life with the greatest purpose and the highest regard for God. Without sin, our Mother came to be and she departed from the earth without sin, by way of her assumption into Heaven.

Saints Emulate Mary's Love

For some people this all might seem hard to believe or understand. That is okay. Our faith is powerful and I encourage you to remember that Jesus reminds us that it is far greater to have not seen and have believed. However, when we begin to experience the magnitude and magnificence of the Blessed Mother in our lives, our hearts for Jesus will forever be changed. When we open up our mind and ourselves to the miracle that took place thanks to Mary's steadfast faith, then Christmas becomes more tangible and it comes alive! Let us recall what the scripture says in the first chapter of Matthew's Gospel:

> *Now this is how the birth of Jesus Christ came about. When his Mother, Mary, was betrothed to Joseph, but before they lived together, she was found with child through the Holy Spirit. Joseph, her husband, since he was a righteous man, yet unwilling to expose her to shame, decided to divorce her quietly. Such was his intention when, behold, the angel of the Lord appeared to him in a dream and said, "Joseph, son of David, do not be afraid to take Mary your wife into your home. For it is through the Holy Spirit that this child has been conceived in her. She will bear a son and you are to name him Jesus, because he will save his people from their sins." All this took place to fulfill what the Lord had said through the prophet. Behold, the virgin shall be with child and bear a son, and they shall name him Emmanuel," which means "God is with us."[114]*

Before we go even deeper into Mary's "yes" to God, it is imperative that we realize that being blindsided in life does not discriminate. You and I are all susceptible to the unforeseen. Even Mary, being as holy as she was, faced great uncertainty and spiritual hardship. There is no telling where or when it will come about or how the unknown will develop. However, one thing is for certain, it did come into Mary's life and the unplanned will sneak up on us too. That is inevitable. As my parish priest, Father Walsh, explained to me, "Life has a way of blindsiding us. But we know that our faith has grown when we start handing it over to the Lord instead of fighting it. This is what Mary did and our Lord asks this of us as well. Mary did hand it over to God and that is so powerful." She said, "Behold, I am the handmaid of the Lord. May it be done to me according to your word..."[115] Could this be your response? The way to get there and to build that trust is through

---

114 Matthew 1:18-23
115 Luke 1:38

relationship and service to God. Our Blessed Mother desires you to be able to have the same unwavering faith and for you to know in your heart that God is in complete control of your life! But in order for this to happen, you must surrender.

Many Christians and even Catholics with strong faith don't quite understand the importance and significance of Mary. This young, uneducated, and poor girl named Mary went from peasant to the Mother of the Savior of the World. How could this be? God knew she had what it would take and believed in her ability to carry it out as a part of her destiny. He saw the greatness in her before she recognized it in herself. He saw the holiness in her from the get-go. Our Lord noticed Mary's willingness to do God's will with the greatest faith, even when uncertainty swarmed around her. Mary was asked to carry out God's plan for salvation because this was her mission in life. By saying "yes" to God's call on her life, amidst being scared, confused, and overwhelmed, Mary became the mother of Jesus Christ and our Mother too.

Therefore, she is the holy Mother of the Church who intercedes for us on behalf of our sinful and sorrowful selves so that we might be aided in our journey to the heart of Jesus, her son. It is for all of these reasons that you need to know her more, understand her role in your life better, and grasp her profound love for you. In the rosary, we meditate on the life and mysteries of Christ and enter into time and space with him as we request the guidance of the Blessed Mother and receive her love. We ask her to "pray for us sinners, now." Why wait or take a circuitous route? If mom says so and we have received her love, let us never stop receiving it because she knows best. We are all Mary's children and she is our Mother. There are many people who would ask, isn't Jesus enough? He is Lord and Savior and there certainly is no one else whom salvation comes from. This is true.

What is also true is that Mary is Christ's mother and she knows him and the depths of his heart better than anyone else. She carried Jesus, raised him, followed him, and believed in his mission from the time the angel came to her. Our Mother's unwavering faith and her humility, as well as her perfect willingness to do God's will is something we can all admire and learn from. What is even more though is her great desire to unite us to the Sacred Heart of Jesus and to bring us fully into his love.

186 | Dan Jason

When we think of the people in our lives who have had the greatest impact on us, our earthly mother is most likely at the top of the list. A special connection and depth is there due to the fact that your mom carried you in her womb and brought you into this world from the start. Whether you have a great relationship with your earthly mom or have a living mom at all, no matter what that looks like, the Mother of God loves you unconditionally as her own child. It is essential to recognize and believe that Mary is not some far off thought or celestial being in Heaven. Her presence is not somewhere unobtainable and distant from us. She is here with us today and has been immersed in the lives of the faithful since the time she walked the earth. At certain moments throughout history, Mary has shown up in profound, intense, and miraculous ways. Before we get into these most renowned happenings, it is vital to discuss how Mary's role as our Mother and our relationship with her is the quickest way to the Heart of Jesus and ultimately the surest road to Sainthood.

At the foot of the Cross there were a few people who remained with Christ and did not leave his side. When everyone else scattered and Jesus was left hanging on the tree at Calvary, the beloved disciple, John, and Mary, Jesus' mother were there with him. When we look back at the scene and transport ourselves to Golgotha it becomes very clear. Just think about all those followers who promised to stick by our Lord's side. They promised to never leave Jesus, only to abandon him. It should not be surprising that the Lord's mother stood with him through it all. Mary was given John as her son from Jesus and John was told that Mary would be his mother; the scripture says, "When Jesus saw his mother there, and the disciple who he loved standing nearby, he said, 'Dear woman, here is your son,' and to the disciple, 'Here is your mother.' From that time on, the disciple took her into his home."[116] Certainly, Jesus initiated the profound relationship between Mary and John as a model for all of us to have with the Immaculata—Mary our Blessed Mother. She desires to guide, protect, and be with us each day. She is the one who knew her Son Jesus best and who can teach you to trust in God's plan for your life, no matter what that plan might involve.

---

[116] John 19:26-27

Discernment Leads to
Trust & Unwavering Obedience

It's healthy and important to contemplate the happenings of life, especially those that are confusing and difficult for us to carry in our hearts. Mary prayerfully reflected, always looking inwardly and establishing a beautiful pattern for her children. As a result of doing this reverently, not only did she remain faithful through it all, she grew in holiness and grace. Mary will guide us in our own personal mission and provide us with strength through her spouse, the Holy Spirit, so we are empowered to live boldly. Sainthood comes through holiness and what better way to receive holiness than from our holy Mother. Mary's deepest desire was the same that day, two millennia ago, as it is for us today. Her heart beats for you and for me. She wants nothing more than to lead us directly to Christ. When we open up ourselves and become united with the Lord, the Blessed Mother will show us the way to receive Jesus' love for us completely. Then and only then will we receive the Sacred Heart of Jesus, becoming one with him.

Through a relationship with Mary centered upon prayer, she promises to intercede for us. Unquestionably, Mary guides her children and protects them unceasingly. By her immaculate and holy blessing on our lives, Mary connects us to the very heart of Christ. At the end of his life, Jesus could have said so many things with his last words before he breathed his final breath. I can only imagine beforehand the type of message we might want to leave with those people we love most in the wake of passing from this world. There is a reason why the Lord's final dozen words that he spoke included giving Mary to the beloved disciple (John) and to all of humanity as her children.

Jesus gave us his mother to be our mother. This is how his life on earth ended, with a present given to us in Mary the Mother of God who became the mother of the Church. Now Jesus is asking us to make her the queen of our hearts. It's not only at the end of Christ's life that we get this powerful presence of Mary or where the remarkable takes place. Actually, think back to the very beginning of Jesus' public ministry. Look no further than the wedding feast at Cana. Mary goes to her son when the wine runs out because she realizes who he is and what he is capable of. However, Jesus tells her that his hour has not yet come and that he is not ready to do the miraculous. Yet, Mary's great faith is what moves the heart of Christ to action. The Blessed Mother tells the headwaters what to do. Her message is direct and it serves as a powerful directive for our lives as believers. The waiters are scrambling, as panic has settled in. There is no more wine, not even the cheap stuff is left and the feast must go on. Mary tells them, "Do whatever he tells you."[117] This word spoken by Mary is an extraordinary message to us as Saints. If you and I can place everything into the Lord's hands and do whatever he tells us, our lives will overflow with the richest blessings and joy. We will have the best wine that was served to the wedding guests on our own journey and it will surely never run out. Our thirst will be quenched because Christ's powerful cry from the Cross where he uttered, "I thirst," will be revered and remembered all the more. By the way we choose to live as devoted sons and daughters who trust Jesus fully on all occasions and in every way possible like our Mother did, we enter into his grace. Mary will bring us closer to her Son and Jesus will give us his loving heart.

Jesus' thirst for our hearts is unrelenting and there is only one who knows how to quench the thirsting heart of God. Christ's Mother has the strongest desire to love us as her children. She continues to lead us to the foot of the Cross. Mary invites you and me to be there at Calvary with herself and John. Inevitably, we will carry crosses throughout our own lifetime, but when we choose to bring our sorrows and pain to the foot of the Cross, we will receive new strength because God promises to lighten our load. When we decide to open our hearts to Mary and allow her into our lives without reservation, we essentially open our hearts up more fully to Jesus. In giving yourself to Mary and asking for her intercession you will grow in holiness. Through consecration to Jesus by way of the Blessed Mother's guidance, you can more fully and more perfectly grow in holiness. To be connected with the Lord who was birthed and raised by the young peasant girl in Nazareth is to enter fully into the mystery of Christ's life as God chose to enter humanity through the Mother of the world.

---

[117]John 2:5

The Power of Marian Devotion & the Rosary

When I was growing up, my great grandmother would pray the rosary. However, I didn't understand what it was or why she took out her light blue strand of beads passing them through her withered fingers as she whispered a single prayer repetitively. It wasn't until I was about thirteen that I said the rosary for the first time. I had learned the *Hail Mary* prior to becoming a teenager, but to me it seemed like a spiritual workout that took a lot of grit to muster through the countless prayers connected to that strand of beads. I walked through the motions, saying the prayers out of obligation. Although I was drawn in for some reason, I did not know the power behind the rosary or what the purpose of this prayer was. Now, nearly two decades later, after somehow a seed of faith and devotion to Mary was planted in my heart, not a day passes without me praying the rosary. Mary has become the queen of my heart. The rosary has become a powerful weapon in my arsenal and the beads that I wear around my neck and carry in my pocket are part of my spiritual armor on the road to Sainthood. The rosary contains such prolific mysteries that are entered into by the faithful, offering an intense meditative way to journey with Jesus and grow closer to the Lord. When we enter into the rosary and offer it up to the Blessed Mother, we are changed.

The rosary is an age-old prayer that was given to Saint Dominic back in 1208 during an apparition. It has been professed throughout the centuries and reminds us how Mary's heart beats for us to know the Lord and enter into life with him in every aspect. By entering into prayer with our whole heart, we enter into the life of Jesus and we journey with him and his Mother toward holiness. We have the opportunity to use each mystery as a way to pray for blessings, healings, and intentions of those in our families and in our world. In addition, the rosary and walking with Mary side by side is a great way to meditate on the love of Christ. It provides time and space for the faithful to enter into the grace of Our Mother who is there to guide and protect us as we venture to grow closer to her Son.

Devotion to the Blessed Mother and consecrating my own life to her and to Jesus has radically transformed my heart and provided me with sustainable inner peace. What do you mean by consecration? Well, to consecrate means to make or declare sacred. To be sacred means that there is a connection with God. So the act of consecrating ourselves and giving our best selves to the Blessed Mother connects us to our Lord in an intimate and exquisite manner. Receiving graces from Mary are common for those who pay homage to her and keep their faith in her Son. Rest in the words... "Hail Mary, full of grace the Lord is with thee. Blessed art thou amongst women and blessed is the fruit of your womb, Jesus. Holy Mary, Mother of God, pray for us sinners, now and at the hour of our death. Amen."[118]

In the beginning of this journey we contemplated some prolific questions regarding giving permission to God to enter our lives so he can change us and show us the way to carry out our mission. Much easier said than done. We have the perfect example and need not look any further. Keep your eyes on Mary. Saints get specific privileges and have their prayers answered more clearly and more quickly, right? What if I told you that your prayers carry the same weight as those who wrote the Bible, the prophets, and the greatest Saints in the Church? Do you believe that? It comes down to your faith. Therefore, the measure with which you believe you shall receive.

Asking for intercessions is powerful and crazy in the best of ways. The intercessions that have personally been received are surely unexplainable at times. This has not been because of anything I did or who I am, but all because of the grace, promise, love, and protection of our Mother. After all, she was promised to you by her Son Jesus at the foot of the Cross where Christ gave himself completely. Mary watched our Lord enter the world and then she witnessed his exit, but this would not be his last moment. Just do it, just believe. Intercessory prayer works because Mary, who loves you and wants you to know her Son, desires to hear you and to lead you to Jesus. Father Michael Gaitley writes about this in his life-changing book entitled *33 Days to Morning Glory* where he states, "The quickest and surest way to holiness and to Sainthood is through total consecration to Mary and Jesus."

When we die to ourselves and devote body, soul, and mind to the Lord we become fully alive. When we thirst for Jesus and ask the Blessed Mother for her most pure heart and to keep us in her heart, then we can be forever connected to the Sacred Heart of Jesus Christ.

---

[118] Hail Mary Prayer

My experiences of prayer and dedication to the Blessed Mother grew exponentially after being the recipient of a number of miracles. Before you discount what I am about to say or for those who think that miracles no longer happen, hear me out. I am sharing this with you because Mary wants to know you and she desires your heart to be one with Jesus. Along with praying the rosary daily, I wear the brown scapular given by Mary to St. Simon Stock in 1251 at Mount Carmel. It was during that appearance to him that she promised whoever wears the brown scapular would be spared of eternal fire. It might sound like magic or some far off weird concept, but let me explain the power of Mary's grace by taking you back to the second most memorable day of my life. For those of you who have journeyed with me through my first book, *Fire Burning Within*, you know my full story and how God spared me from taking my own life when I was a teen. Fast forward nearly a decade, removed from that first miraculous moment, I would soon be the recipient of yet another time where she came "full of grace."

It was a long four hour road trip from my home in Albany out to Buffalo. On a cold December Sunday, the exact date was December 18, 2016. I was looking to have some fun with my best friend. Just a week before Christmas, fully immersed in the advent season and fresh off of weekend mass, I was on my way to pick up Andrew who lived in Syracuse for the Bills vs. Browns game. As I often do on many car trips I took out my rosary. This particular rosary was special to me as I had received it as a gift while being in Rome having visited the Vatican a few years prior. I started to pray for family and friends while meditating on the glorious mysteries. Three decades (strands of beads) into saying the rosary, the weather had turned from mere rain and 43 degrees to freezing rain and ice in a matter of seconds. My small black Toyota Corolla traveling at 65 mph on the Thruway hit a patch of black ice and my car began to skid. My vehicle was fishtailing and then slid directly toward a massive tractor trailer adjacent to me. In a blink of an eye everything changed. It would be only another second before I would be totally engulfed by this big rig, having my car squished underneath the eighteen wheeler. My heart sank and one thought ran through my head, my life was soon to be over. Instinctively, my hands yanked the wheel of that car to the left, pulling it in the opposite direction of the truck to avoid being crushed. What happened next was something hard to explain. It was an occurrence that you can't even make up.

Thinking about it alone is bleak. Considering the probability of survival leaves me dumbfounded about how I am still alive to tell you this story today. In a matter of less than five seconds, a time frame that moved in slow motion seeming to last an eternity as it played out, my car did two complete 360s. As it spun like a top across the interstate it then hit more ice and rolled two and a half times. Finally, the vehicle halted after landing upside down in a ditch. I had rolled across the highway like some dice, luckily being stopped by a massive snow bank which kept me from continuing into oncoming traffic that would have obliterated me. I remember as clear as day the thought that shot through my mind like a rocket as this all transpired, "Lord if I don't survive please let my wife and my family know I love them."

When the whirlwind of events came to a close, I was hanging upside down from the roof of my vehicle. Surely this wasn't a dream, or nightmare rather. In my mind thoughts came flooding in so I knew that I was conscious. However, I didn't know how badly I was injured or if the car was in danger, or even worse, caught on fire. The roof was completely smashed in and the windshield destroyed. All of the doors were demolished except the rear passenger exit. I knew I had to try to get out and it had to be fast. I sat there frozen, dangling from the ceiling after a near death experience. My heart was pounding a million times a minute and the scene replayed in my mind like an old cassette tape on rewind.

Coming to my senses, I crawled out of the car with my rosary in hand. It was as if God had placed an angel there at my feet at that moment protecting me from all harm. When I managed to emerge and stumble out of the demolished vehicle, a State Trooper was right there beside me. She said, "I watched that entire accident and I cannot believe that you are alive, let alone that you don't have a single scratch on your body. You are lucky." I had no real words to explain this to myself or to anyone else for that matter. All I could muster up in that moment of sheer disbelief that my life was spared was, "Me either, except I had some protection." Still clenched in between my shaking fingers was of course my rosary—my protection. Coincidence, no way.

This was God's divine mercy, grace, and protection. Trust fully and receive.

An event like this on an average day in December, while praying the rosary in route to a football game, ended up being life-saving. When you experience supernatural graces and protection in your life, certainly it is much easier to have faith. Belief becomes truth and fact, which no one can deny. When you are the recipient of divine assistance and assurance through Mary's intercession how can you not be changed? My relationship and devotion to the Blessed Mother has greatly shaken up my world and it has radically altered the course of my life. This life-sparing incident was the most profound physical experience and sensation I have had during my lifetime. In addition, there have been others since then which include and are not limited to being saved by the Blessed Mother's grace while scuba diving in a lake after getting trapped under a dock. With no light coming through and the oxygen having run out of the tank, I thought my life was over yet again. During this experience, I recall praying, asking Mary to take my hand and lead me to an opening so my life could be spared. I remember praying the words "NOW," the same *now* that is in the Hail Mary... "*Now* and at the hour of our death." When we believe, we receive. When we ask and it is God's will for our lives, big things can happen.

Not only will protection come upon us, but also blessings for the lives of other people and positive experiences that occur due to divine assistance. Praying for the healing of numerous sick members of my family, including those riddled by cancer, turned into remarkable recovery. There was even a baby that the doctors said was going to be born without arms and legs. Science and reason said that she would be lucky to survive and have all sorts of mental retardation. Many people prayed for this little girl. I specifically prayed a rosary every day for a period of six months for this child. She was born a perfectly healthy kid who now lives a full and happy life. Many other miracles have taken place including the blessing of faith upon so many I know and love that have come to receive the Lord in their hearts.

The point of sharing these experiences and answered prayers is to relay a message that Marian devotion and faithfulness go hand in hand. God's love for his children is showered upon us through amazing graces that we receive through the Blessed Mother. As much as we need air to breathe or food and water to consume for survival, so too do we need love to satisfy our hungry hearts. You and I are malnourished and starve spiritually without knowing the Lord Jesus through the intercession of the blessed Mother in our lives. Can we survive without knowing her more deeply and allow Mary to know us at the core? My answer is actually a follow-up question. Why would anyone ever want to? Why would you ever want to not know your Mother and feel her warm protective love and care? Is it our aim to not be merely alive, but to live fully in order to share the joys of the Lord with others! One of the greatest joys includes the ways Christ fills our hearts with the radiant love of his Mother. Always remember that Mary is our Mother also.

So why does Mary care so much for us? It is because as our Mother she wants us to be filled with true and lasting joy. She knows that in this world only one thing will make us fulfilled, namely only one—Jesus. A relationship with her Son and receiving his abundant love is the only way for us to have joy that never ends. God gave Jesus to Mary and now she wants to bring us to him—give us to Christ. Before we continue to learn and reflect more on Mary and the important role she plays in our lives, I invite you to pray with me for a brief moment:

> *Oh Blessed Virgin Mary, guide us and protect us. May the light of your immaculate grace shine upon your people. Help us to have the unwavering trust you had in the Lord and allow our faith to deepen. Show us how to trust and to love as you did and live in our hearts so we are inspired as your children to walk closely with God. Be with us and move us to say "Yes" as you did in order to carry out God's plan for our lives. Lend us your heart oh Mother so we may draw closer to the Father and are united with the Sacred Heart of Jesus. Amen*

– Our Lady of Guadalupe
Mary's Appearance to Juan Diego

Apparitions are rare. By definition, an apparition is an unexpected sight, typically the vision of a person who is no longer living. We are not talking about ghosts or chasing fictitious creatures here.

Apparitions, for those of faith, have occurred over the centuries. They have had massive impacts on situations as the divine spark of God is present in the miraculous. Apparitions have led groups of people and individuals to conversion of heart and to great faith. The four most famous and well known apparitions include Mary's appearance to children at Fatima, her unveiling to those at Lourdes, to teens at Medjugorje and to a peasant in Mexico City. There are many others that you can read about and that the faithful of the Church have experienced. Mary is alive not only in our hearts, but in the world as she watches over the Church as only a mom can do. And no, you do not need to have an apparition—vision or physical sight of Mary during your lifetime to become a Saint. However, we can learn from these experiences and the holy moments because they carry great purpose and meaning for the lives of the faithful and the body of Christ on earth.

The first miraculous event that connected Mary to me on a deeply personal level was receiving a brown scapular that I wore during my horrific car accident. Six months or so before my life flashed before my eyes and death nearly came knocking, I received the brown scapular from Father Justin. I remember being at the chapel on Mount St. Mary's campus in Newburgh, NY when the Franciscan priest gave a vigorous homily about Mary's love and protection of her children. It was there, on that seemingly ordinary day, that an extraordinary protection was issued. Father spoke about Saint Simon Stock who had an intense vision—apparition. Simon Stock encountered the Blessed Mother about 800 years ago and she gave to him the scapular to wear as her promise of protection.

Father Justin explained that she continues to work miracles through to this day. The promise was that anyone who wore the scapular would be spared from eternal fire. It has been noted countless times that men, women, and children have survived insurmountable situations by receiving the protection of the Blessed Mother because they wore that brown scapular. Some people would say that it's coincidence, others name it as luck. For me, I experienced it first hand and I can tell you that Mary was with me. Her intercession and God's divine power spared my life. Call it what you want, but I know it was supernatural grace. Why are people so afraid of the miraculous? Did not Jesus tell his disciples over and over, "If you believe..." Sometimes what transpires is so magnanimous that there is no explanation. In the end, holy moments come from one source, God.

The second apparition I learned of that has had a significant influence on my life during my spiritual journey was one I heard about when on mission a number of years ago. It is interesting that God tends to appear and send the Blessed Mother to those who have a heart for him despite the difficulty of the situation that is faced. The year was 1531. The setting takes us south of the border in Mexico, near today what is known as Mexico City. Juan Diego, a simple peasant and member of the Aztec tribe had great faith. Living amidst a culture and within a society that was sacrificing upwards of 9,000 people a day was torturous to his people, let alone his soul. This included women and children being brutally murdered as their blood was spilled as offerings up to the sun, moon, and other gods. Needless to say, seeing this daily was very difficult for Juan Diego.

His heart was stirred up to seek Christ and his love for the Lord was profound. The events that took place remind us of how powerful one person's faith can be. It shows us how they can be the *Saint Next Door*; faith being used to spread love and hope, which conclusively leads to life. Juan knew something had to change and he believed in the power of prayer, especially giving thanks to God. So he walked miles each day to attend mass in secret because he desired to receive Christ in the Eucharist where he did so at a small chapel atop a steep hillside. Diego's heart was pained by his people and his soul suffered agony. To see the innocent children slaughtered daily was too much to bear. So Juan took it to prayer and laid his sorrows down at the feet of Jesus who then sent his Blessed Mother.

It was a typical day when one morning Juan Diego was walking to mass. The date was December 9th, 1531, and he hiked up toward Tepeyac Hill trekking through the rough terrain. When Mary first appeared to him, she showed up as a young girl. Juan was naturally startled and did not know what to make of this apparition. Mary even spoke to him in his native Nahuatl language, asking him to ask the Bishop to have a church built in that area. I can only but imagine the thoughts that must have gone through Juan's head. First of all, he probably was doubting whether he was seeing clearly or if it was a dream. Then what came to his mind was what would come to most people's minds in this unusual situation; Who would believe him? After all, he was a poor man in his 50s and part of a tribe that was not well received.

But this is the beauty of Mary's grace and the Lord's power of her working in the lives of the faithful. There is no requirement of status, wealth, career position, or any other criteria. Faith and trust are all that are required of us. An open heart to love is all that our Mother asks for. Nothing else is necessary besides being present. Am I saying that it is normal for Mary to appear to people? No, I am not. Nor will I suggest she has appeared to me or to anyone I know in the same capacity as she did to this peasant man who later became Saint Juan Diego. Yet, I do believe that she is in our midst and it is possible. I hope that she will appear again soon to her faithful children. Back to the apparition.

The next day, Mary appeared again and asked Juan to speak to the Bishop at the time, Juan Zummaraga. Still not knowing how to explain what he experienced, Juan Diego went his way. It would have been awfully difficult to get a meeting with the most esteemed member of the Church hierarchy for anyone, let alone a peasant. What made matters even more challenging for Diego was that he was from the Aztec tribe that was brutally killing its own people. Being part of a heathenistic culture made him far less than popular. By December 11th, Diego's uncle was very sick and he had to leave at once to care for him. This was Juan's only hope that his beloved family member would survive. The morning of December 12th, while Juan Diego was trying to take another way to intentionally avoid Mary, the Blessed Mother sought him out. Juan basically told the Virgin Mary that he didn't have time for her because he was in a hurry to get to his sick uncle. Imagine that!

Instead of getting mad, Mary, being full of grace, told Juan that his uncle had already been healed as a result of his great faith. Mary then told Diego that she needed him to bring a sign to the Bishop at once. So at that moment Juan Diego agreed and the Blessed Mother provided him with Spanish roses as a sign to provide to the Bishop. This happened at a time during the winter when no roses at all could possibly grow in that elevation there in the mountains of Mexico City. Our Lady asked Juan Diego to take those roses back to the Bishop and to show him them. Little did Juan know that Bishop Zumarraga was a great botanist of his time. He loved roses, just another sign that our Mother knows what her children need. Juan's "yes" to Our Mother changed the course of history, as her great power and the miraculous working of the Lord shone forth. Juan Diego put the roses in his tilma (cloak), made out of a rough sack like material, and started a long journey to the Bishop. After walking several miles, Juan arrived and was permitted entrance to the Bishop's quarters. He knelt down and something miraculous happened.

As Juan was on his knees opening his cloak to present the roses to the Bishop which was a sign from Mary to build the church, what took place could have only been engineered from the Heavenly Father. Unbeknownst to Diego, inside his tilma (cloak) emerged the image of what is Our Lady of Guadalupe. Her image and beauty appeared on the very burlap sack fabric of Juan's cloak. It was not artwork or manmade. No one had drawn it or sewed it into the fabric. This was a miracle that not only convinced the Bishop to build the new church there at Tepeyac Hill, but it led to the conversion of millions in Mexico and all across Central and South America. Upwards of 8,000-9,000 Aztecs per day were being baptized and brought to faith as were others throughout the continent.[119]

The greatest conversion to Christianity took place because of the sweet love and grace of the Virgin Mother. A small, simple "yes" uttered by one poor and humble servant who had great faith changed the world. Our Lady asked Juan Diego, "No sabes que soy tu madre? Do you not know that I am your Mother?" Not only is Mary our Mother, she is the Mother of all children. Her love and mercy, as well as her tender care and desire to connect you with the heart of Jesus is her deepest longing. Oh Blessed Mother I ask that you lead your children closer to the Lord and keep us always protected in the mantle of your grace. Give us your heart and keep us in yours so that we might come to know Emmanuel and be given his Sacred Heart on our road to Sainthood.

---

[119] A Handbook on Guadalupe: Mary, Francis

Our Lady & the Powerful Symbols of the Tilma

There is great symbolism and divine meaning behind each of the intricate details on the tilma of Juan Diego. The image of our Lady of Guadalupe speaks volumes to the miraculous and how God continues to bring alive the faith. Remind you, it has to be stated again that this is not a work of art or some type of religious creation. It is the working of a miracle through Mary composed by the greatest artist of all, God! Mary appears to be about 14 or 15 years old on the tilma and is pregnant with the savior in her womb. The black ribbon that is tied around her waist indicates her pregnancy. Take notice of her solemn face and how she is holding her hands in prayer, as she reflected upon all things in her heart. There is a bright sun around her head, signifying the glow of the Aztec sun and radiance of Heaven on high. Below the Blessed Mother's feet is the moon. This was an important symbol for the Aztec empire and the Mexican people as the moon holds great power in their culture. Near her feet is a Franciscan priest that looks like an angel figure holding up Heaven and Earth. The garb that Mary is wearing is a teal color, which was symbolic of Aztec royalty, fitting as she is the Queen of the Church. The star pattern on her robe was studied by astronomers and is the exact star formation that was in the sky above Mexico City and Tepeyac Hill the night of December 12th, 1531. This was the exact day when our Lady appeared to Juan Diego and gave him the sign. The roses that are imprinted on her robe are Spanish roses, the same which our Lady gave to Juan Diego to bring to the Bishop.[120]

Certainly, through God's divine power, Mary coming onto the scene in a profound way transformed the Mexican culture and converted millions. Her abundant grace bestowed upon Juan Diego, a peasant, reinforces that she is the Mother of all who call on her name. So what does this all have to do with our road to Sainthood? Well, each of us is called by God to carry out a unique mission. We have all been blessed with a different measure of faith and with talents to utilize. No matter what that measure of faith is or where we are called today by the Lord, one thing is for certain: Jesus is asking us to lead people closer to him. Being a disciple is what this life is about. Who

---

[120] A Handbook to Guadalupe: Mary, Francis

better to learn from and to guide us than Christ's mother. Our Lady
will aid us, protect us, and show us the way to the foot of the Cross
and the loving heart of her Son.

I hope you take comfort and feel the power of this beautiful
Memorare prayer which reminds us of why Mary is to be revered and
why we as believers must open up our hearts to her and her Son.

> *Remember, O most gracious Virgin Mary, that never was it*
> *known that anyone who fled to your protection, implored your*
> *help, or sought your intercession, was left unaided. Inspired by*
> *this confidence, I fly unto you, O Virgin of virgins, my Mother.*
> *To you do I come, before you I stand, sinful and sorrowful. O*
> *Mother of the Word Incarnate, despise not my petitions, but in*
> *your mercy, hear and answer me. Amen.*

Do you not know that you are her son, that you are her daughter?
Having been blessed to see the tilma with my own eyes and to
pilgrimage up to the top of Tepeyac Hill I can attest to Our Lady of
Guadalupe's power in my own spiritual journey. Setting foot on the
ground that Mary appeared to Juan Diego nearly 500 years ago, I can
say that I have been changed. Sure, having gone numerous times and
desiring to go back again has great power in my life. Regardless, if you
ever go to one of these holy places of apparition, whether or not you
have your own miracle happen to you or to someone you know, one
thing remains constant. Our Mother loves you and will never stop
pursuing your heart.

As you continue to journey on with me and learn more about
Sainthood, we will discuss how to impact the world. We have much to
discover with regard to the ways that God is calling us during our time
on earth before we arrive home. My hope is that you will open up your
hand to Mary, your Mother, who is reaching out. If we would have
just a single drop of her thirst for her Church, as she does for the
world, the inspiration and faith we have would grow vastly. Surely,
there is no limit to what you and I can do with Jesus and the Blessed
Mother in our lives. My challenge to you right now is to give it a
chance. You don't have to understand it all. You don't have to know
how it will happen. Just trust and believe.

Allow your faith to come more fully alive and invite Mary into your heart. Below you will find a prayer that I wrote. It is a consecration prayer and my personal devotion to Our Lady. This prayer is something that I say regularly and it is why I not only believe, but know with full conviction in my heart that Sainthood is possible. Holiness is obtainable not because of what we have done or what we will do, but because of God's grace. Becoming whole—holy—happens because we have the most loving Mother who wants nothing more than for us to experience the fullness of God's love. Invite Mary into your life so she can become the Queen of your heart. No one can lead us closer to Christ than the Holy Spirit and its spouse—Mary the Mother of God. Your spiritual mother loves you and as the bride of the Church, she promises to bring you closer to Jesus.

Oh blessed Virgin Mary, my Mother and the Mother of Jesus, consecrate me to your son Jesus and to you. Holy Spirit, living in Mary, live in my heart. Grant me your most pure heart oh Mother and keep me in your heart that I might be connected to the Lord and Savior Jesus Christ. Sanctify me and help me to die to self, offering up my life to you. Bring me to holiness in body, mind, and spirit so that I am connected to and given the Sacred Heart of Jesus. Oh Mother of God, lead me ever closer to your Son through divine intercession and protect me. Help me to listen to Jesus' thirst for his children. Help me to respond and to do what you ask of me. Give me the love I need to take care of the little ones and bring them to you Oh Lord. Guide me and show me the way to you my God, this day, and every day so I do all things to build up the Kingdom. Help me to never cease leading others to Jesus. Give me the strength, the words, the thoughts, and the actions of eternal life that I live out my baptismal call and become a Saint for your Church. Amen.

Challenge 12

Today's challenge is to think about and pray for your relationship with the Blessed Mother. If you haven't considered this or prayed a rosary in a while, I encourage you to do so. But when you pray, I hope that you will invite Mary into your heart. Meditate on the mysteries of Christ's life and ask Our Lady to guide you closer to the heart of her son. I encourage you to open your heart to the Mother of Jesus because when you do, your life will be changed. She will help you and show you the way to have unwavering trust in Jesus.

DUMPSTER DIVING WITH JESUS

CHAPTER 13

*"Begin now... Believe me, don't wait until tomorrow
to begin becoming a Saint." – St. Thérèse of Lisieux*

Everyday Saints are Commonly Uncommon

Each day the world is in need of people like you to live life in an
unordinary way. Every morning with the rising of the sun, society
craves people I like to call *everyday Saints*. Throughout this book we
have discussed some noteworthy canonized Saints and people in
history who have made a significant impact. The term *everyday Saints*
has come up in the previous chapters from time to time, but it's
significant for us to now dive more deeply into this holy concept.
Today is the day that you and I put on our own armor and get out
there to fight the good fight for the faith. Remember that Jesus came
to serve others and to spread God's love to open up the Kingdom for
us all. If we are to live out our own call of discipleship and walk the
road to holiness, it is paramount that we don't lose sight of becoming
everyday Saints.

So what is an *everyday Saint* and how do you get there? Well, it is
actually not overly difficult or involved. It really comes down to you
and I being who we are authentically at the core. This means us

blazing our own trail and doing things with extraordinary love and vigor. It involves embracing each day as a blessing and seeing our time as a prime opportunity to go out into the world and love fully. The scriptures remind us that Jesus called his disciples to the abundant harvest that is out there in our world. This message wasn't just to be heard and acted upon by the apostles and followers of the Lord 2,000 years ago. It remains today and when lived out creates such a radical change in our world. So what exactly are the *everyday Saints* going out and harvesting, you might be wondering. Well, they are committed to working in God's mission field in order to plant seeds, share love, spread hope, and in consummation help bring souls to Christ.

Throughout the three or so decades of my lifetime on this earth it is pretty clear when I come across someone who is different. When I meet a person who has something about them, a fire, a light, an attractive beauty that radiates from within, I want to know them. It is as if we are amongst an angel whom God sent our way as our daily bread of encouragement. The scriptures say, "Man ate the bread of the angels; food he sent in abundance."[121] Not only do we pray for the daily bread of the Lord in the prayer Jesus taught us, but unexplainably God provides these men and women we need at the exact moments we need them. We will touch on this concept of divine connections a little later on, but, without a shadow of a doubt each person desires to understand who these people—angels are. We want to spend time with them, and join forces with them.

Everyday Saints exist throughout the world. They are the men, women, and children whose faith shines and who embody the anthem, "He would love first." That saying is something that is aligned to who Jesus was and who he calls us to be. The *everyday Saint* is the person who gets up and works hard and goes the extra mile. They listen to their co-worker who is having a tough day, they take a minute to point out the great efforts of a colleague, and they celebrate the promotion of someone in their department. The *everyday Saint* is the mom who rises early to make her kids lunches for school and writes notes of encouragement for them to read. She kisses her children and tells them that she loves them before they get on the school bus. The

---

[121] Psalms 78:25

everyday Saint is the husband who calls his wife during his coffee break or shoots her a text just to say hello and let her know that she is his queen. He is the man who comes home and helps out with things like making dinner or doing the laundry to lighten the load of his spouse. The *everyday Saint* is the kid who cleans their room and puts away their toys without their parents asking. It is the big brother or sister who helps their sibling with their homework and allows them to tag along when playing with older friends.

Everyday Saints are the people who send handwritten letters or cards to their amigos throughout the vast seasons of life. They are the people who help the elderly into their car or to cross the street. They are the humans of this world who come in a variety of ages, races, ethnicities, cultures, religious affiliations and countries who forgive others and believe in second chances. *Everyday Saints* are the humans who listen first, are slow to speak, contain their anger, and think about others. They ask God, who in this world needs some love today. *Everyday Saints* smile at others and are the smile of God on others. They are humble, honest, hard-working, and most of all faith-filled people who want to impact society by allowing God into their lives. *Everyday Saints* preach the Gospel to their greatest ability by living out the good news through their daily affairs and routines in a loving manner. You are the *everyday Saint*.

Saints Lead by Example & Seek Encounters

We all have people who look up to us. There are people right now who desire to emulate characteristics and qualities that you have. Yes, there are members of your clan, cohort, or circle that crave your attention. They need you and desire what you have. You are a Saint to someone in your life right now, whether you know it or not. Chances are there are numerous people who are inspired by you, have been impacted by your life, and who admire your ways. Your life has great meaning and by authentically living it, you are changing the world! *Everyday Saints* all have one thing in common, they are different. Yes, you heard that right. The one thing that all people who are *everyday Saints* have that is similar is that we are all dissimilar. What I mean is that you are cut from your own cloth. The beauty is that there is no mold, as each person is one of a kind. There will never be another human that can do what you can do or will impact the world with their personality, demeanor, talents, and passion like you can. Just be you. If you are the best version of yourself each day and you go out there and love to your greatest ability good things are bound to happen. You will be a difference maker and you will change lives because you will change the worlds of those you spend the most time with.

Enough cannot be said about how *everyday Sainthood* spreads. It simply takes each of us doing our part. Nothing other-worldly, miraculous, or profound is required of us. What is required is that we give our all, be our best, and love like Jesus would to our greatest capacity. Go *ALL IN*! What is required is that we ask God and the Holy Spirit to give us the grace, the patience, the understanding, the opportunities, and the ability to continue to be manos y pies—his hands and his feet. It continues to amaze me all of the people that God brings into my life, especially when I go out of my comfort zone. It tends to happen quite often when I do something totally different. These people tend to magically appear on the scene when I say "yes" to the call Jesus places on my heart.

Over a dozen years ago, I went on my second overseas mission. The first had been a three week trip to some remote communities outside of Nairobi Kenya where we served children at Nyumbani Home and Village, an orphanage and community where hundreds were inflicted with HIV/AIDS. The experience was profound, eye opening and made me realize how blessed I was. Destitute poverty, filth, shacks, dirt floors, piles of garbage and raw sewage surrounded that orphanage in the slums of Kibera and Kariobangi. Normally I would have run the other way, but this time I heard Jesus calling. It seemed as if he was asking me to dumpster dive with him. By doing so I was jumping into the most spectacular and gigantic pool of love. The joy that followed was transformative.

The love shared, human connection established, and heart to heart encounters were all-powerful and life-changing ways that changed me. The beautiful people I met and the children I was so blessed to spend time with have been sewn into my inner soul and it's the great love exchange that occurs every time I experience Christ in others that continues to fire me up to serve Jesus through loving the poor today.

It was so powerful and profound, far more than simply traveling across the world to serve. Undoubtedly we can experience God anywhere we are, but on another continent was where I truly started to meet Jesus in other people. The poor that I encountered in Kenya were so rich in spirit, having such a strong faith. They radiated joy amidst the most abhorrent situations including hunger, thirst, disease, and disastrous living conditions. I recall a moment that struck my heart and when thought about over a dozen years later still moves me to tears. I am forever grateful.

While in Kibera, I went with medical professionals throughout the slum where over one million Kenyans and refugees from other surrounding countries resided, especially war torn nations like Sudan. The people there lived in small dilapidated wood shacks with a scrap metal roof. My initial reaction was an ache for these families who would never escape such grave destitution. Some of the group members on the trip had a very hard time experiencing the sights, sounds, and smells that we entered into by stepping foot in that slum. It was never a question whether I should be there or not, let alone if I wanted to because it was the place I had to be. I did not know it at the time, yet that became very clear with all that transpired over the three week mission, especially on this particular day. Being there was truly a matter of who Jesus was going to lead me to and where he would show up to me. After a few more minutes of traversing the dirt paths between the countless rows of thousands of these wooden huts, we came to a small cluster and began to visit the people distributing what we had to offer including medicine, provisions, and some clothing. Having been to three or so places where we were met outside of the small structure that stood before us, we took a left and then another right down the path and the doctor and translator motioned and pointed to yet another shack just a few feet away. It was at that moment when I would have an encounter with the Saint next door.

Greeting us like the others did, just outside of her home, was a grandmother of nine. The old withered woman looked at the doctor and translator. She then looked at me and smiled. Her wrinkles and frail frame showed the years that had taken their toll on her body. She had cared for all of those children solely after her own daughter and son-in-law had died due to the AIDS pandemic, which killed millions across the continent in decades prior. After she met us at the door, like the others had done, she motioned to have us come inside, which had not been the case prior with the first three visits we did nearby. We entered through a narrow opening, the door being a small tattered sheet. I went inside to find five of her children sleeping on a mat. Standing on her dirt floor, I looked around, the structure was no more than 80 square feet. There was nothing inside except for a single chair, a large pot over a small fire, and a jug of water that had been recently fetched from the Nairobi river numerous miles from our present location. I had to do everything possible to not allow my jaw to drop to the floor in sheer amazement. Never in my life had I seen anything quite like this. I wanted to cry because my heart was broken. However, the conditions actually would pale in comparison with what happened next.

Shortly after being invited inside with the doctor and translator, I began to distribute the items we had brought for her family. The elderly woman, named Zawadi, once again gave me the biggest and warmest smile. She said, "Jambo," which means hello in Swahili. She then pointed to the old rickety chair that was there and said, "Karibu nyumbani kwangu, tafadhali kaa," which the translator told me meant *Welcome to my home, please sit*. I was completely overwhelmed with emotion, feeling like a great King taking the throne of a palace because her love, generosity, and hospitality enriched my life in just a few minutes. It was unlike any I had ever experienced before. Zawadi had nothing. Yet, she insisted on giving me the one thing she owned that she was most proud to offer. As I took a seat in the chair, Zawadi then took a long wooden spoon and scooped a large pile of porridge out of a metal cauldron that was on the fire. She handed me a bowl and said, "Kula," *Eat*. How could I possibly eat when she had nine other mouths to feed, not counting her own. I accepted this most generous offering of a meal and ate. With each bite I felt the love that had made that meal and my heart grew three sizes that day because of her willingness to open up her home and life to me. I looked at Zawadi, smiled at her and said, "Asante Sana," *Thank you a lot*. Our eyes locked and reflecting on this moment, I can still see her beautiful face looking back at me. Her smile was glowing so magnificently. After finishing the porridge I asked the translator to tell Zawadi that I would pray for her and her family. I then wanted to know what she would like me to do when I got home. I was told that she asked that I tell others about the conditions her family and people were in so that if possible they could offer a prayer or provide some help.

Zawadi was not so concerned with her own situation, explaining that many others had it far worse than she did. How could that possibly be? In any event she desired that others would learn and know about her fellow Kenyans so that more hope could be brought to her people like had been provided to her on that day. The interesting thing is that I did not feel as if I had brought her hope at all, but she assured me that I did. I do know with full certainty that she gave me hope because anyone who can have faith and continue to love God and neighbor through those conditions has a heart focused on love which is life's greatest treasure. She taught me an immense amount that day. Later on before we left and went on to the next location, I learned that her name was Zawadi. The native who was with us told me that it was one given to girls in that region meaning "Gift."

Zawadi was the saint next door. She literally showed up in my life and was a beautiful gift to me. I feel so blessed to have met her and was left forever changed by her love. Jesus was alive in her heart and our Lord—the suffering Christ, loved me through this elderly woman in the slum. Zawadi was a gift to her nine grandchildren who were left orphaned after their parents' lives were robbed due to AIDS. Her love for me, a complete stranger, overflowed my cup. Zawadi was a perfect expression of holiness, her love flowing from within her soul to mine. She left me knowing that God was fully present. That tiny shack which was far worse than any condemned or abandoned residence I had ever seen in my life, was truly a home. It was home because home is where the heart is and even more powerfully where love is shared with others. Zawadi clearly was the heart of God for her family and the love of Jesus who smiled on me, as well as everyone who would be lucky enough to meet her.

So often we hear cynical comments such as, "Why go all that way, what good is it going to do anyway?" Or the remarks that suggest that we aren't really going to make a difference as *the problem*—referring to the poor as a problem that cannot be fixed. The real problem that lies here is not in any person, but in that mentality. The poor are not a problem at all, they are beautiful and beloved Children of God. They also do not need fixing! Let's do our best to echo the loving approach of Jesus himself who gave that prolific sermon on the mount saying, "Blessed are you who are poor, for the kingdom of God is yours. Blessed are you who are now hungry, for you will be satisfied."[122] There is something to be said about being poor materialistically and rich in spirit. Surely, it is not good for children and those in our human family to face starvation, unsuitable living conditions, and loneliness— the greatest poverty of all. However, there is great power in having less attachment to the world and a boundless connection with Christ. How gorgeously attractive it is to cling fully onto faith, treasure family, and place complete emphasis on the love of Jesus. Presently and eternally, God's love is the only satisfying, lasting, and refreshing remedy for the human heart. Let alone what we learn about love from experiencing it in such a profound manner with the poor not only alters your perspective on life, but changes your heart. Love is gorgeous and that beauty cannot be missed when we look into the eyes of the poor and stare straight into the heart of the Lord.

That day many years ago, in a place far away, I learned what real hospitality is all about and what true love looks like. Zawadi showed me that hospitality is an invitation into a time and space where the deepest trust and safest environment is created. It's making someone feel at home with you. Yes, the food, drinks and physical location, namely the things we do for others is important. However, it's even more important to cultivate such a relationship with our brothers and sisters on this planet where people can open up and share whatever experience they are in and the things on their heart. The most beautiful hospitality comes with the willingness to listen, to accept others, and in allowing them to enter your life and you entering theirs just as we are—free of all judgment.

You love them and see them as God would, rid of any criticism or expectation and full appreciation, grace, and in doing so make the person in front of you so comfortable that they can be who they are today, not having to be concerned with who they might want to be tomorrow, or even worse, pretend to be someone they are not. It's in this type of unconditional and perhaps dare I say crazy love that Jesus greets us where we are. It is this type of love that leaves you and I, as well as our neighbor healed because wounds are bathed with tears as

---

[122] Luke 6:20-21

we weep with those who weep and mourn with those who mourn. It's the heart that we see, the depth that we feel, and the love that we share that allows us to take part in the Heavenly Father's love—God has loved us by giving us the gift of life and brings us to holiness through Jesus.

When we look each other in the eye and see the divine spark that is within every woman, man, and child created by God, we have a *Namaste* moment. Our spirit and light connects with the other person we meet and honors the spirit and light within them. When we love in this manner, lives are changed because chains are broken, walls come down, and hearts are healed. The soul in me sees the soul in you and we rejoice together in seeing God who is in us and with us. During these explosions of love, we see the Lord fully present in the person who is in our midst. Love is all that every human spirit needs and it's the greatest and most powerful gift that we can provide when someone shows up in our lives. Their presence is a great present to us and ours to them. Essentially we leave with a piece of Jesus because loving in this way will undoubtedly change both people in any eternal fashion.

As I sat in the airplane gazing out the window I left Kenya far different than when I had arrived just a few weeks prior. God had chiseled away some layers, working on my heart. But even then I did not know how these encounters would so radically impact me. I now fully realize that it's more about how you connect with a person's heart by being there as you meet one another. By graciously accepting them into your life and accepting you into theirs, you can be present and love can flow in the way God orchestrates it, mystery and all. Similar to the two neighbors from the beginning of the book, Rose and Amelia, we garden together in the journey of life uprooting the weeds together and planting deep seeds of trusting love. Over time this springs forth renewed hope for the future and blessings that we could have never imagined. The hope is that we will always see the beautiful flower in one another.

Seeds of Faith

Sometimes that flower has not even broken the soil, but will come into full bloom later on in life. That is how God sees us—beautiful just as we are. This is the way that Jesus comes to us when we allow him to enter our lives fully and often by means of other people. Christ comes to us in the great garden of the universe, amidst the thorns and the thicket, the weeds and the multitude of other plants that are there, grafting us to his vine where we grow and bloom like a rose. As the saying goes, no rose is without thorns and neither are we, as each of us has things that have hurt us in life. We have pricked ourselves and others at times. Yet, as God makes his way past those prickly areas in our own lives, so should we, being his Saints, dig deeper into the heart of our brothers and sisters. By watering them with the Lord's generosity, patience, acceptance, and belief in them, we can love as Jesus loves us.

The more time passes, the greater the understanding is of what life and outreach are all about. It's a matter of the heart's fullness that only comes from showing up. Your existence on this earth calls you to do so, especially when you take time to pray on life, your mission, your purpose, and what makes your soul sing with true joy. You never know where Jesus will find you or who he will appear as. He might be just one person or door away. The doing really wasn't what mattered at all on those mission trips or any service oriented work done for that matter, but it was and is in the being—being present with and to the others. Maybe you have had your own "coming to Jesus moment," as the saying goes. Whether you have or haven't had that intense experience, it is okay either way. One thing I will guarantee you is that if you keep living love, your heart and the people around you inevitably are changed.

God planted a renewed seed of faith in me through these beautiful life experiences with the poor, as he revealed his presence to me in a new way. I was ministered to by the poor as God planted in me—a seed of endless love. Without love we are nothing as Paul says, "If I give away everything I own, and if I hand my body over so that I may boast but do not have love, I gain nothing...At present we see indistinctly, as in a mirror, but then face to face. At present I know partially; then I shall know fully, as I am fully known."[123] Doing anything and even everything is pointless without love.

What is meant for us to recognize and live out is being a mirror of God's love, a reflection of Christ in and for the world. We look inside and we see Jesus in the other.

They look back at us and see the risen Lord gazing back at them. The blood, the nails, the sweat, the piercing; all of this is the external physical existence and layer of the love. That is only magnified inside by the heartbeat of God that is within the spirit. When we are open and willing to look at the external and see it, recognize it, and then look through that to the heart of the poor and see them as God sees them, everything changes. By entering into Jesus' love fully when being with people and showing up for them, we are fully known and become aware of who we truly are! Remember, we are all *Niños de Dios*—Children of God.

To serve, especially the poor and marginalized, is a great privilege and honor. It is the *everyday Saint's* duty. Later on we will visit this call and our commission to service specifically, but for now I want to emphasize relationships and the Saints that God puts in our lives. During my next global mission I traveled to Dominica, a small remote island in the Caribbean, just north of South America. Little did I know that it would be there, on this tiny island, that I would encounter a living Saint. Every once in a while you might hear a person use that term, "He/she is a living saint." It's not something thrown around lightly nor should it be. The guy that I would really get to know on that mission trip is someone who has been changing countless lives for years, and has revitalized an entire community in Syracuse, New York. Let alone, he changed my life and heart for service radically.

I believe it's extremely imperative to share the good news and hope, largely that is a great portion of what the premise of this book is grounded in. I would be remiss to not spend adequate time on sharing some heartwarming stories about the *everyday Saints* that have crossed my path. What is probably even more important than the stories themselves is the example that these men and women have shown by living out their faith and carrying out the greatest love in a challenged world. Why I have been so blessed or fortunate to be in the

---

[123] 1 Corinthians 13:3, 12

right place at the right time to be in their presence is a mystery. My only hope is that you and I would realize that we are these *everyday Saints* as well. When we show up and just are our best selves, when we have hearts wide open, people see the reflection of Jesus in us. They then come to believe in hope again and lives are changed.

Comparisons must not ever cross your mind even for a second. Don't be someone else or worry about anything other than staying focused on being the Saint God made you to be. The one thing that matters today and the solely important element which remains every single day of our lives is that we love. Love is all that is required and there is no measuring stick when it comes to love and God!

It was toward the tail end of the ten day mission in Dominica that I really got to know this young man who was an *everyday Saint*. Our group had spent a good portion of our time working in a handicapped school for teens, assisting at a youth center in the poorest part of the island, as well as visiting the homeless.

During one evening as I cleaned up after dinner, I could feel a lightness and the warm spirit of God coming to my mind and heart from that day's events. I had the privilege of serving alongside many wonderful people, but there was this one particular member of the group who I had witnessed loving on the poor that day so authentically and openly. He was different. There was an aura and a glow, a twinkle in his eye and a never stop motor to love those that others deemed "unlovable." I was doing the dishes and reflected on the experiences we were having on the mission and couldn't get Andrew out of my mind. I kept replaying in my mind the impact he was having on the poor, especially the children and elderly. I could tell there was real depth to this young man who I didn't know that well at all, but only by name and rightful reputation. His heart for service back home in Syracuse was unlike anything I had ever heard of or witnessed before. I really wanted to know what made this mysterious and selfless college kid tick. Why did he care so much about people he had never met and those labeled as "outcasts" by the rest of society?

The next morning, during breakfast, I learned that we would have a couple hours free in the later afternoon once we got back from the teaching in the school for children with disabilities. Andrew, the guy I had done dishes with the night before said, "Would anyone be up for a hike to the boiling lake?" I don't know about you, but I certainly never had seen a boiling lake before nor thought much about them existing. Yet, no one in our group even showed the slightest interest. After all, it would be over 100 degrees and the hike would require a professional guide, as well as serious gear that we did not have. I looked around the room, people just shrugged off the question. Something stirred up inside me and I felt a tug. I said, "I will go with you." Little did I know that the hike to the boiling lake on the island of Dominica back in 2009 would change my life forever. Traversing some steep terrain, navigating around many extremely dangerous cliffs, and free climbing perilous areas of the mountain was exhilarating to say the least. The view was worth every second of the trek. After about a four hour hike to the summit, what we saw and took in was incredible. We literally stood at the summit of the island and looked down upon such stunning aqua blue water boiling from volcanic activity below.

The hike that day was much more than a mere memory of a spectacular natural phenomenon, it was all about meeting an *everyday Saint*. This *everyday Saint* would go on to be my best man in my wedding and the person I look up to as a role model, an inspiration, and someone I get to share loving service with during the course of life. See, when your eyes are open, there are living Saints all around you. During the nearly seven hour venture we were on, I got to know the heart of my best friend, Andrew Lunetta. There is no one on this planet like him. I truly believe that he is the second coming of Mother Teresa in male form. I say that with all due respect and sincerity. The conversations I had with him during the hike and what he shared from the heart radically changed me. I realized that I had to do more. Not because I had to in order to be loved by God or to earn his love. I had to do more because God was calling me to more. He thirsted for my love. Remember, with God leading the charge, we are all capable of greatness.

Saints Attract Other Saints & Are Stronger Together

As I think back about life changing moments, really getting to know Andrew and allowing God to work on my heart through him is something that has set me on a beautiful course of service. For him and for experiencing Jesus in him I am forever grateful. Sometimes in our lives God will bring people to us when we least expect them. It could be a best friend, a spouse, or a stranger that impacts us in a way that is profound. You never know. The thing about it is that these encounters and life-giving experiences happen more often when you and I go and are open to new opportunities along the way. The times when you trust, take a chance, and go where God is leading you, even when you don't know why; these are times that will shape your heart. These are the moments that God really is chiseling away the excess to uncover the beauty within. And sometimes these can be the very moments that you will run into a living Saint. This was the case for me in Dominica.

Over the next dozen years, my friend Andrew and I would do countless service ops together. Seeing him love the homeless by providing them with somewhere warm to stay in his own apartment, witnessing this man give his own winter coat off his back to someone on the street during a blizzard, and the dozens of houses he has built for those in need in Syracuse through his nonprofit A Tiny Home for Good has been amazing. It shows that one person can make a radical difference when they love and allow God to work through them. Andrew has changed the scope for the homeless in central New York, he has provided hope for hundreds of people, and he continues to shine brightly. My hope is that you will channel your inner *everyday Saint* Andrew in your own special way. You are an *everyday Saint* in the making. You have greatness to share and to offer this world.

The *everyday Saint* stays true to who they are and they live a life that is unapologetic. Over my years in ministry and in missions both local and abroad, I have been so greatly blessed to meet even more tremendous people who are doing beautiful and powerful things for God. The common denominator for each of them has been their great love and desire to share Christ's love with those they meet. You probably have not heard of any of these people, but that is okay. I am sharing them with you because they are the new age apostles. These men and women do what they do not for notoriety or praise. They care not for recognition, but purely to take action because their hearts desire to bring love, goodness, and joy to the lives of people. Each of these men and women are Saints. They are *everyday Saints* on the move, building up the Kingdom one person and one encounter at a time.

Everyday Saints are people like Craig Johring and Danny Leger of *Hope of the Poor* who bring love and hope by spending time with and serving the poorest of the poor in the streets and dumps of Mexico City. They take Jesus' love onto Native American reservations in the US singing songs, building community, and sharing tacos on piles of trash. *Everyday Saints* are people like my closest faith-filled friends Nick and Garrett Bernardo and Sean Finan of Novus Clothing Company who spread the good news by embodying the "Claim Your Crown" motto every day to be Christ-centered through their business. Witnessing the loving approach they take and how they utilize the clothing industry as a platform to share their faith and their love with others is special. *Everyday Saints* are people like those I serve with at Baseball Miracles Inc. which provides baseball and softball instruction, bringing hope and love to underserved children around the globe through a game.

The uncommon and beautiful generosity of *everyday Saints* like Derek Bevan are changing the world one child at a time. Derek's selfless humanitarian efforts in eastern Africa have been remarkable. This *everyday Saint* founded Village of Hope Kenya, to provide a way for girls to be educated in the rural region of Gwassi near Lake Victoria. His nearly two decades of work in Kenya is bearing great fruit as he helps to rescue Kenyan girls from sex slavery and empowers them to live life on their own terms so they can have a future. The Saintly efforts of Derek and his family are reshaping the mindset of young boys and men in Kenya so they learn to value women by treating them with love and respect.

Furthermore, the *everyday Saint* is Savannah Mlot of Southern California, who with her family created and operates Brooke Orphanage which has helped rescue and rehabilitate formerly enslaved children in India. She and her network provide these kids with a loving home, education, and a bright outlook through knowing the Lord. These Saints are people like Eric Newman and all the volunteers of Roc Solid foundation which builds playgrounds for children with pediatric cancer. Talk about showing up in a time of need and giving happiness to a child and their family who is battling a dreadful disease. These *everyday Saints* show us what hope looks like. They turn a nightmare into a dream come true, as love eases pain through outreach and the connection of the human spirit!

Being an *everyday Saint* is about being your best in a common world, by living each day with uncommon love. The list of these great and holy people cannot be exhausted. Serving alongside *everyday Saints* and watching their powerful witness to the faith has been special and inspiring. When you see someone light up when an underserved child gets their very own new baseball glove and a dream come true day takes place on the ball field, you know that the love and joy of Jesus is real. When you join people like Savannah or Derek who connect you on a zoom call with your sponsor child in India or Kenya, you know the power of Christ's love is alive. How could you not believe when you see the radiant smiles and the sheer excitement in the girls and boys rejoicing at the orphanage and being educated at school?

Saints witness the good works of others and are motivated by them to get involved. You know Christ is present when you observe Craig and Danny walk up a mountain of garbage to do a dumpster dive in Mexico City to hang out with the poor. Observing this moves the spirit and fills you with gratitude for other *everyday Saints* who are agents of love in a hurting world. It puts a smile on your face to join the efforts passing water and tortillas out to a mother who works tirelessly digging through trash to find recyclables to gain a few pennies to feed her hungry family. You are left changed because that is what Jesus would do. When you put a hammer to the nail and watch your best friend, Andrew, build countless homes for the homeless to bring purpose and dignity to their lives, it reminds you that the Kingdom is near. *Everyday Saints* love and live a life that shares love with others no matter where they are and who they are with.

Everyday Saints are the grandchildren who visit their lonely grandparents. They are the children who take care of their aging parents and the little boy who shares his toy with his classmate. Later on as we journey together, we will explore and expand on the importance of loving service. However I mention these acts of genuine goodness that come in many forms because these people are true Saints living among us. They show that all that is required is your personal best to impact others by just being the faith-filled disciple you are inside. You are the living gospel, which literally means you are the "good news."

You are the breath of God and you bring hope to the world. You are *everyday Saints*. The person a house down in your neighborhood might be the next *everyday Saint* that you meet. So why not you? And why not me? The world needs Saints. The world needs heroes and heroines. Be heroic in your own way. Live out your deepest call and love to your fullest potential. I greatly admire the people that I have included above and their humility, willingness to serve, and desire to impact others in a positive manner by never counting the cost. And now I look forward to meeting more on the journey together toward Heaven!

Whether we are speaking about the great works and impactful love of famous Saints like John the Baptist, St. Paul, St. Ignatius of Loyola, and Mother Teresa or the *everyday Saints* whom the world does not know on a grand scale, that does not matter. What matters and is most essential to hone in on is how they all lived. The focus must be on that and why they continue to go about life in an uncommon manner. Saints and holy people are not perfect. Like you and I, they are striving for greatness. Above everything, they desire to positively influence others and through their loving impact to change lives. Saints allow God in and embrace the holy moments, especially the small happenings in the daily occurrences. When we learn to do the same and when we begin to seek out more opportunities to love, we too will change the world. I continue to stress this because it is so true and it will happen. It needs to!

As you continue to voyage on and while contemplating *everyday Sainthood*, rest in these words of the Buddha. His name Siddhartha Guatama is actually Sanskrit meaning, "he who achieves his aim." After all isn't our call to sainthood about achieving the aim that God has placed on each of our lives? The Buddha is sure to point out that love is about the depth of connection and in the purity which is exchanged. The Tripitaka is a holy text and collection of sacred scripture sayings that leads to enlightenment and emphasizes the Buddha's desire for all individuals to live a life of loving-kindness. Within the Buddhist scriptures and those like it he is known to have stated, "Love does not need to be perfect, it just needs to be true. Love is a gift of one's innermost soul to another so both can be whole."[124]

---

[124] Siddhartha Guatama Buddha

It's fascinating the parallels that are drawn when examining the teachings and scriptures of various religious traditions. Certainly there are fundamental differences that exist, but when we can remove ourselves from the dogma for a moment we can at least appreciate the cross-cultural human desire for community and love. These qualities are those found in the *everyday Saints* and in the canonized Saints of our Church. Assuredly, all human beings need love and every person in our world has the ability to love. The *everyday Saint* says "yes" to love regardless of the external and then he or she loves the best they possibly can without restriction. This takes the limit off of any situation and allows the time and space for God to do his magic—for the spirit to come alive and for him to be in our midst.

In his exceptional literary work entitled *The Art of Happiness* the 14th Dalai Lama, Howard C. Cutler, powerfully speaks of the necessities of love and connection. He calls to mind our desire and need to be part of a loving community that is void of criticism, full of tender kindness, and loving acceptance by saying, "Love is the absence of judgment. Love and compassion are necessities, not luxuries. Without them, humanity cannot survive. We can live without religion and meditation, but we cannot survive without human affection."[125] Unapologetically and inexhaustibly, where love exists God is fully present! Saints live out love with no constraint.

Challenge 13

Go look at yourself in the mirror. Take a long glance at the person who stares back at you. Speak out loud and tell yourself, "I am an everyday Saint." Now, make sure when you wake up each morning you remind yourself that you are a Saint who is made for greatness. Believe it and allow God to work through you in whatever capacity the Lord calls you to each day. Keep your eyes open this week for people who you witness responding to holy moments. Don't be afraid to applaud them when you see acts of love, charity, and beauty taking place. Remind others that they are everyday Saints on the journey too. Through love we can build a beautiful world for God! In all circumstances, never

---

[125] *The Art of Happiness*, Howard C. Cutler (14th Dalai Lama).

forget that Jesus would love first. Ask the Lord to live through you to do hard things so you can love others, especially those who have been forgotten.

The Saint Next Door   Dan Jason | 221

forget that Jesus would love first. Ask the Lord to live through you to
do hard things so you can love others, especially those who have been
forgotten.

HIS HANDS & FEET
CHAPTER 14

*"Life's most persistent and urgent question is: What are you doing
for others?" – Dr. Martin Luther King Jr.*

Mission Field of Love

When I boarded an airplane headed for Mexico City in April of 2019,
little did I know that in a number of hours I was going to see the face
of Christ. Years of my life had involved searching for the Lord. I had
little glimpses of his presence when doing local volunteer efforts and
community service. Going on missions abroad was something that I
had first experienced with the Jesuits, having served in Kenya and
Dominica. I definitely recognized the presence of Jesus then and had
encounters with God on those missions. These experiences were
incredible. Having the opportunity to serve and work with orphaned
children with HIV/AIDS was powerful. When I went to Africa I
thought I was going to bring Jesus with me and love to those I met. I
certainly did. Despite my initial thoughts and what I hoped would
happen, I received far more from the children there who changed my
life. The love and grace those little ones gave me was a gift I will
always treasure. The same was true when traveling to Dominica and

serving the poor and kids at a school for the handicapped. Both of these experiences helped me to grow spiritually and formed my matured heart for serving God's people.

Each time we go on mission, whether near or far, it is an opportunity to share the heart of Jesus with others and receive the Lord through his abundant grace. However, this experience in Mexico City was something different. Sometimes in our lives we have a radical encounter. It is during these few mystical moments that God changes our hearts and transforms us completely! After a long plane trip from New York to Mexico City, we took a bus to the Basilica of Our Lady of Guadalupe. What a way to kick start the mission and experience Christ. This set a real tone for what was to come. We celebrated evening mass and had the opportunity to view and pray before the Tilma, the burlap sack of Juan Diego which contained the miraculous image of Our Lady on it. I truly believe that it was at that moment praying before the Tilma and asking the Virgin Mary to take me closer to the Lord that my eyes began to see things differently regarding the poor.

Prior to that specific mission to Mexico City, I prepared by praying daily and asked to see the face of Christ in those I would serve on mission. I hoped God would show up and show out in a profound way and he sure did. The next few days we hit downtown Mexico City, meeting the street kids and homeless. By means of tortillas, beans and some broken Spanish, we spent time with those on the margins. Father Gregory Boyle, the author of *Tattoos on the Heart* and director of HomeBoy Ministries in LA said, "It is not enough to take a stand on an issue. We must rather be like Christ and stand with those facing the issue, being one with them." By sharing in that meal, trying to piece together a few words, and most importantly in recognizing the humanity of those we met, we had an intense encounter with Jesus. Because we shared love, God shared his love with us. In loving them and walking with the poor, I saw Jesus and really felt his presence like never before.

Three days into the mission, kids who were strangers that I hadn't met a mere 72 hours prior now were like family. The love of Christ that was shared between us and the relationship that was established through our human connection became so strong in such a short amount of time. When I decided to go on mission to Mexico City my finite mind did not realize that Jesus would show up as a street kid. The homeless, orphaned and abandoned children who had been rejected, looked down upon, and written off by society were completely forgotten about by our world. But the wounded and scarred Jesus, who has holes in his hands and wounds in his side, brought me closer and showed me what true unconditional love looks like.

Jesus was ministering to me through the poor. I never would have imagined finding Christ in a drainage ditch twelve feet under the ground, but he was there. Those children who were deemed outcasts and the downtrodden did the most important uplifting of my heart and spirit. I was filled with joy because the love I received penetrated my inner soul and my heart. Christ's love has a way of flooding you with great peace. How could the hurting and the poor show me the face of our Lord? A few years later as I plan to go back again and approach a half dozen missions there, I have a new family—mi familia de Mexico. Jesus led me to them and the joy he gave me continues to fuel my fire within.

On the final day of the mission we headed on a long bus ride to the edge of Mexico City. As our bus began to slow and turn onto some side dirt roads, I wondered where we were headed next. The smell that infiltrated my nostrils was wretched and the fumes began to consume the bus from about two miles away. We were told that no one comes to the city dump unless you lived and worked there. My immediate response to that was, why would any live or work there? If someone had to go in, they certainly made sure to wear a full hazmat suit. Hearing that some people in our group started to look around for gloves and masks, but we didn't have any.

That day we were going into a garbage heap and we were going to have an "explosion of Jesus," as Craig, the director of Hope of the Poor put it. As I took my first step off the bus I wondered what was about to occur when I stepped foot on the grounds of the dump. A swarm of flies immediately attacked me and the smell was even more horrific. All that I could see for miles was heaping piles of trash. I mean the mounds were so gigantic that from the road they looked like literal mountaintops. How did this happen? Why was I at a dump in Mexico City? The answer to these questions that raced through my mind was simple and quite direct, yet not easy. This is where Jesus would be. This is where our Lord would come to visit the lonely, the sick, the poor, the uneducated and the orphaned. This is where love in its purest form would be found.

I started walking a few hundred feet and watched some men working sorting trash. I said a quick prayer and asked God to lead me to someone who I could help, but more importantly someone who would show me the face of Jesus. I took a quick turn to the left and walked a few hundred feet further. Back, way back behind a huge pile of trash was Jesus. He appeared. It was the face of the risen Lord that I saw in Olga, a 30 year old mother of three. Olga was quietly sorting cans and glass bottles, as well as plastic containers into massive trash bags. I later learned that this had been her job since she was old enough to walk. What a lot in life. What a short straw to draw. Imagine never knowing that an outside world exists except for possibly an old tattered newspaper clipping. In actuality, this was the place she was born and this was inevitably the place she would die. I went over to her and introduced myself.

Olga smiled ear to ear. I started to help Olga with her work. Before you knew it, we were talking about her kids, her faith in Jesus, and she was asking me about my job as a teacher. Learning Spanish did come in handy after all. I met Olga's children and saw the small dilapidated shack they lived in. Her kids were beaming with excitement when I spoke to them in Spanish and later we would play some soccer in the dump. A game that consisted of an old half torn basketball and two metal coat hangers for goals seemed to turn into a World Cup Futbol match. The kids loved every second of it. The highlight moment was when Joshua scored a goal and we all shouted GOAL, running around wildly! We sprinted through the trash and cheered, high fiving one another because our team had won the game. The biggest victory was love and that filled us all with joy. The joy we shared together in that soccer game, in the human connection by placing bottles into bags, and through conversation was life changing.

Surely, these were moments I would always remember and I pray that my presence brought a glimmer of hope to my new amigos. Later on that day, after some more tortillas and beans, I asked Olga what made her smile and why she was so happy. I couldn't fathom how she could live in this horrid environment, arguably the filthiest and stinkiest place on earth and be joyful. Her response was something I could never have expected in a million years. Olga told me, "I have everything I need. I have my kids, my faith in God, and you came to visit me. My life is good" When I looked into her eyes, I saw Jesus Christ. She was so poor, as poor as poor can be. Yet, she was so immensely rich, rich in the spirit. Her heart and her entire being was centered on the things that actually mattered. Looking into Olga's eyes in that moment when she said, "Tengo todo. Tengo a Dios y a mi familia. Viniste a visitarme. Mi vida es buena," was beyond profound. This is what love looks like and this is what love sounds like. Olga's life was a love sermon lived out daily.

After praying and reflecting on this experience it is clear that Olga's life was gold tested in fire. She saw our Lord and understood the Cross well. She was glowing and peered back at me with such a loving gaze because she was the face of the hidden Jesus. I gave Olga a hug and then met some other Saints in the dump. We played some more soccer with Juan, Jose, Chili, and Joshua and then we left. Boy was it amazing to hang out with Jesus. See, there is a reason why Jesus said in the beatitudes, "Blessed are the poor in spirit for theirs is the kingdom of Heaven."[126] Some of us face physical poverty.

Sometimes Saints are angels that come to us in powerful ways when we least expect them. A number of years ago, as I continued on mission in Mexico City, I met a woman named Sandra. She had the cards stacked against her from the get go to say the least. This woman's mess became her message and her testimony that she shared at the park was profound. Upwards of one hundred homeless and street kids gathered around a lawn space just off of the busy intersection in the middle of the city. Sandra began to speak and to tell those seated on the grass as well as all of us her story. When you meet someone you can sometimes tell there is a special quality about them. Right away everyone in her presence could feel this aura that radiated from her. I was captivated by Sandra's passion and willingness to be vulnerable. Becoming an orphan at two years old, she had been abandoned by her parents. She lived in one of the many orphanages in Mexico City until she was seven. At that point her aunt took her into her home. Abuse followed suit, and Sandra was forced to do all the chores, cook, clean, and work continuously. If a mistake

---

[126] Matthew 5:3

was made, the little girl was burned with hot knives, irons, and cigarettes. Unfortunately things turned even worse as Sandra was sexually abused by her older cousin. One day, at age eight, she escaped and ran away.

As if she had not faced enough trauma, Sandra was found on the street by a woman who told her she would help the small child. Little did Sandra know that she was actually being kidnapped and sold into sex slavery. She was dressed up in skirts, had makeup caked on daily and she was forced to drink alcohol in extreme proportions until inebriation. Sandra had hundreds of men take advantage of her as the darkness continued. After six months of this horrific situation, she escaped to the streets. Eventually Sandra was found by the police in the park who threw her into the mud and raped her. They even lit her hole in the ground where she lived on fire in an attempt to kill her. That was where Sandra joined the countless other street kids for the next decade trying to stay safe from gangs, keep warm during the winter, and away from abusive men. Needless to say, her pain continued. The only way Sandra ate was by digging through piles of trash, rummaging through garbage cans, and taking food, as well as half empty water bottles off the ground to survive. Her jobs consisted of washing car windows in the streets. The agony of her situation consumed her and Sandra ended up addicted to drugs. As an addict she covered her pain with substances in an attempt to escape the demons of her past and her present reality.

By age 15, Sandra became pregnant only to have her son taken from her. She was abused even more before she gave birth to her daughter. Sandra's second child became the love of her life. God was the furthest from Sandra than he had ever been as her life was completely enveloped by trauma. The emotional, physical and spiritual wounds Sandra had were too much to handle. How could God exist. If he loved her he would not have allowed this to happen. In her great torment, Sandra broke down one day after people stole the blankets that were being used to keep her daughter warm. She cried out, "God, if you exist, help me!" Saints are angels on earth that show up in people's lives when they least expect it. Sandra's life was about to change, although she could never have seen it coming.

One day this white man from Nebraska showed up at the park. He purchased all of Sandra's rosary beads that she sold in order to make enough money to feed her daughter. A number of days later that same guy came back to the park and told Sandra that he would help her and her daughter. The man gave them some food and tried to conversate. By this time Sandra had gotten her son back, and she told the man that her kids had never had a birthday before. The man's name was Craig. He told her that on January 16th he would be back after returning to Mexico City. Craig told Sandra to meet him at the Basilica on that date, the day of her son's birthday. Sandra disbelieved that this stranger would come back, but low and behold, he did. Not only did Craig come back, but he took Sandra's family out to a Chinese restaurant, the very place that her son had always dreamed of going. This was the first time they had been in a restaurant without being thrown out and treated like garbage. It was the only time Sandra's family had cake with candles to celebrate a new year of life. As the relationship continued to be built, Craig eventually went back to the park day after day, and he provided an apartment for Sandra and her kids to live in.

Fast forward six years later and Sandra is helping to run Hope of the Poor in Mexico City. Through the loving act of a Saint, Sandra's life drastically turned around. Craig showed up and loved Sandra and her children, building trust through being with them in their darkest hour. As a result, Sandra encountered Christ's love for the first time. Through meaningful work, being treated with dignity, and learning about the faith, Sandra was restored. Craig taught Sandra how to read the bible, he got her kids into school and continued to pay for her home. Through rehabilitation, Sandra became clean, beating her drug addiction. With Craig's support, her depression turned to great joy and an enthusiasm for life. Unfortunately Sandra contracted cancer. However, she is able to remain positive and hopeful, knowing that God is on the throne of her life. The most beautiful thing is that Sandra has dedicated her time on this earth to sharing her story with others on the streets of Mexico City. She preaches in the park, makes home-cooked meals for the poor and homeless at the city dump, and provides encouragement for young people who battle addiction. Sandra had every reason to give up, but she kept fighting. Any child that does not have a place to live, Sandra brings them into her home until she can find them a safe and loving permanent residence. Moms that are out on the street are found by Sandra who gives them a room in her own house so they and their children are safe and she loves them back to help. Sandra is a Saint and her holiness was uncovered thanks to her friend, Craig Johring, who accompanied her on the journey years ago.

See, you never know who you will meet, the story you will hear, or how someone will radically change your life. God's grace and love can do all things, even when it seems impossible. I have never heard of a more powerful or greater story of redemption. The beauty that exists in Sandra and Craig motivates me and gives the world hope! Today Craig and Sandra work side by side to help countless mothers, homeless children, and street kids. They pour out God's love on everyone they meet. They lead missions in Mexico City, many of which I have participated in where people encounter Jesus in the poor. Undoubtedly, their great love continues to transform lives. Poverty exists all around us and the mission field is massive. What Craig and Sandra have shown me is that Saints are angels among us who embrace the "other" and lead them to the heart of God's merciful love. Sandra's story indicates that the Saint is Next Door and her life is a living testimony that love always wins! Her victorious story makes us realize that there truly is no greater love than laying your life down for someone else. From the pit of hell to the promise of eternal life, it is all made possible because someone decided to show up and grace was received. No matter what, do not give up because breakthrough is just one encounter away. It all comes down to love and grace. Like St. Thérèse stated, "Do not fear, the poorer you are the more Jesus will love you. He will go far, very far, in search of you, if at times you wander off a little."

Sandra, like all Saints, learned to trust God. She and Craig both answered the call to enter into where God was calling to love as he loves us. In trusting we receive a true gift from the Lord. Trust is the first step toward redemption, a comeback, and eventually victory. Trust lives in love. Sister Faustina Maria Pia discussed the crucial nature of trusting the Lord in her book *Jesus I Trust in You: A 30 Day Personal Retreat with the Litany of Trust*. In this powerful work of literature she professed that trust gives God permission to recreate us. Sister Faustina Maria powerfully stated, "Transformation happens as we trust that his [God's] love is deeper than anything that besets us." This makes me realize that when you and I trust, anything can happen. When we follow the ways of the Saints by becoming a man or woman for others, we create a time and space for trust to occur in the life of someone else. This allows God to really go to work. Without trusting Jesus fully, we cannot overcome the darkness, sin, and despair of this earth. Our own failings and the weight of the world can be far too much to handle on our own. Certainly, we can miss the Saints who appear in our midst if we don't have eyes opened to see them. Poverty is something we all face in many different ways, but trust and love can help us embrace that poverty and conquer it. God can use anything we overcome as a 'we' to bring goodness to the life of another person.

This is what hope looks like. Hope comes in the form of everyday Saints like Sandra and Craig. As we journey on and face grave hardship or know of others we meet who embrace such difficult circumstances, our call is to remain fascinated with Jesus who is hope. Be fascinated with Jesus because he is fascinated with you. The Lord wants you and me to become empty. It is in emptying ourselves that our brokenness and our fallen nature can lead us to holiness and fulfillment. How can this take place? Well, you see it is in our poverty that we become rich. This is so counter cultural and hard to fathom, but so it was true with Sandra and it is true for all who depend on the Lord for his strength.

By emptying ourselves we open up our hearts to the wealth of God. It is in our emptiness that a space is created for the Lord to come into us and make his dwelling within us. Jesus wants to live in you. The Holy Spirit will find you and lead you to God each day. It's in the invitation to enter into the mystery of God's love that we find ourselves embracing our own poverty and growing closer to his heart. When we are totally dependent on God and rid ourselves of the thoughts, worries and "stuff" that clutter our spirits, we can, by God's grace, rest in Christ's peace. The Lord desires this because he first loved us and wants us to receive this joy which is found in a new life in him. Jesus tells us in John's Gospel such profound and encouraging words of truth, "I am in them and You are in Me. May they be made completely one, so the world may know You have sent Me and have loved them as You have loved Me." [127]

---

[127] John 17:23

When things go sideways in life and we can't make sense of anything, that is when we are asked by our Lord to trust him. You cannot practice trust so to speak, but you just have to arrive to live in it. The relationship with your Father in Heaven and love are what bring trust out of us so we no longer have to rely on ourselves, but we can rely on God. And that's why we have to become like a child in the Gospel, to depend on God for everything. The beauty is that wherever you are today, that is not the end. You are not finished. I once heard the Friars discuss how the beatitudes are a beautiful way for us to understand the depth of God's grace and love working in the world.

Therefore, it's all about the comma. Take a look at the beatitudes. Why do you think each statement is followed by a comma and then God's answer for what he will lead us to? A period would equate to permanency, whereas the comma leaves this space open for the Lord to keep working and ensures us that there is more on the other side. Only one thing has permanency, and that is the love of God which will never end or be outdone. Where God's love exists, forgiveness, grace, and transformation can be found. As we journey closer to Sainthood, may we emulate the trust of Sandra. Hopefully we can, no matter what we face today. We must receive it, believe it, and breathe it. Living out trust, embracing the cross, and allowing God to enter in changes everything. Sandra gave the Lord permission to take over her life, and not only did he lead her out of the greatest suffering and poverty a person could face, he has shown her how to utilize the hellish life she has had to overcome to bring hope and inspiration to innumerable women, children, and homeless men in Mexico City. Before we continue to unpack poverty, let's take a moment to prayerfully reflect on the beatitudes.

The Beatitudes:
1. Blessed are the poor in spirit, for theirs is the kingdom of heaven.
2. Blessed are those who mourn, for they shall be comforted.
3. Blessed are the meek, for they shall inherit the earth.
4. Blessed are those who hunger and thirst for righteousness, for they shall be filled.
5. Blessed are the merciful, for they shall obtain mercy.
6. Blessed are the pure in heart, for they shall see God.

7. Blessed are the peacemakers, for they shall be called children of God.
8. Blessed are they who are persecuted for righteousness sake, for theirs is the kingdom of heaven.

Like those on the streets or at the dump in Mexico City, the poorest of the poor lack material goods. Some of us face emotional poverty, lacking joy and peace inside due to pain, loss, or some other *Friday moment*. And still others face relational or spiritual poverty, facing a scarcity of human connection or not knowing God. As my friend Craig so often has said, "The greatest poverty in the world is loneliness." All humans need love. When we visit the poor and spend time with them, we get to hang out with Jesus. When we hang out with the Lord and share his great love with our brothers and sisters, it changes us radically. The love of God is so radical and so crazy that it can transform you in an extreme manner. Being a Saint really comes down to loving others and serving those in need. We are all capable of doing this and the reward will be great both in this lifetime and in the world to come.

That night, after my first experience at the dump, I went back to the Basilica to pray. I felt a call to missions in a way I never had before. It reminds me that when we take a step out of our comfort zone and "shock" our faith it is then that God causes great growth and an awakening to occur. The impact it has on us lasts for years to come. A simple "yes" when asked to go on mission with a bunch of good friends from my hometown parish turned into one of the most impactful and radical experiences of my life. I got to see and hang out with Jesus and his homies in Mexico City. The cool thing is the Lord is all around us. He awaits you. Christ is in your home within your children and your spouse. He is raking the leaves outside on a brisk fall day and he is at the corner store working the register. No matter where we go or who we meet, God is with us and within those we encounter. There is a Saint within each person and what is asked of us all is to love and see the Saint in others.

The road to Sainthood and our journey with God to holiness is not easy, yet the reward and joy you will receive is immeasurable. As we have talked about throughout our time together, love is the most important component you have. It's the ultimate litmus test of your faith. Saints love others and they go out of their way to do so—it's that simple. Your capacity to love is extensive and God desires you to share that great love with others. Saints change the world through love. As disciples and *everyday Saints* you and I are called to this. It's the reason why Jesus gave the great commission before he departed from the apostles after the resurrection. God is love and where love remains there is hope, there is light, and there is the promise that will last forever. Love and service go hand in hand. You cannot have one without the other. Think back to your childhood and call to mind a time when your parents or grandparents did something for you or when another family member impacted someone. That required great love and selflessness. What is your earliest memory of someone serving with pure love?

In life, especially during the *Friday moments* that we face, love comes to the forefront and with it comes charity, namely acts of service. Recognizing the way that people love their spouse, seeing a mother pour out everything within herself to her children, and witnessing the way a neighbor opens up their home to the family and friends in hospitality is beautiful. Service comes in so many ways, shapes, and forms. Our Lord calls each of us to a life of service. Jesus lived this life of service to the highest degree and his love is what he asks we share with those we meet. It is in living this way that we are able to not only do the will of the Father, but we become the will of the Father as he is immersed in love. This takes place when we abide completely in God.

A commonality amongst all Saints is the desire to love, to do what is right, and a drive to impact people in a unique manner. One of the greatest blessings we receive from reading about and reflecting upon the lives of the Saints is the way they carried out love. Each Saint is loved in a unique manner and their love of God and neighbor is a prime example of how love can radically change people's lives. You and I are Saints in the making, again not because we are perfect, but because we are willing to say "yes" to love. Sharing Christ's love is the ultimate gift we can offer the world. Serving others is the greatest testament of love and this is the power that has and will continue to renew the face of the earth. After all, "Faith without works is dead."[128]

---

[128] James 2:17

When we look at the lives of the great Saints it is beautiful to see and be motivated to know how they dedicated their time in loving service.

Giving yourself completely is the greatest act of love a human is capable of. We know that Jesus did this on the Cross. Over the centuries there have been martyrs who were creative enough to die for the faith. Saint Maximillian Kolbe is a prime example of a person who lived in a mission field of love. Kolbe voluntarily traded places in Auschwitz concentration camp during World War II with a man who was a husband and a father. He did so in order to save the stranger's life. This calls to mind that Jesus discussed the magnitude of love with his disciples after explaining to them that the Ten Commandments really all fall into loving God and neighbor. Our Lord went on to share that there is no greater act than the heroic nature of laying down one's life for his friends, let alone someone we don't even know.

Maximillian Kolbe was known to be a great writer, an encourager in his day, and someone who transformed lives. By the way he lived without fear, ripe in his devotion to serving those in need and willing to share all he had with those he encountered, the Franciscan Friar lived out the gospel message. Certainly Kolbe lived out the Saint's lifelong mission—loving at all costs, especially for the sake of souls. As we continue to uncover the truths regarding Sainthood, we look at our own lives to see how we can grow in holiness by engaging in acts of love. Contemplate these potent words from Saint Maximillian Kolbe, who left hearts forever better by living out the message he shared on the redemptive power of love by professing, "Let us remember that love lives through sacrifice and is nourished by giving. Without sacrifice there is no love... A single act of love makes the soul return to life." Imagine what Kolbe's act of love did for the man he died for that dismal day during the Holocaust, not to mention how his example resounds to the multitudes who venerate the Saint decades later. This reminds us that each time we love, no matter how large or small that deed is, it impacts the inner being. The person we love receives Jesus in that very moment. Simultaneously, God's great love radiates in the soul of the one who gave selflessly. Each person involved in the love encounter grows in holiness, as we both get one step closer to Heaven.

Love is the Answer

St. Frances Xavier Cabrini, better known as Mother Cabrini, is known for starting the Missionary Sisters of the Sacred Heart of Jesus in 1880. Her call to holiness and serving God's people was exemplary. When she took her vows as a young lady, she also took on the name of Xavier in honor of the great Francis Xavier who is the patron Saint of missionaries. Mother Cabrini was moved by the spirit and called to put love into action. Although she desired to serve as a missionary in China, the Pope asked her to go to the U.S. to serve the poor. For the next 35 years of her life, despite great challenges, Mother Cabrini founded 67 institutions including hospitals, schools, and other terrific organizations in the U.S., South America, and all across Europe. Mother Cabrini dedicated her life to service and her love for those in need was profound.

She was a missionary to the poor, disenfranchised, the sick, and the uneducated. St. Mother Cabrini traveled across the Atlantic Ocean over 30 times in order to continue her efforts globally. She inspired thousands to join her which brought hope and love still remaining today to so many cities around the world. There are countless shrines and dozens of churches that bear her name. What is most significant is not the accolades or the fame, it is that Mother Cabrini said "yes" to loving service. She did so the heart of Jesus could be brought to countless people. This shows us that you do not have to have it all figured out, God has a plan. The one requirement is that you accept the invitation to serve and the Lord will be the one who uses you and me as his instruments.[129]

Loving service comes through the gift of time. St. Francis Xavier understood this well. However, the patron Saint of missions was actually converted by another Saint, Ignatius of Loyola, after an invitation to join the Church. Francis Xavier's "yes" then led to a lifetime of service where he traveled throughout India, Malaysia and Japan. His service to the poor became his heart beat. Xavier often would not sleep, but continued to heal the lepers and care for the sick both day and night. He brought God's love and hope to hundreds of thousands during his days as a missionary.

---

[129] Franciscan Media-Saint of the Day (Mother Cabrini)

Regardless of the difficulties, the horrific conditions, and the tireless work, Xavier is known to have radiated joy. Some people might wonder how someone who gives up their life to go and serve others, especially the poorest of the poor could be so joyful. It shows us that the human heart thirsts for love and when we give that love and others receive it, a powerful encounter with Jesus takes place. Xavier's impact and prime example of charity paved the way for countless Saints like Mother Teresa of Calcutta and is the pattern that missionaries around the globe carry out today.[130]

What is important for us to not lose sight of while on our long journey to holiness and Sainthood is that we have Xavier and Cabrini inside of ourselves. You and I are no different than anyone else. Loving service does not require us to go to foreign lands, yet some are called and they will go. Loving service does require you to give of your time, to selflessly care for those in need, and be the hands and feet of Jesus Christ. Loving service is about being the smile of God on people who are in need and going where the Spirit of the Lord guides you. Whether it is charity toward children like St. Nicholas, service to the destitute like Francis of Assisi, or any other act of kindness, love is all we need. Many people wonder what it would be like to see the face of God. What if I told you that Jesus is in your midst? What if you did not have to wait another day, let alone until your time on this earth came to an end to see the face of Christ? For Jesus himself said, "For behold, the Kingdom of God is in your midst."[131]

Christ's first apostles and his faithful over the past two thousand years have been called to love and share the good news with others. However, this is a law of nature. Service and love goes even beyond the realm of human life and is witnessed in the natural world. Pope Francis illustrated this well when discussing the joy love brings by stating, "Rivers do not drink their own water, trees do not eat their own fruit; the sun does not shine on itself and flowers do not spread their fragrance to themselves. Living for others is a rule of nature. We are all born to help each other. No matter how difficult it is...Life is good when you are happy, but much better when others are happy because of you." When we give we receive and when we love, the love

---

[130] Franciscan Media-Saint of the Day (Francis Xavier)
[131] Luke 17:21

of God fills our hearts with abundant joy.

Serving the poor and homeless is something that I have been involved with since my college days in Syracuse, New York when I met Andrew. Every week I looked forward to going to the local soup kitchen on South Salina street with my best friend and another incredible guy named Anil, from the Bronx. We established and ran a group called *The Le Moyne College Sandwich Makers*. Twice a week we were joined by a dozen or so friends on campus and made hundreds of sandwiches to bring down to the Samaritan center. There we served breakfast and passed out the lunches to the guests. Building community and giving love to others was an extremely important part of my life then as a Jesuit student and it is even more ingrained in me today. The heart of St. Ignatius of Loyola and his desire to bring Christ to others dwells in me.

Not only had Ignatius founded the Society of Jesus in 1534, but he vowed himself to serve the Pope and the needs of the Church. Ignatius developed the *Spiritual Exercises* known as the Examen Prayer which one part involves a person reflecting on their day and calling to mind where God showed up or where they received or gave his love. He also was known for educating the poor and finding homes for orphans.[132] The man who founded the Jesuits and gave of himself so willingly made a lasting impression on me during the formative maturation that I underwent as a college student on the heights at Le Moyne. Being with those in need and walking alongside them was something that was desired. My heart was and still is filled with joy each time I serve. I mention this because any time is the right time to get involved and share your love with others. And there is never a moment where we have a love encounter that our souls and the soul of the other is not impacted or changed.

Love is Presence

Showing up is the first step and allowing God to enter the encounters we have with people radically changes the human heart. The hidden Jesus is important for us to find in our own mission field of life. Being

---

[132] My Life With the Saints (James Martin)

with the poor and those who reveal Christ's face is significant because that is what God asks of us. It is truly who God is. It is beautiful because it leads us closer to the Lord and it allows us to experience him in others. Our goal should never be to try to fix things when we are serving and working with the poor. Instead, we must have the approach of sharing Jesus through our love by entering into the lives of the marginalized.

Through giving the love of Jesus and receiving his love from them, both of us are changed. What I have learned by serving alongside my friend Craig in Mexico City is the powerful example of love, which is manifested in our never ending pursuit to encounter Jesus by experiencing the suffering in people and in places that no one else is willing to go to. Craig explains that we are instruments of God's love and grace, taking the Gospel message to heart and living it out by loving and serving those who are unloved. What is so beautiful about this approach and call to respond to love is that all we really have to do is simply show up. Our presence and faithfulness to go is all that is required. Then, God will do his work through us. Just be. With regard to transformations and breakthroughs Carig has seen in the lives of street kids in Mexico and the poorest of the poor, he powerfully stated, "It wasn't anything that I did or said, it was the power of God working through me and through other people. I always feel like I am hanging out with Jesus when I am hanging out with someone who is rejected and they are alone, and they are lonely. I feel like I am hanging out with the suffering Christ.

My approach is to just love them. And people heal in that type of environment." Certainly this reminds us that love binds our hearts together as we journey on toward Heaven. Being connected by God's love, sharing in the suffering, and by giving ourselves to those who carry their cross, this ultimately is giving our hearts to Jesus. When was the last time you hung out with Jesus in this way? I guarantee you that if you hang out with the poor and the outcast, the lonely, the handicapped, and those who are unaccepted, you will see the hidden face of Christ. Jesus is there in the loving encounter, especially amidst the lowly of society. Your heart will be filled with joy. Jesus loves you and needs you to spread his love.

Where Jesus is, there is love; and where God's love is, there is hope. Where hope remains, there is light. The light of Christ leads us all to everlasting joy. Saint John of God put our role on earth beautifully and explained the purpose of each human being's call to loving service in the Lord by saying the following:

> *If you come here, it is solely in order to work, not to sit idle, for the most beloved son is entrusted with the greatest tasks and labor...And love our Lord Jesus Christ above everything in the world, for however much you love him, he still loves you more...I have nothing else to say to you, except to express the wish that God may save and keep you and lead you and everybody in his holy service...and hoping in God, slave of our Lord Jesus Christ and with a great desire to serve him.*[133]

In answering the call to serve we answer the Saint's call to love. By heeding this call we live out the twofold commandment that Jesus proclaimed to the world, namely to love God and love our neighbor. So, will we slow ourselves down and open our eyes to see the face of Jesus in others and respond with love? If you do and you open your heart to serve those in need, your life will be forever changed. It is time for us to seek out the poor in our own communities and to share Christ's love with them. Remember, Jesus "came to seek and to save what was lost."[134] So I encourage you to spend some time with the poor and in doing so you will unveil the face of God. The Kingdom is among us and although it won't come to complete fulfillment until we are with our Lord in Heaven, he does want you to have snippets of paradise here on earth. Abundance doesn't mean material goods, a fat wallet, or stuff that will lose its luster. The abundance and full life that God offers you is often found in the cross, the pains, and the sorrow. The moments we know we are truly alive are in the times we experience Jesus in others and these mysterious encounters of powerful conversion of heart lead us to such richness. When we seek first the Kingdom of God and we look in the right places, Jesus is there and his love leads us to receive gifts that come in the form of a fuller spirit, a heart for others, and a joy that no one can take away. Now it's clear that the joy and love of Jesus will fill you up even on a mountain of trash.

---

[133] Saint John of God
[134] Luke 19:10

Corporal Works of Mercy

As you know, being a Saint requires us to live differently and to carry out our faith in a manner that never ceases. Jesus called the disciples to perform works of mercy and he is asking you and me to do the same. It's through these holy and charitable acts that we bring the Lord to those we encounter. Growing up Catholic, I had often heard about the corporal works of mercy. However, these works seemed far off and only things that really holy people did. I admired the Saints I read about and how they were continuously blessing the lives of people they met by living out these corporal works. I even hoped that one day I too would follow suit. I sometimes wonder why people hesitate, or even worse, deny themselves from taking a leap of faith when it comes to serving God. What are we afraid of? As I began to see the fruit of the labor as a teen getting involved in more charitable acts, it became clear that the corporal works of mercy are at the very core of what it means to be a disciple.

The corporal works of mercy symbolically illustrate the seven acts of loving service including to feed the hungry, to give drink to the thirsty, to clothe the naked, to give shelter to travelers, to visit the sick, to visit the imprisoned, and to bury the dead. If you have engaged in one or more of these works, you know why mercy is the center of them all. The word mercy literally is derived from the Anglo-French "merci" meaning benevolence, forgiveness, and kindness. Is not every one of us in need of mercy at some point or another throughout our lives? Compassion is a beautiful gift that must be shared and cannot be denied.

When praying on the corporal works of mercy and thinking about our journey to Sainthood, we must reflect on Matthew's Gospel. His powerful words at the end illustrate and call each of us to love—faith in action, through selfless service. Although mercy and living out our faith is central here, we must not lose sight of the greatest message of all. This can ignite the flame of love in us and has the power to change the world. You might be thinking, *Why all of this talk about changing the world? Isn't that a little arrogant or cliche. What can one person do that is so significant anyway?* Well, first of all, the Gospel cannot be chained. If we go and live out the missionary call that Jesus makes through these works of mercy and carry them out to our best ability, undoubtedly the world will be altered for good. And yet, that is not even the most significant part. Merciful acts of heartfelt service and spreading the love of Jesus opens him up to us. Living in us and through us, Jesus refines our hearts. In doing so we fully turn our lives over to the Lord and we cannot remain the same. As St. Paul says to the Galatians, "Yet I live, no longer I, but Christ lives in me; insofar as I now live in the flesh, I live by faith in the Son of God who has loved me and given himself up for me."[135]

Service and the corporal works of mercy are a gift. Not only are they a gift to those you serve and share your love with, but they are a gift to your Heavenly Father. You can truly serve and love God best by serving and loving your fellow brothers and sisters. When I was in college, my spiritual director and mentor, Father Maldari, shared with me some of his experiences regarding prison ministry. Back then I thought to myself how amazing and noble it was for people to go and share the Lord with criminals. The majority of society would never think to give the time of day to a murderer or someone who has intentionally hurt or sinned gravely against humanity. It wasn't until I had a close family member who was about to face upwards of a decade in prison due to a horrific event that it dawned on me. I had to get involved.

Until you step foot into a prison and go beyond the steel bars, you don't know what life inside locked up is like. Not to mention, sitting inches away from some of the most dangerous people known to man is nerve racking at the surface level to say the very least. So why even go in and risk it anyway? What good can come of your time inside and what does anyone owe people who have hurt our community? These are all very rational and depth-filled questions.

However, the answer became clear to me. Sainthood is not about comfort, it is about greatness. The person who overcomes themselves, their ego, and their safety net will find that God can transcend all the anxiety, he can win victory over fear, and he can dispel the darkness of the cell. High fives, hugs, big smiles, and lots of laughter. What the heck do these things have to do with prison? No one should be having fun or enjoying any of their time of punishment. Laughter must be the sign you are in an insane asylum. Let's go beyond the surface level.

---

[135] Galatians 2:20

This certainly is not the case for many incarcerated individuals who spend their time behind bars, but faith is alive amongst some. Nonetheless, this was the case at Greene Correctional facility in Coxsackie, New York when I went with a number of volunteers from the Albany Diocese to a REC (Residents Encounter Christ) weekend retreat. God's love and joy were present.

Before entering the barbed wire fenced yard, we went through numerous metal detectors, were patted down, and had to leave everything besides our clothes behind. Hearing the heavy steel door slam shut behind me when I was inside did make my heart jump a little. My mind began to race and I felt my skin begin to crawl as I passed by cells of inmates. I started to wonder why I was there. As I walked a little further and could see the green bus pulling up inside the prison circle, I knew there was no turning back. We were greeted by the bus driver who opened the door with a friendly smile and a welcoming "hello." Soon we were dropped off at the community center inside the prison where I could hear music and singing. Curiosity began to come upon me with great fervor. After taking a step inside, I was rushed by numerous men in green jumpsuits. My initial inclination was to run the other way, but I did not. The men were clapping, offering fist bumps, and literally shouting with joy. I thought for a moment that I was in the wrong place. I couldn't believe it.

That night set a precedent and it left a massive impression on my heart. Stepping out of my own comfort zone and accepting an invitation was all it took. God did the rest. Having now served for nearly two years in prison ministry, I can tell you that the only real difference between me and the people inside the prison wall is the color of the clothing those men wear. Certainly I have not committed any atrocious crime, but my point here is that we all bleed red. Every human being desires love and each of us needs mercy. Lest we not forget the merciful love of the great St. John Paul II who on December 28th, 1983, a mere 18 or so months after being shot by his would-be assassin Mehmet Ali Ağca, deliberately went into this man's prison cell to forgive him. Later on the Pope's request for this man's pardon was granted. Imagine the radical nature of that type of love and how it could emphatically change a cruel man's heart. And so it did. Mehmet converted to Christianity and in December of 2014 he visited Rome and laid two dozen roses on the Pope's tomb. Divine Mercy

Sunday, which is celebrated the second Sunday after Easter each year, was initiated by John Paul II as his example of Christ's mercy reflects the divine love of the Father.

I could go on and on about why Jesus calls us to the corporal works of mercy and particularly prison ministry, but what is foremost to embrace is that we all need human connection. This especially holds true with people who have fallen off the beaten path. As the thirteen-time NBA champion player and coach Phil Jackson known as the *Zen Master* put it, "No man is an island. No man goes his way alone. What I put into the lives of others, will come back into its own." Humans do not thrive in isolation, they can barely survive in it. The human heart desires relationships. People were made for relationships. Most of all we were created for a relationship with God. And where relationships exist, forgiveness and mercy must be present because we are all broken.

The love of Jesus has no bounds, certainly a prison wall cannot contain it. I began to understand this saying by Coach Jackson when Drayton, a lifetime convict, summoned me to his table during the prison retreat shortly after I arrived. This man who was in his 60s had been incarcerated for well over 25 years. The outside world thought of him as a bad and dangerous man, rightfully so. What they did not know about Dray is that despite him having done some horrible crimes, his heart had changed and he had repented. I will never forget what Dray told me the first time I met him. He said, "Dan you know coming to prison saved my life. See, sometimes God uses a hammer. Other times God uses the sledgehammer, but for me he used the jackhammer." My hope is that you too will allow God to chip away at your heart. I know that I entered prison wondering how I could possibly impact the lives of the men there or provide them with some sense of hope. I left being so filled up, not because of anything that I did, but all because of the willingness of men to share from their heart, admit their faults, and desire to change. The Saint is willing to listen. He or she is willing to look at even the most abhorrent and unattractive situations differently. As you and I strive for holiness and grow closer to Christ, my hope is that we can ask Jesus to help us to have his Sacred Heart for others. Let this be the anthem we live by and how we faithfully follow the Lord as it says:

The King will say to those on his right, 'Come, you who are blessed by my Father. Inherit the kingdom prepared for you from the foundation of the world. For I was hungry and you gave me food, I was thirsty and you gave me drink, a stranger and you welcomed me, naked and you clothed me, ill and you cared for me, in prison and you visited me.' Then the righteous will answer him and say, 'Lord, when did we see you hungry and feed you, or thirsty and give you drink? When did we see you as a stranger and welcome you, or naked and clothe you? When did we see you ill or in prison, and visit you?' And the king will say to them in reply, 'Amen, I say to you, whatever you did for one of these least brothers of mine, you did for me.'"[136]

When we encounter Christ in the poor, we embrace our own poverty. We are filled with great love and are able to allow the love of Jesus to flow from us to those we meet. It is not enough to simply take a stand on an issue. We must stand with others and be one with them in what they face. When we do this, then the walls, the stigma, and the barriers are broken down. Human to human, life to life, a personal encounter cannot be replicated. The depths of the human heart and connection with people is what life is all about. The love of Christ is here with us always and present in the little ones. The greatest poverty in the world is being unloved. It is a tremendous blessing to have the opportunity to share with others on this journey of life and meet people where they are. Love transforms all and Christ Jesus gives us lasting fulfillment.

Where Love is Absent, Jesus Invites Saints In

Having the opportunity to go to spend time with people who are the "unlovable" outcasts of society is important. When you go and simply show up, blessings and immense light comes flooding in. The encounters that you have with the poor, the suffering, the imprisoned, and the disenfranchised is something that is purifying. You bring joy

---

[136] Matthew 25:34-40

into the lives of those you meet and they lead you closer to the Lord, radiating the love of Christ. Sometimes the situations we find ourselves in when surrounded by the poor are messy and less than pleasant. Various encounters might even be uncomfortable to say the least and we might have experiences that make us question again why we are there.

Remember to enter fully in and instead of taking offense or looking at your own interest, try to ask, *How does Jesus want me to show up for this person right now?* When we can look at it through this lens of love, our Lord gives you and me the strength, courage, and ability to see the encounter as he sees it. Most of all, we then can allow him to work through us and *be love* for those we meet. This intense experience and the love that is transmitted between those we encounter and ourselves is what continues to keep me going back to places that nobody else wants to go. I return because God keeps calling me to be there because he is present in all of his creation, especially in the margins of society. God has a way to humble our hearts so we might more fully rely on him and allow his love to flow through us. These encounters ensure that we might decrease and Jesus might increase.

The fact is that the poor are all around us. They are in our workplaces, our communities, and in our schools. Poverty tends to mask itself behind various walls. There are all different forms of poverty albeit physical, spiritual, emotional, social, and financial. Whatever form of poverty someone faces, it can drain them, sucking the very life out of their inner being. When you and I show up in someone's life, we give them hope and these seeds germinate. There is no telling how much this renewed hope will do for a person or a community and in fact it is not up to us to decide. We continue to plant the seeds and God keeps causing the growth. In the words found in her private writings St. Teresa of Calcutta beautifully explained why serving God matters so much:

I am leaving my old friends. Forsaking family and home. My heart draws me onward to serve my Christ...Oh God, accept this sacrifice as a sign of my love. help, please, thy creature to glorify thy name! In return, I only ask of thee, O most kind

Father of us all: Let me save at least one soul—One you already knew...The life of a missionary is not strewn with roses, in fact more with thorns; but with it all, it is a life full of happiness and joy when she thinks that she is doing the same work which Jesus was doing when he was on earth, and that she is fulfilling Jesus' commandments: "Go and teach all nations."[137]

As long as we remember that we are workers in the Lord's vineyard, we will stay connected to the vine. This will allow us to do God's work that he calls us to and our labor will bear much fruit. Think back to the ministry and times of Jesus. He certainly performed many miracles and all of these impressed the crowds. Giving sight to the blind, healing the lame, and raising the dead is quite remarkable. It is not an everyday occurrence that these happenings transpire. Surely it's extremely important to recognize that as much as Jesus wanted to bring healing to people's lives, what he desired far more was to draw them into his heart so he could have an encounter with them. Jesus was not merely a doctor for the ill, but one for the broken hearted and those who lacked faith.

Our Lord shows us time and time again that physical healing was important to show the power of God, however there was something much greater taking place there. The spiritual connection of souls and the internal health is most critical. After all, that lasts forever and knowing God intimately is the only thing that can truly sustain the human soul. The bottom line is that Saints serve and they do not count the cost. Answering the call and showing up will revolutionize your heart and it will affect the people you share Jesus with. During the many times we show up in another's life and we have the consciousness to not focus on "doing," but instead we concentrate on being present, this causes change.

Being present is a gift, a far more impactful one than most understand. Do not get me wrong, there is great merit in providing food, water, clothing, and hope through tangible works of mercy and aiding through necessities. This is important. However, these are mere vehicles for us to enter into the human situation of our fellow

---

[137] Teresa, Mother. *Come Be My Light*, p.16 & 19

brothers and sisters and share with them their journey as we bear the Cross together on the road to Heaven. Don't worry about how it will all work out, just go, trust, and see how God will use you! My hope is that you will seek out opportunities to encounter Christ in the poor. It is often the best way to find ourselves because we realize that life is most meaningful when we give our hearts away to others. As Ghandi powerfully put it, "The best way to find yourself is to lose yourself in the service of others."

So think about what you will do in the coming months to take a step out of your comfort zone. Remember, the poor are all around you. Invite someone into your conversation. Take a few minutes out of your day to be present and love someone like Jesus did. Your willingness to love and show up in the lives of another person will sprinkle light and make this world a better place. There is no doubt that you will go away feeling whole. Engaging in such encounters are truly holy moments. We are called to be Saints and we spread the Kingdom one person, one kind act, and one relationship at a time! The ripple effect is profound. You are the leader and the change that the world needs. Mother Teresa lived out service and loved with the heart of Christ. Rest in these words from Mother and know that your time to shine is now as she said, "Do not wait for leaders, do it alone, person to person, today...I used to pray that God would feed the hungry or do this or do that, but now I pray that he will guide me to do whatever I'm supposed to do, what I can do. I used to pray for answers, but now I pray for strength. I used to believe that prayer changes things, but now I know that prayer changes us and we change things."

My Prayer is that you and all the Saints who journey on toward Heaven can keep this vow to serve Christ and love completely without denying him anything. Whether big or small, miraculous or mundane, let's always continue to have the love of Jesus at the center of our lives and burning in our hearts. The good news needs to be spread to his people and the best way is through love. There is nothing that satiates the thirst of Christ and our hearts than to walk humbly with the Lord and to share his joy and love with the world.

*Prayer & Vow to Jesus to Serve Him
and to not Refuse Him Anything:*

Lord Jesus, I am in awe of your blessings and goodness in my life. I love you above all things. I vow not to withhold myself from serving you no matter how small or large your ask is of me. May you, my Jesus, live through me and give me your Sacred Heart so I have the capacity to love others with your love. Fill me with your holy presence each day so that I can share your joy with everyone I encounter. Please use all of my life and my being to serve you completely without any reservation. Thank you Lord Jesus for loving me and for looking past my flaws. Send down your Holy Spirit and dispense your amazing grace upon me. Allow me to trust in you always. I implore the intercession of the Virgin Mary and all the Saints. Intercede for me. Jesus, my life is yours and you are mine. Make me your Saint. Without you Lord, I can do nothing. But with you, I believe through your power and grace I can bear much fruit and do everything you ask of me. Lord Jesus, I trust in you. Amen.

Challenge 14:

Reflect on the beatitudes and where you feel inclined to serve the Lord today. How can you trust God more and empty yourself so that Jesus can fill you up with his goodness? What is it that fires you up and what do you enjoy doing with and for others? Line up a few acts of service within your community or area to take part in over the next couple of months. Invite a friend or family member to serve with you and remain open to how God will use this to deepen your faith. Remain open to where Jesus leads you and those he asks you to love, even in the most random or smallest situations. Don't worry about what you should say or even what you will do, just be present. Show up and realize that love is the only thing you need. God will take care of the rest. Trust fully that Jesus will love others through you and participate in his joy!

FILLING GAPS
CHAPTER 15

"No one can replace you to do what you are destined to do until you totally fail and leave an empty gap that God will fill." - Israelmore Ayivor

Imagine being at the edge of a canyon. You have to decide what move to make and time is running out. If you stay where you are, surely nothing will change and eventually you will run out of water, not to mention forget the view that might await you on the other side. However, if you decide to descend into the depths and then make the steep upward climb, there is tremendous risk. Any number of factors could cause serious injury and you might not make it. So what do you do? You have run through each scenario thoroughly. The sun is blazing, the sweat is pouring down your face, and you can make out what appears to be some kind of water on the other side.

Finally, you manage to have enough gall to take the initial step. Your footing isn't secure and some small rocks plummet hundreds of feet to the bottom. You hesitate and look back for an instance. Then you say to yourself, I can do this, it is worth it. You begin again. The journey takes hours upon hours. Fortunately you have someone else with you to rely on. Your pack that you are carrying is starting to weigh you down and your legs are growing weary. But now you are more than half way there and in the middle of the valley. There is no stopping and you have to finish what you started. You grind your way through and begin the ascent. Each step it gets harder as you seek out the proper footing and stretch for solid rock to hold onto. You are nearly there. Your heart is racing and the adrenaline is flowing like a river through your veins. A few more feet. You made it!

Would you have made it alone? Certainly not. The hole in the earth that you just traversed through was massive. Looking back it's almost unimaginable that you got to the ground you are standing on currently. And before you, there is a beautiful lake with enough water that your cup will gush over thirty times. So what does this all mean for the Saint? How does this leg of a journey relate to you and me? Well, God never said life would be easy. This holds especially true when he asks us to take the leap of faith and go to the other side. There is much planned for you and sometimes our own plans become eroded. When they are washed away it can be excruciating. But never forget that love will fill the void in your heart. It might be a hole that's as big as a canyon, but when received it is an oasis of peace and mercy.

Love is a word that we have discussed often on our journey thus far. It's difficult to quantify. Father Pierre Touissant of the Franciscan Friars of the Renewal, who spends most of his time at the St. Joseph Friary down in the Bronx, powerfully reminds us that "Love is free, faithful, fruitful, and total." Father P.T. is often heard reminding the postulants and people he encounters how vast God's love is. He explained to us that God's love is so open, it's as big as the hole in the side of Jesus inviting us in, just like the Lord did with Thomas when he doubted and told him to put his entire hand in his side. This is such great imagery because we can picture the scene from the Gospel as Jesus is with the other disciples in the upper room and they are beyond excited to be with him again. At first they were afraid and thought he was a ghost when he entered through the walls because the doors were locked. But then they are amazed and fired up to be with the Lord. Thomas hears, but lacks faith. Then he comes, sees, and is still unsure. Eventually Thomas enters into the love of Christ fully when Jesus invites him to stick his arm into the wound which overflows with love. At this moment Thomas, called Didymus, believes and says,

"My Lord and my God."[138] The human heart bursts when it is filled completely with love.

So the question is, are we living love this way? Are we totally open and are we willing to have enough faith to enter into the wounded side of the Lord who invites us all the way in? Even if it takes a while to get there, go. Saints allow God to fill in the gaps with love. Loving is the way and having steadfast faith as to descend into the unknown and voyage over the most difficult terrain with trust that an oasis awaits us builds a bridge to any crevices or canyons our soul faces. Based on the seed God planted in your heart, you respond with great effort and our Lord does the rest.

It's loving in this particular manner that we emulate the chastity of St. Joseph, Mary's spouse. He purely loved God with all his heart. What I admire most about St. Joseph goes beyond the fact that he was Jesus' earthly Father and a great husband to the Virgin. He trusted and loved so deeply that it led him to change his plans radically. He lost control and gave permission for the Father to be the gap filler. Joseph allowed the Lord to stretch out his hand and he was willing to climb the mountain of faith that the Father put in front of him. Lest we forget that Joseph was a simple carpenter from Nazareth who became the human stepfather of the savior of the world and the patron Saint of the Universal Church, families, and fathers everywhere. Not bad for a guy with a hammer and some nails in his tool belt. The bottom line is Saints stay the course when life goes sideways on them, continuing to trust and love the best they can.

Into the Unknown and to the Other Side

For Antonio, he was unsure if the canyon was worth traversing. If it was, how would he possibly do it? The young man had his head bent and rested his arms on his knees. As he prayed in the small chapel, thoughts swirled in his head. Tony had come to ask the Lord for help in his life. This was certainly not the first time and it would not be the last. As he poured out his heart to God, he could only think about his shortcomings and the mountain that remained ahead of him. The

---

[138]John 20:28

questions started to spin out of control like a tornado in his mind. The angst of life was drying up his thirsting heart at that moment. Tears began to cascade like a waterfall down his face. A small pool was forming beneath Tony's feet. As he cried out to the Lord pleading for grace, he did not know how he had gotten to where he was. Why had he buried this dream and called for such a long time?

Running away from it was not the answer. Antonio understood that there was so much that was out of his control and yet his faith remained. Although the tough road of life had hardened Tony's heart a little, being there in the presence of Christ was what his aching soul desperately needed. The uncertainty of the future, his next move, and ultimately where he was being called to next seemed so heavy because facing reality was tough. The young man knew that he was not alone in the journey and had never been forsaken or abandoned through it all. What carried Antonio on during the trek was evident to those who knew him best. It was more so who carried him. Faith was what allowed him to even consider this again, let alone give real merit to the situation.

Why did Tony face this particular situation some would call an "Everest" on his path? Certainly, it was tearing him up inside. Why now? How was he supposed to navigate through it and make an enormous life-altering decision at this juncture in time? Staring down the crossroads of life at a massive fork in the road was not easy. Tony knew that either way, pain and disappointment would come. He realized that understanding and acceptance would be lacking from many and that could remain forever. If Antonio stayed where he was and kept living the way things had always been, happiness would be there partially and perhaps little pockets of joy to an extent. However, the lack of ultimate fulfillment would remain. Tony's soul thirsted for more and he felt God calling him stronger than ever before to the priesthood. To flip the script on life now would not be easy and the unknown still loomed. Whether he decided to take the leap of faith or not there were consequences to bear. Staying rooted in the situation was somewhat comfortable because it was the life that Tony knew and the one everyone expected of him.

For the most part it would also be a far easier road. Keeping things the same was the path that basically set Antonio on auto pilot. His family and his best friends had known that he discerned the priesthood earlier on, but that had surely passed—so they thought. Undoubtedly, staying neutral was a much simpler path. After all, his life had been really good and he was blessed. But to deny the soul of what it thirsts for and to not heed the strongest call on his life could be detrimental with cataclysmic implications on his internal and eternal being. Tony believed burying "it" again, once and for all, would sell himself radically short of his fullest potential. How could he continue to deny God and the plan established for his life? Although the young man constructed this hardened outer shell, while authentically living a life that projected happiness and joy, there was still something missing. The element was nothing that Tony could fill nor any other person for that matter. The piece to the puzzle he needed to be whole—holy and complete was out there and attainable. Since it had not yet been put into place, it left a sizable hole in his heart that he knew only the Lord could fill. But it wouldn't be filled on its own. This would occur only if he went down that winding and uncharted road.

Grace would be the glue that would hold Antonio together, especially when contemplating the more challenging path. And so is true for you and me when we are up against radical changes, have to make difficult decisions, and contemplate matters of the heart. This is because we are moved by the one who made us and knows us most. Our souls long for more and will remain uneasy until they settle into God's will no matter how long or hard of a path we must take to get there.

As Antonio fixed his eyes on the Cross in the chapel, the young man knelt before the blessed sacrament. He was alone, but not really. There in the silence, the world seemed to stop for a brief moment. He knew he was in the complete presence of God. Tony sat there hanging out with his best friend, the Lord Jesus. There is something to be said about fully entering the presence of the Savior. By taking time to quiet our hearts and all the noise that surrounds us, we can finally listen. The questions that had been whizzing around madly in his brain and the anxiety of a gargantuan decision began to calm. The storm and raging sea of Antonio's heart was now entering the depths of more peaceful waters. He laid it all out there at the foot of the Cross. In prayer Tony asked God to take it and show him the way. He knew what he had to do. What was left was for Antonio to do the most courageous thing possible—to say "yes" to Jesus even though he was afraid.

Gaps existed, there were many questions left to be answered, and the unknown was vast. However, the trust and faith Antonio had in the Lord was able to bring peace to his tense heart. Most people would ask how could this young man be so torn up inside? From the vantage point of the world, he had it all. Look at his life and tell me what could be better? Even Tony, himself, would agree that the blessings were countless. The financial stability, the friendships, an amazing family and most of all his loving fiancé, Mariel. Clearly, he was rich in the things that mattered. Antonio had traveled the world with her and they had built a beautiful life together. They understood one another at the core and their love ran so deep. There was a real soul connection and a love that was powerful beyond measure. And yet, Tony kept wrestling in his heart because the spirit was calling him to something more. This young man who had built the fabric of his life on honesty, integrity, faithfulness, and love was facing inner turmoil. Nobody else knew besides for the two he loved most, his fiancé Mariel, and the Lord.

What was the next move? Where would Tony go and how would the future unfold? The move was crucial, but listening to his heart and the message God was placing on it was most essential. Like the young man in the Gospel, could Antonio part ways with the earthly riches? After all, "What good is it for someone to gain the whole world, yet forfeit his very soul?"[139] There is something to be said about the heartfelt connection and depth of knowing the soul of another person so deeply that you want what they desire. When your love is so rich and unconditional that you want the people you love most to be free to spread their wings and soar, this allows them to thrive. You want them to be at peace. Your heart wills that they feel so at home with you that they know your love will never cease because you desire their joy to be complete. The soul connection with the Lord is boundless. God understood Tony's heart better than any person ever could and having his fiancé Mariel believe in his call, as much as he himself did, ignited the fire within him. The hatchet no longer needed to be buried.

---

[139] Mark 8:36

As tough as it would be, she was on board. She loved him unconditionally and wanted what was best for his soul and for the world which was awaiting him.

It was time to sharpen the ax and cut down the tree that had overgrown and been a tough obstacle for the majority of Tony's life. Some questions remained. Would he be brave enough to actually take the leap of faith? Would he have the humility to fully turn over his life to the Lord and admit that there was no way he could do this alone? How would Tony's story end if he did take the road less traveled? What would his future look like and how would this magnanimous decision and massive change impact everyone he loved most? The good news was that like the *everyday Saint* on the road to holiness, Antonio understood with complete certainty who held his future. However, only time would tell the outcome and how his story would truly play out.

Saints Endure & God Turns Question Marks into Exclamation Points

In life there are situations, moments, and seasons we experience where the answers are not all figured out. Having a plan is great, but often the roadmap of our lives involves hidden twists and detours that were unforeseen. We zig and zag, we go backward and forward, eventually landing on the path of our destiny. Could we get to our final destination alone? I don't think so. It takes a lot of humility to come to a place in your mind and more so within your heart to ask God for help. Many times people can be too proud to admit that they don't have it all figured out.

Life is not supposed to be tied up with a bow and ready for perfect delivery all the time. It is okay not to know. Although this is not easy by any means, it is crucial for our spiritual well-being. It's important to ask others who know us deeply to pray for us and with us. Moreover, it is even harder at times to let go of what our will is, in order to embrace what God's will is for our life. Having a humble heart does not come naturally and it is not comfortable to lose control. And yet, when you quiet yourself by listening intently to the Lord you can then receive his grace. Through the humility God provides, you carry out the plan which the Lord lays out and this will bring you true and lasting joy.

St. Faustina is known in the Church as the "secretary of Divine Mercy." Having experienced numerous visions of Jesus and his Sacred Heart, she was in tune with her spirit and listened to the Lord. It must have been difficult for Faustina to attempt an explanation to people where she shared her visions of Christ. Initially she probably wrestled with these visions. I can only imagine how hard it had to be for her to believe what she saw was a reality, let alone to disclose it to others. Although doubt can creep in and the weight and expectations of the world slam down upon us, we must continue to walk humbly with God. The Lord knows the fullness of your heart. He will make a way when there seems to be no way so long as you trust in his ocean of mercy. St. Faustina did so and she lowered herself to the point of keeping things in her heart and listening to God despite the doubt and rejection of those around her. In her diary entitled *The Divine Mercy of My Soul* she shared her experiences of the visions.

In her writings and evidently her vocational work, she lowered herself to trust Jesus fully when he called her to become a nun. After multiple attempts to join religious orders, Faustina did not give up and finally was accepted by the Sisters of Our Lady of Mercy. The road was difficult for her because she had to work as a housekeeper and a cook. She continuously traveled around trying to earn enough money to pay for her religious habit (clothing) and earn the respect of her superiors. Faustina's unwavering faith and her humble heart continued to attract Jesus to her. She said, "I will make every effort to obtain that place unnoticed by others. It is enough that God sees."[140] This remarkably humble woman and servant of Christ kept pursuing him and remained open to Jesus working miraculously within her. One can only admire Faustina's courage, humility, and trust in God's plan. The master was at work again. Not only did she experience God's grace, she saw Jesus face to face. In her diary, St. Faustina writes:

In the evening, when I was in my cell, I became aware of the Lord Jesus clothed in a white garment. One hand was raised in blessing, the other was touching the garment at the breast.

From the opening of the garment at the breast there came forth two large rays, one red and the other pale. In silence I gazed intently at the Lord; my soul was overwhelmed with fear, but also with great joy. After a while Jesus said to me, "Paint an image according to the pattern you see, with the inscription: Jesus, I trust in You."[141]

No matter what we are facing today, trusting in the Lord like St. Faustina is what we need to do. Believing in God's great love will help calm your soul when there is something stirring in your heart that causes you to stay up late at night. When you face difficult choices, like was the case for the young man, trust will guide you through. You might be combating uncertainty right now on a large decision or it could be something else that is burdening your soul. A gigantic mountain might seem immovable and too much to handle. Something you can't quite wrap your mind around could be causing an inner jihad—holy war and struggle in your soul. I encourage you to heed the example of St. Faustina and to repeat the five powerful words that will radically change your life, "Jesus, I trust in you." When these words are spoken aloud and believed within, the unstoppable force that has powers to move mountains is commenced due to our great faith.

Thanks to Faustina's openness to Christ, we now celebrate Divine Mercy Sunday to conclude the Octave of Easter every year. Not only was Maria a great witness to the faith, but she accepted God's grace and mercy. This allowed Jesus to work through her so his endless mercy could be emphasized and shared with the world. Like St. Faustina initiated, we must emulate her approach to rest in the Lord and fully trust in him. When we go to Jesus with a meek and trusting heart, Christ will embrace us fully. We are wrapped up in his warm, merciful love.

Mercy is an answer to our prayers. Mercy will restore our brokenness and God's love will repair our souls so that we can be made whole—holy—again. When it comes to thinking you must have all the answers, this is the furthest from the truth. Ultimately, you and I will come to grasp that only God knows what is inside the deep waters of our hearts. He alone understands your greatest desires and

---

[141] The Diary of Saint Maria Faustina Kowalska : Divine Mercy in My Soul

needs of grace. After all, the creator of the universe knows us even better than we know ourselves. As David wrote in the Psalms, "Delight yourself in the Lord and he will give you the desires of your heart."[142] Gaps in life exist. Occasionally these can feel as monstrous and extensive as the Grand Canyon. At other points we come to notice the seemingly endless tiny crevices that exist in our foundations as well. Regardless of how large or small the gap is, God finds ways to fill it and provide what we need. But we must trust the Lord fully. Life has taught me some tremendously compelling lessons. In my walk of faith and the journey to Sainthood, God keeps paving the way. I encourage you to have full confidence in knowing that God is doing the same for you. We just have to keep going, even without fully knowing. God fills in all the gaps. Trust and believe!

Angels Among Us

On our road to Sainthood and as we respond to the call that God has put on our lives, there will be divine connections that occur. It is interesting that the Lord already has the right people lined up, the Heavenly encounters, and the angels to light the path we are on. Believing that God truly fills in the gaps that exist in our lives is an important step, but equally significant is remaining open to the people who come to us, especially those who appear when we least expect it. If you look back at your life, you can probably think about some people you have met and friendships that have been gained that came out of the blue. We often hear about putting ourselves in the right position, the power of proximity, and being surrounded by good company. I get all that. However, there are some moments and some people who are just different. The power and grace of them entering your life at exactly the right juncture is seemingly unexplainable. These "angels" came when you needed uplifting, a listening ear, or a boost of confidence. Their presence to us is exceptional.

There are divine connections that God orchestrates in your life that are not mere coincidences, but "godcidences." Looking back at some life changing moments in my own life I can see the hand of the

---

[142] Psalms 37:4

Lord at work. When some big decisions needed to be made at various crossroads, God put in front of me some amazing people. As the scripture says, "Do not neglect hospitality, for through it some have unknowingly entertained angels."[143] I don't know about you, but I believe in angels. As a kid, I always imagined the scene of the 1990s sports classic movie *Angels in the Outfield* playing out in life. For anyone who knows the movie, there are times when the ballplayers have no chance of making a play on the diamond. Yet, they are miraculously lifted up by the angels on the field, gaining the unusual ability to do the spectacular.

What is more impressive about the scenes of this fictional movie is that it shows that there are happenings in life that are baffling. Angels do exist and come our way. Perhaps they even draw us closer to the Saint who is living next door or stir up our hearts to become that Saint for others. The friend who appears on the scene when you are going through something tragic in your life and is there for you when you need it most might be an angel that God placed in exactly the right moment and with perfect timing in your life. Who are the angels who have come into your life and lifted you up in your moment and time of need? Who swooped in lately and provided that spark and vigor that your spirit so deeply longed for? At times these people are met once and then they are gone. The encounter lasts only for an hour, a day, or a year.

Concurrently, there are angels who keep flying with us. These people are the Saints who invest in our lives not because they want something from us, but because they desire to see us fulfilled. These angles have been divinely connected, their souls and ours are melded together from the beginning. The fusion shared has no end. The communion and connection is heartfelt and it runs deep. There is no need to try to explain, but we just are and they know how we feel because it is a holy connection. Although rare, these angels do come among us. The Saints are living in our day and age. Keep your eyes open and understand that God is going to fill in the gaps. He promises to do so through the love of Jesus, but also by speaking to us, moving in our midst, and giving us the hope we need through the angelic *everyday Saints* we encounter along the way. Moses was the great

---

143 Hebrews 13:2

leader of our early faith. He, the father of the Jewish people who God entrusted with his commands wrote in the Psalms:

For he commands his angels with regard to you, to guard you wherever you go. With their hands they shall support you, lest you strike your foot against a stone. You can tread upon the asp and the viper, trample the lion and the dragon. Because he clings to Me I will deliver him; because he knows my name I will set him on high. He will call upon me and I will answer; I will be with him in distress; I will deliver him and give him honor.[144]

Allow that holy and beautiful message to submerge into the depths of your heart. The angels are being commanded by the Lord right now. Believe this and receive this. You have nothing to fear and the Lord promises to keep you safe. Not only will you have protection, you will meet those along the way—the angels in your outfield who will elevate you even higher to God. These angels sent by our Father will guide us, provide the help we need, and be God's presence that fills in the cracks. So the next time you meet someone and are left "wowed" or thinking there is something extra special about them that you can't put your finger on, know that God arranged that divine connection. You feel that magical presence because the mystical power holds true. These holy men and women are the *everyday Saints* and "angels among us."

Each summer I drive down with my family to Ocean City, New Jersey. Having gone year after year, the route is nearly second nature. Entering the fully packed car is exciting. I don't even mind sitting wedged between beach umbrellas, stacked coolers, and other countless items. It is actually quite pleasant because it leads to a week of memories with those people I love most. The smell of the ocean becomes more pronounced as we approach the sandy shore. Every time we travel the highway down state and cross the Jersey border there is construction going on. Huge dump trucks are moving dirt, buildings are being erected, and throngs of workers are continuously hammering away at the highway. The 95 plus degree heat is enjoyed

---

[144] Psalm 91: 11-15

by us during those summer months because the great northeast is riddled with such cold hard winters. Unfortunately, this drastic change in weather does not bode well for the roads. So like clockwork, construction crews each summer show up. They spend a few months resurfacing and repaving the streets. The potholes, divots, and other gaps are filled in and before you know it, the car is cruising effortlessly toward vacation.

Such is life. Your journey will have bumps, detours and gaps along the way. Yet, if you remain the course and allow God to be the GPS, you will reach your destination. Smooth sailing is desired by humanity. However, I like to think of the gaps in life as the way that God reminds us that we can't journey alone and we must trust him fully as he reconstructs our hearts. Knowing what the future holds is one thing, but knowing who holds your future is far better! This cannot be said enough. Understand my friends, that God knows you well and his love for you will never cease. Life will send you many question marks, stop signs, and roadblocks along the way. There will be people who try to throw you off course and many distractors will fly by. Be still and know that God already knows. He is God and he will help you navigate through it all. The journey becomes a little easier and much more manageable when we trust and turn over the wheel of our lives to him. We are co-creators and co-pilots with the Creator. We will enter desert moments from time to time, after all Jesus faced 40 days of his own hardship in the wilderness. When you and I stop worrying so much and start turning that angst into prayer, the Lord will help calm us ever more. Your faith and trust in Jesus alone will settle your restless heart. Never forget that God's amazing grace is abundant and it is his grace and love that fills in all of the gaps.

Challenge 15

The next time you are at the beach, fill a bucket with sand. Afterward, get some larger shells or some rocks and try to add them. They don't fit because the sand has been packed tightly and has hardened. Empty out your bucket. This time, fill the canister with rocks or sea shells first. Then dump the sand in and watch it filter around the larger objects. Notice how easily the sand is now able to be added because it flows through the bigger pieces already there. The sand is no longer hardened since there is space inside. Let this little experiment sink into your heart as you look out at the deep ocean. As the waves crash at your feet, understand that God asks you to trust him fully and to not harden your heart. The rocks or shells represent the most important pieces of your life; family, friends, career, desires, hopes, and dreams. The sand resembles the many experiences, opportunities, people you will encounter, and the life happenings that are yet to take place. Trust fully that God is the bucket that holds it all together. Allow life and Jesus to flow through you like the sand does as it reaches the most important elements. In doing so you will be left filled and everyone who knows you will feel Jesus' loving presence, just like the sand is felt and supported by those rocks and shells.

BE CHURCH
CHAPTER 16

"Holy communion is the shortest and safest way to Heaven."
– St. Pius X

There are many things that lead us inside a Church and draw us closer to Jesus at the foot of his Cross. The Eucharist is the pinnacle and cornerstone of our faith. It literally means to give thanks and the holiness of communion illuminates our hearts. Unquestionably, the Eucharist is the climax of all sacraments for believers. The word sacrament means "to make holy." Sacraments fill us with God's holiness and allow us to truly *Be Church* for others each day. In a little while we will discover the power of the Church that exists far beyond the reaches of the four walls of the steeple that people head to on Sundays. In order to *Be Church* for the world we must be filled up with Jesus who gives us the power to do everything. Then we can truly be his disciples, namely being him—Christlike to everyone in all circumstances.

The spiritual connection with Christ that takes place for the soul by receiving the Lord in the Blessed Sacrament is life-changing. After all, Jesus is fully present to us and with us in the Eucharist. It is there that our Lord gives himself fully through Holy Communion that we are filled with the gracious power of his body and blood. With Jesus at the center of our lives, we cannot go wrong. The Lord's power is made manifest in our inner selves when we open up our hearts. Jesus is the one who will quench your thirsting heart for the living God. Christ floods you with his oceans of mercy and abundant grace so that your soul will be refreshed in the Lord's presence. He fills you so that your hungry heart is satisfied, as you and I are fed with Jesus' great love.

Every time that we gather around the Lord's table and partake in the Eucharist, we enter into his life, death, and resurrection. By receiving the Lord in this manner we celebrate with our fellow brothers and sisters in the faith. This changes us from the inside out. Bishop Scharbenger suggested that Holy Communion is the way for people like you and me to essentially practice Heaven. He explains that Jesus, in the Eucharist, invites us to participate in God's goodness and beauty. Since we cannot deny the presence of the Lord being at home with us during the mass, we enter a place and celebration that is real. It is during this jubilant moment all across the world where believers of many races, ethnicities, and tongues become one in Christ. This unification and partaking in the feast of Thanksgiving through the Lord's body and blood allows you and me to receive a sliver of what awaits the Saints and God's people in Heaven. Bishop Scharfenberger explained the power of the Eucharist by saying:

> *The Mystery of the all-high God, Creator of the universe being present among creatures in the elements of bread and wine no less is clearly a matter of supernatural faith, not explained by natural means. Believer or non-believer, no one denies this. Also, agreed upon by most Christians is that Eucharistic presence, however understood or characterized, is sacramental...the bread and wine become the Body and Blood of Christ. We also say—we proclaim—that "when we eat this bread and drink this cup" WE become the Body and Blood of Christ, which the Church truly is. By consuming Christ in the Eucharist, we celebrate what we are, and we become more fully who we are...It is a participation in his life, death, and resurrection that transforms us into becoming who he really is NOW, in our lives, in the present. To receive Jesus in faith is to*

be changed by him. We become whom we consume, transformed into who he really is.[145]

Saints RSVP to Jesus' Invitation

Like the woman at the well, Jesus invites you to come to him. This
happens by receiving the Lord sacramentally and spiritually. Jesus
desires your thirst for him. He will fill you up, heal you when you are
empty and broken, and give you true life. God already knows your
every need. And yet, when you meet him there at the altar, he accepts
you just as you are. When we understand this gift and partake of the
mystery of it through the sacraments, our souls are filled and we
receive a cup overflowing with blessing that is poured out to us with
never ending love. This is why the faithful followers go away more
than satisfied from Jesus' well because out of Christ's heart flows
streams of life-giving water. In the words of Saint John Paul II, "The
Eucharist is the secret of my day. It gives strength and meaning to all
my activities of service to the Church and to the whole world."

My friends, understand that each time we receive the Lord in the
Eucharist, Jesus lives in us again. When we come before Christ in
adoration and spend time in front of the Blessed Sacrament that is
exposed in the monstrance, he is there in our midst. It is there that we
can give ourselves completely to him and live out the prayer *Totus
Tuus* which means "Totally Yours." There is nothing more that our
Lord wants than for you to receive him into your soul. When we do,
we are filled with true and everlasting life! Recall Jesus' words found
in scripture, "I am the bread of life; whoever comes to me will never
hunger, and whoever believes in me will never thirst...Amen, amen, I
say to you, unless you eat the flesh of the Son of Man and drink his
blood, you do not have life within you. Whoever eats my flesh and
drinks my blood has eternal life, and I will raise him on the last
day."[146] Do you believe this? Jesus Christ fully present in the Eucharist
will change your life and heart for God forever.

As I grew older into my twenties, there were many questions that

[145] Practicing Heaven (Bishop Scharfenberger)
[146] John 6:35, 53-54

came to mind and I often wondered why. I understood that the sacraments, especially Holy Communion, were paramount. However, I still contemplated if our Lord was truly present in that host and how could it be so? By prayerfully taking it all to God and spending time with him in front of his Son, the Holy Spirit revealed the mystery of the Eucharist to me in this way; God is truly present in our lives. Jesus is fully there, body and blood, soul and divinity in the Eucharist. Our Lord veils himself and his immaculate presence is hidden behind the essence of mere bread and wine. He does this because seeing him in his fullness would be too overwhelming for our human hearts. This is why we can feel Jesus' presence as he enters our body and soul, yet we must wait until we are made new with him in Heaven to share in the fullness of our Lord's majesty.

The point here is that the more we receive Christ in Holy Communion and with great reverence, the more holy—whole we will become. Ultimately, it is God who changes us from the inside out, taking our heart and giving us the Sacred Heart of his Son, Jesus. When the power of God is in us, not only are we transformed, but we then have the ability to go out as his Saintly disciples to change the world. Franciscan Friar of the Renewal, Father Francesco put it this way, "Prayer allows God to give what we don't have so we can have what he wants to give, his love." We can't do much of anything out in the world if Jesus isn't fully inside of us.

Undoubtedly we receive the Lord through the highest form of prayer, the mass so that we can *Be Church* which we will fully deliberate further on in this chapter. Love and God himself enters us through prayer and this only happens when we make ourselves available. Without God we can do nothing, but with Jesus living in us we truly can "do all things through Christ who strengthens."[147] Prayer is our communication with the Lord, it is the foundation of relationship, and it's the essence that makes the sacraments and the Church come alive. Father Pierre Toussaint of the CFRs described it in the following manner, "Prayer allows us to go past the obstacles that come up in our own lives." He explained that it's a journey of freedom to set us free so we can give ourselves away completely to God and others in love. This spiritual element and nourishment helps

---

[147] Phillipians 4:13

us accompany each other which strips us of the hindering blocks, allowing us to grow together in holiness. Those we pray with, namely our community of faith become a gift to us and encourage us to see each other as God sees us. That's why Jesus tells us numerous times in the Gospel that we have to pick up our cross and deny ourselves in order to find true life in him.

We know that the world is in need of hope, joy, and most of all love. The world needs your prayers and you and I who live in this world need Jesus. We are called to prayer daily. This is the very reason why going to church, celebrating the mass, and receiving our Lord in the Eucharist is so powerful. Furthermore, this is why *being the Church*—the living body of Christ can transform humanity one person at a time! Listening to these words of Mother Teresa, she paints a clear picture on how essential the Blessed Sacrament is by saying, "In an ever changing world, the holy Eucharist is a constant reminder of the great reality of God's changeless love." Thirst for your God, be filled with his Son, and live out the gospel message by sharing the love of Jesus with all you meet.

Jesus Lives in & Through the Saint

Realize that God alone can change your heart. He will reveal to you the mysteries of the Eucharist and the amazing power found in him through this sacrament, as much as you need to understand. Trust in the mystical power and little by little or "poco a poco" as the Franciscan Friars of the Renewal explained on their podcast, Jesus will come alive in you. Father Angelus of the CFRs in the Bronx, New York articulated that humans all have a desire for more and we approach this by trying to shape our own identities. As human beings it is natural for us to fill our schedules, use our energy, and pursue a variety of things, many of these very good. However, our true identity is found when we uncover our spiritual selves by entering into the Lord's heart and inviting him into ours. In the podcast episode entitled *You're Not an Outsider*, Father Angelus suggested that the Blessed Sacrament is the best way for us to become fully alive, whether we are in a state of grace, a time of struggle, or a season of prosperity. God has crowned us all from the beginning with his divine love and favor as his blessed sons and daughters. Father Angelus relayed this message as a matter of the heart by saying:

> You recognize life is demanding, but we find our identity in Christ. We live in this place, receiving the relationship from God our Father and living with Jesus inside of us and we inside of him. Then we become instruments of God and of blessing. There is something divine here and there is an anointing because the believer lives in prayer. We come to live in an anointing of our calling. There is something happening here and the Gospel is alive here.[148]

This makes sense. Jesus is alive in the Blessed Sacrament. We are his anointed. When we receive him physically into our bodies and spiritually invite him inside our souls, we cannot remain the same. In this moment you and I enter into our Lord's heart and he lives inside of us. There was a woman named Janie Tinklenberg in the 1990s who started the W.W.J.D. movement—*What Would Jesus Do?* Amongst her teenage youth group in Holland, Michigan she desired to inspire young people to live and embrace the world differently. This grassroots platform caught fire and spread throughout the nation and world. I have worn a bracelet with those letters on it for most of my life. It's powerful to actually think about what Jesus would do if he was in each situation we face or within the happenings of our 21st Century world. What's even more compelling is to consider that when we enter into life with the Lord by taking part in his body and blood in the Eucharist, he truly abides in us. As he enters into our hearts we then can do what Jesus would do and that is to love first. Jesus allows us to take on the powerful attitude and Pauline mindset that occurs when you and I receive him: "It is no longer, I who live, but Christ who lives in me," as Paul relayed to the early Church.

So what? You are telling me that simply eating the host at mass or praying in front of the Blessed Sacrament is going to change my life? Yes, actually as long as you fully enter into communion with him by not withholding any piece of your heart, God not only enters your

---

[148] Father Angelus (CFR), Poco a Poco Podcast

body, mind, and soul, he lives through you. This is where faith comes in. Trust can only be built on the relationship we have with our Father. And if that is not too strong or is fading away at the moment, just go back to him. Therefore, it's good to think W.W.J.D. but even more powerful to be present to Jesus in prayer, to receive him as often as possible in Holy Communion, and to allow his grace to filter through our lives so he is in our hearts and we abide in him. Father Mark-Mary Ames is a priest who is as real and as holy as they come. He is down to earth, relatable, and committed to sharing tangible ways for us to grow closer to the Lord. Father Mark-Mary recently wrote the book *Habits for Holiness* and he helps to lead the Community of the Franciscan Friars of the Renewal down in New York City. He described prayer in a powerful way stating, "It's about remaining connected to the vine. We must remain in him (Jesus). We are doing something wrong if we aren't doing it from a relationship, from the right place, from the pocket. Through him, with him, and in him."[149]

Father Mark-Mary and the CFRs so often says that the pocket is where Jesus is found and where Jesus enters. He calls that the pocket of your heart. Your pocket and mine is loaded up when we build on our relationship with the Lord through reading scripture, living out love, and most importantly through prayer. After all, is not prayer spending undistracted time with God? As we share our lives with him and even more importantly listen to him, we become like Jesus.

Undoubtedly, the greatest prayer comes in the form of the holy mass where we are closest to Jesus because he comes fully to us. So the next time that you are celebrating mass or you hear the Gregorian chant of the priest saying the Eucharistic prayer, "Through him, with him and in him," know what this is all about. It's soul food indeed. Jesus comes into our life physically and spiritually which empowers us to go out and allow him to love and live through us. Accept this great invitation and enter into the depth of your Savior's heart because he longs for you to enter in. As St. Teresa of Avila suggested when receiving Christ in communion, "Close your bodily eyes so that you may open the eyes of your soul. Then look upon Jesus in the center of your heart."

---

[149] Father Mark Mary Ames (CFR), Poco a Poco Podcast

Saints are the Church

Every Sunday, millions of Catholics go to mass and Christians enter places of worship throughout the world to celebrate and give thanks to God. This tradition and rite of faith has been passed down over the centuries as the Church was built on a firm foundation. It has been carried out by the early followers of Jesus. Shortly after the last supper and with the conclusion of Christ's passion, death and resurrection, it began. Throughout our journey to Sainthood, the Church and actually to *Be Church*—being the body of Christ in the world, is highly important. Holiness occurs when we receive the Lord into our lives wholeheartedly and then bring that love and share it with the world. Having a place to go and worship, somewhere to pray, and a communal home to celebrate the sacraments is pivotal. It provides structure, a community of support, as well as accountability for our life of faith.

Building on the rock and relationship we have with the Lord and sharing in this unity with other believers is essential to our personal growth as disciples. As we discussed earlier, nobody will ever become a Saint in isolation. The beautiful liturgy, the songs, the readings, the traditions and customs all enrich our experience as we enter the physical building known as church and participate in our great faith with our brothers and sisters. And yet, God must not and cannot be contained to a single building or for one hour a week. We serve and are in communion with our Lord who is the God of the universe and desires to know us deeply. He wants to be part of every intricate detail of your life and you are called by him to ultimately *Be Church*.

So how do we *Be Church*? How are you and I the living body of Christ on this earth? We are to become and live out the hope of Emmanuel which means, "God is with us." Although this might seem like a very complex or considerable undertaking, it is actually quite simple. As we opened up our minds and hearts to service and selfless love together already in this book, the concept can be built upon. Loving service of others and being the hands and feet of Jesus in the world must be utilized when we contemplate and then most importantly carry out this call to Sainthood. There is a reason why Jesus first called the apostles, walked with them, taught them, and transformed their lives. Then, he sent them to the ends of the earth.

Along with the many disciples and followers, the Church was built to share and spread the good news.

Growing up in a small town in the Catskill Mountains of New York State, I routinely went to mass with my family every Sunday. I was engaged and participated at a young age as an altar server. This was enjoyable and as time marched on I began to have thoughts about the priesthood. I remember being there with my great grandparents in the back of that small church desiring to have inner peace and a joy-filled heart, something they certainly already had. Although I cannot speak for everyone in that church, I can attest to what I saw outside of that one hour per week we spent together on Sunday mornings. As a kid I often wondered how the same people who were there worshiping together and praying with each other could be the very ones to lose their cool at the red light or cut someone off in traffic. These church goers were also spewing gossip like a firehose around town. This might seem familiar to you. Years later, I realized that even intense and heartfelt prayer for an hour could never be enough for my soul, let alone what God is calling each of us to on this road to holiness.

It fires me up to think about the Church in a different manner. I liken it to the coach who gives the pregame speech. The players are all there, gathered around in the locker room. Each one is fixed on the man or woman at the center who is laying out the game plan. The blueprint for defeating the opponent has been heard and absorbed by every player. The team knows that it will require great effort, a no quit mentality, concentration, and teamwork to get the win. There is electricity flowing through the player's veins and an intense feeling is in the air as they come together. They put their hands in and shout out their battle cry just before exiting the locker room. Finally, just seconds prior to sprinting into the arena for the big game, the coach or team captain utters one more word of encouragement. They are pumped up and ready to take it! The fans are going wild and the game begins.

Going to church and celebrating mass requires intense participation. The team is there together in community as we gather in prayer and worship. The Word is proclaimed and it fills our hearts. It excites us and provides life to our souls. The pastor gives a homily, preaching a message of hope to the congregation that listens intently to it. We then celebrate and receive the Eucharist, being empowered with the body and blood of Jesus Christ. We come together and pray again and then go out to proclaim the gospel by our lives. It is this hour together, similar to the pregame locker room speech for any team, that we—the body of Christ, are only beginning.

Like any great athlete, preparation, practice, a game plan, and comradery with teammates is key. However, you can't stop there. It must be carried over to the game. If not, you lose. As Saints we must not allow ourselves or our fellow believers to fall into the trap of compartmentalizing life. This is especially true when it comes to our great faith. The reason why the Church was created and the keys were given to Peter to build on the rock was because each member of God's family is called to live out the mission of love and share it with others. Enough cannot be said about how imperative it is for us to *Be Church*.

While my life continues to unfold and my faith grows it becomes more and more clear that "church" is not so much a noun as it is a verb. It's more about action, namely the doing, than going to a specific place. Certainly, we need a physical location and the space a church provides, especially to receive the Eucharist. Undoubtedly, the sacraments transform our lives. These elements of church empower us and provide nourishment to go out and to *Be Church*. After all isn't that the goal and commission spelled out by Jesus to the disciples? The body of Christ going to work in the world is a powerful thing. It calls to mind the great words of St. Francis of Assisi who was all about doing and being a person for others as he professed, "Preach the Gospel at all times and when necessary, use words."

You are the living Gospel. You are the message of hope and the beacon of light. You and I are Saints called to spread love, share the faith, and truly be the hands and feet of Jesus. This is not just a nice saying or some beautiful idea. No! It is our call and by *being Church* and living it out every day of our lives, we will be transformed by God. His great power and grace will flow from us. The Lord will provide all that we need to faithfully carry out his ministry and to proclaim the Gospel by our lives. My hope is that you are fired up and that zeal for being men and women for others is stirring within your heart. If you are unsure of how to go about it, don't worry. You are not alone.

Continue to engage and participate in the Church. Allow the grace of Jesus and his infinite love to shine upon you and provide you with the answer to your prayers. Keep walking by faith and receive the

Lord sacramentally, especially through the Eucharist and reconcili-ation. In doing so, your life will be changed and you will have the living God inside of you. You will be equipped and ready for battle as St. Paul writes in his letter to the Ephesians, "Therefore, take up the full armor of God, so that you will be able to resist in the evil day, and having done everything, to stand firm. Stand firm therefore, having girded your loins with truth, and having put on the breastplate of righteousness, and having shod your feet with the preparation of the gospel of peace; in addition to all, taking up the shield of faith with which you will be able to extinguish all the flaming arrows of the evil *one*. And take the helmet of salvation, and the sword of the Spirit, which is the word of God."[150] It's true that the one living inside of you is greater than all contrary forces that exist in this world. At this moment I invite you to welcome Christ into your heart wherever you might be scattered throughout the world.

Prayer of Spiritual Communion:

My Jesus,
I believe that you are present in the Most Holy Sacrament. I love you above all things,
and I desire to receive you into my soul.
Since I cannot at this moment receive you sacramentally,
come at least spiritually into my heart.
I embrace you as if You were already there
and unite myself wholly to you.
Never permit me to be separated from you.
Amen.

Challenge 16

This week after you go to church, reflect deeply on the Gospel message and homily. Ask God to show you how to Be Church in the world. Take the love and promise of Christ with you to your home, your neighborhood, and your workplace. When you are hanging out with

---

[150] Ephesians 6:13-17

friends, Be Church. Allow the power of Jesus that lives inside of you to flow through you and share him with the world. Your acts of love, charity, kindness, and forgiveness are the good news that is to be shared with those you encounter each day!

KINGDOM BUILDING
CHAPTER 17

*"Seek first the Kingdom of God and all these things
shall be added onto you." – Matthew 6:33*

Who are You and What Will Your Impact Be?

Picture yourself at your own funeral. What does it look like? Who is there and what type of emotions are coursing through people's veins. Is there celebration in one regard for the life that you led or is it only sorrow? What kind of stories and memories will be shared around the kitchen table today or in the years to come when friends, children, and grandchildren talk about you. In your community, will there be a loss or will life just march on like nothing happened at all? People have buildings named after them and even streets that bear their name. There are parks and scholarship funds, as well as other tributes to honor the fallen. None of this is bad, but these too will become part of everyday life and mundane over the years. However, what lasts is the way we loved by the way we lived in touching the hearts and souls of everyone we encounter.

When you look at yourself in the mirror what do you see? More importantly, who do you see? Maybe you haven't taken a good hard look lately. If not, my hope is that you will. Not to judge or condemn, but to seek and to find. Life is very much like sailing a boat. You are in the open water. The choppy sea comes and rocks the boat from time to time. Then it is on to smoother waters and the wind eventually propels your sails. The energy and force thrusts you ahead and the light filtering through the clouds rushes in. A wave might come crashing upon you from time to time, but you remain strong and endure the storm. Remember, Jesus is always in the boat with us because he loves us. He has the power to calm the storms we face and take us to the other side.

Like a good sailor, you continue to navigate the vast ocean paying attention to what is in sight and hoping to find fortuitous land ahead. If you were to stay at harbor there would be no exploration or growth. An anchored boat never finds the unforeseen treasure that is out there buried in the distant future. Unfortunately, so many people go about life and die without their dreams coming to pass. Cemeteries are filled with bodies that never reached their fullest potential. Let alone, many humans never experience the greatest riches of a peace that can fill the spirit and the joy that comes from truly giving God's love away to the world.

In our lives, there awaits us a treasure that can be found in the depths of our hearts. This occurs when we build up the Kingdom and spread love. The gateway to it is found in genuine compassion, hope, and peace. As we spread this to people the universe grows in holiness. It is in laboring for the Lord and the tireless ways we seek to find him that we are filled. When you and I share Christ with others in the daily fabric of our lives, we build up the Kingdom of God on earth. You might have heard the saying known as "the dash." Among the innumerable uncertainties of life, there is one thing that is a guarantee, we will all die.

Saints Use Mortality as Motivation

Mortality is as real as the ticking of a clock. What happens after our time is up, however long that may be, is hanging in the balance. It's an age-old philosophical and spiritual query. My faith and most likely yours has led to the belief and hope in Heaven. As the saying goes, "On your tombstone it will have the year you were born and the year you died. There will be a dash. That dash will represent all the things that you do, whether good or bad. That's how you're remembered. What do you want your dash to represent?" Who you were, and the impact you had on other people's lives will matter the most. The more people you impact and the more ways you influence situations, you are changing lives.

Think for a moment about someone who has enriched your life and in what ways they have done so. Hopefully you can remember at least one person and what they did to make you feel differently. They certainly played a large part in changing the scope of your existence. Saints are the people who tend to come along and appear on the scene. They pour into the lives of others so much that they leave the person more full, better off, and feeling more whole. Saints lead others to holiness. Death might be inevitable and inescapable, however there is another guarantee. What I am talking about is one that we can control based on how we use our time, talents, and the faith that has been granted to us. You and I can love and make a difference.

Jackie Robinson was an MVP, World Series Champion, and a man of great faith. Robinson showed that one human could take a stance on an issue and do something constructive to work toward reaching solutions regarding the problems in our world. Certainly, a single life can inspire other people to be great. A massive impact occurs through how you treat others. Showing up in people's lives and sharing in an encounter with them is crucial to fostering a healthy soul and a sound well-being of the human spirit. Taking a stance on an issue or doing something is good, but it's not enough. Love and being present is what people need. Love is primarily about standing with people and journeying alongside them whether it be in their time of need or in their season of plenty. Life must be centered upon impacting others and sharing the love and faith we have in a genuine manner. Positivity begets positivity and hope breeds hope. Love is the greatest force in the universe and we don't have to look any further than the Cross to grasp that. The Saint practices Heaven daily by loving.

Sometimes we get overwhelmed with the feelings of insignificance or not being "good enough." We might even wonder what difference we are making if any at all. How could I be like Jackie Robinson, St. Paul, Mother Teresa or any of the other Saints? But it is not about making a name for ourselves. It isn't about fame or glory. God does have a mission for you. That mission is for you to do your best to build up the Kingdom here on earth. You and I are called to lead as many souls as possible to the Lord so that they can share in great joy both now and in the world to come. It's easy to fall into the rabbit hole of comparison. In a day and age that is littered with social media postings, a get-ahead mentality, and keeping up with a high class lifestyle we constantly look over our shoulder. If you are to become the best version of yourself, it is important for you to stay in your lane and be the best you can be. Being your personal best every day will be what makes changes happen where we are for as long as we are there. Kingdom builders are the Saints that go to work every day with a tool belt filled with love and positivity.

At any given moment we have people around us who take note of our choices, the way we treat others, and how we love. When we put our faith in action, when we do the uncommon thing, and make sacrifices it can be a game changer. Mother Teresa loved bringing Jesus to the healing hearts of those in distress. She became a great Saint and left an imprint on the world. She did what she could do. If we live with great love and embrace this attitude, Heaven will be made manifest to those on earth. Kingdom building is about loving others where they are and for who they are. Who you and I are is a people created to impact this generation in our own way. We do not know when our time will run out, but if we trust in God's plan for our lives and are receptive to holy moments each day we will be remembered. What is much more compelling and significant than making a name for ourselves is making a name for the one we represent, Jesus Christ. Holy Scripture reminds us, "And whatever you do, in word or deed, do everything in the name of the Lord Jesus, giving thanks to God the Father through him."[151]

Saints choose to be the best version of themselves each day. Simultaneously, they live one day at a time working to aid others to become Saints. Understand that your life is a platform to share the love of Christ with and through the way you interact with people they will know what you stand for, namely who you stand for; you are in the army of God. This dictates how you go about your day and what

---

[151] Colossians 3:17

you devote your life to. As the age old song says, "and they will know we are Christians by our love."

Becoming a millionaire, acquiring fame, acceptance, status, and power; none of these will provide the joy in knowing at the end of your life that you made an impact with unremitting reward. The world needs *everyday Saints*—heroes of faith who live for an audience of one, God. When we live for him everything changes and people will see Jesus in us. It is then that they desire to know him more because we love as Christ loved. So what will your impact be? How you share love and Jesus with the world matters. Remember, our Kingdom is not of this world. This life is not the end, it is only the beginning. What greater thing can we possibly do throughout our lifetime than to live for God and lead others closer to him? Each of us has to discover how to best manage the time we have been blessed with.

Your life is a gift to be shared with the world. Saint Faustina reminds us, "Act in a way that all those who come in contact with you will go away joyfully. Sew happiness about you because you have received much from God." Souls are at stake and it's up to you to carry out the mission. You are called to complete the work you were put on this planet to do. Now it's time to get started. The voyage involves unmatched effort by each Saint and the great commission is to build up the Kingdom brick by brick. This happens one person at a time when you focus on finishing the race you have been called to run!

Challenge 17

Reflect on the ways you feel called to build up the Kingdom. What talents or abilities has God blessed you with? How can you utilize these gifts to bring people closer to the Lord? Now, go out and be brave. Don't worry about how, just be present and allow God to move you to action. Be yourself and watch the manner that Jesus will use you to lead others to him. Allow the Lord to live through you and he will maximize the treasure he gives you. Then you will have what it takes to build up others, pour out positivity to the world, and share a little slice of Heaven here on Earth.

JOURNEYING ON
CHAPTER 18

"The feeling remains that God is on the journey too."
- St. Teresa of Avila

Kingdom Come

The woman was racing back and forth and couldn't believe all she still had to do. Another day was waning and a multitude of tasks were left like stones unturned. As time faded like sand disappearing in an hourglass, Martha felt anxiety creep in like a cockroach drawn to a morsel in a dark hallway at midnight. The day took a stronghold over her like a vice grip. Why were there so many burdens coming down and numerous lists that she hadn't even touched yet? Martha was overwhelmed once again. She was doing everything possible to get ready for the dinner guests who would be arriving soon. Frustration grew as she frantically swept the house. Martha whipped up a number of dishes, and ferociously cleaned everything in sight. The preparations seemed to be endless. Meanwhile, in the next room over, her sister Mary was just sitting there. How could she be so aloof? What was her problem? What nerve her sister had. Mary sat and waited. Meanwhile, Martha frantically attempted to get everything done in time. As Martha stressed, Mary simply was present and listened.

Who was she listening to and why was she not helping her sister? A great lesson was learned that day by Martha and it is one for each Saint to listen to. What Martha would eventually realize was that Jesus cares more about our presence than he does about the lists of doing that we create. So often in our journey of faith it's not going to be in the doing where we grow, but it will be in us showing up and just being present where our relationship is built. Saints are able to be present and not get distracted. Saints listen. Mary was listening to the Lord. She sat at his feet.

The Gospel passage in Luke tells us specifically that Jesus directly shared a word on presence with the sisters. They had been on opposite ends of the spectrum when it came to their approach toward life so the Lord said, "Martha, Martha, you are anxious and worried about many things. There is need of only one thing. Mary has chosen the better part and it will not be taken from her."[152] Upon hearing these words, Martha must have stopped in her tracks abruptly. I can imagine her pausing and taking a deep breath. She may have even closed her eyes or possibly shed a tear. Distress must have come upon her and then she would have to face a reality check as well.

Being a taskmaster and a doer is not a bad thing at all. In fact, we know that "faith without works is dead," and that this world needs us Saints to take bold action. However, Jesus seems to be relaying a pertinent message to Martha in this teachable moment. While the Lord spent time with the two sisters he was showing them and us that we mustn't get so busy in our lives as to lose touch with God who loves us most. In the doing, in the balancing of schedules, and all the everyday tasks, we cannot become so distracted that we forget what provides us the greatest joy. Rather, who brings us true life, lasting happiness, and fulfillment to our soul. Jesus is the one. Through it all, like Martha, you can have these important reflective moments in your life where God shapes your heart and shows you a "better part." On your journey to Sainthood and while traveling the road to holiness which ultimately ends in Heaven, you and I have to fixate our eyes on the Lord. Therefore, when we do this and Jesus is truly the center of our lives, we will be fulfilled. When Jesus is our universe and

---

[152] Luke 10:41-42

everything we do and who we are begins to orbit around him, we recognize that the life trek we are on is moreso a prolific pilgrimage of faith. It actually has no end because he is the Alpha and the Omega, the beginning and the end. Heaven is forever.

Sometimes when you take time to be in his presence, the Lord will speak to your heart. You're reminded, "Come to me, and I will give you rest."[153] Life is a balancing act that can be tough. At times the weight of the world is pounding down on you and it can be easy to turn to a million other things to distract us from reality. All you have to do is to turn to Jesus like Mary did. Even if it takes you a little while and you do so later on like Martha learned to do after the Lord spoke to her heart, that is more than okay. In Jesus we find rest for our weary souls. It might seem like we can never get ahead or even catch up to where we are "supposed to be." Working tirelessly for that promotion, getting the kids to practice, and having to do the many daily tasks of paying bills, household chores, and keeping everyone in the family situated is burdensome. Step back and breathe. Don't forget, Saints need rest in order to journey on.

The many things that must be done, people we feel we have to care for, or the business affairs of life shouldn't and mustn't take us away from what this life was given to us for, namely who we were made to be with—Jesus. Saints have no problem telling the Lord they are tired. Saint John XXIII as Pope used to pray, "It's your Church God, I'm going to bed." God understands the expedition is tiresome, Saints keep journeying on however that looks.

In the best situations and amidst the many positive aspects, life can be draining. Working to advance ourselves, give to our family, and provide for our future is important. These are all things to be held in high regard. However, the Saint keeps a focused perspective realizing not even family and the best things we are involved in cannot take first place on the podium of life. If Jesus isn't on top and if he isn't receiving the gold medal daily, whatever you elevate higher will rob you of what you were made for. After all you and every Saint was made for Heaven. That is again why you and I must turn to the great Saints, apostles, and disciples of the Church who continue to show us

---

[153] Matthew 11:28

the way. St. Paul writes, "But our citizenship is in Heaven, and from it we also await a savior, the Lord Jesus Christ."[154] The Saint learns to trust and comes to understand that we are pilgrimaging on to our Heavenly homeland.

Earth is a Mere Pit Stop for the Saint

Lazarus is someone in scripture who we can learn from in a number of ways when it comes to our universal call to Sainthood. It is refreshing to know that our Lord experienced the pains of losing a best friend. Christ wept when Lazarus died. If we unearth the meaning behind the events that transpired in the miraculous raising of the dead man, we will see the compelling nature that holds great power for us as believers. First, Lazarus was significant to the Lord. Not only was he Jesus' friend, he was a child of God. Jesus had a close relationship with him and our Lord shared a common bond with Lazarus' sisters, Martha and Mary. Christ's heart ached because he understood and felt the pain these two women were feeling. This reminds us of our Saintly call to be one with people, to invest wholeheartedly in them, and to foster bonds that even death cannot break. Then, there is the big event—the act of Jesus physically raising Lazarus from the dead. Oftentimes people are enamored by this mind-blowing feat. Although we all know that Jesus was God incarnate and had the power to do anything, it still leaves our jaws hanging on the floor as it did for all the witnesses during the 1st Century. However, what is even more is the particular manner in which Jesus brought him back to life. It happened and it's directly linked to the unshakable faith of Martha and Mary. Imagine how deep they must know and trust the Lord.

After hearing of her brother's passing. Martha goes straight to Jesus when he is in town the next day and she says boldly, "Lord, if you had been here, my brother would not have died."[155] That's true faith and the solid belief of a Saint who grasps the power of God which can't even be contained by the snares of death. The story of Lazarus

---

[154] Philippians 3:20
[155] John 11:21

doesn't end there though, more ensues. Jesus tells Martha to not be worried because Lazarus is going to rise. Her faith was so strong she knew this to be true. The only thing that is left to uncover is that Christ was going to resurrect Lazarus to show everyone God's almighty and infinite love. Martha had experienced enough during her time with Jesus to know and believe in eternal life.

She rested in the presence of the hope-filled promise. Again, that would have been a great ending, but God wanted to do more as the Gospel tells us that Martha continues her conversation with Jesus by saying, "I know he will rise, in the resurrection on the last day. Jesus told her, 'I am the resurrection and the life; whoever believes in me, even if he dies, will live and everyone who lives and believes in me will never die. Do you believe this?'"[156] It makes me think that Jesus knew that Martha believed and because of her great faith and her trust in the Lord's promise, he rewarded her in getting her brother back.

At that moment the two sisters and Jesus go to the tomb. A gigantic rock was there blocking the entrance. Jesus who was troubled by the aching hearts of his friends and those gathered said, "Did I not tell you that if you believe you will see the glory of God?"[157] Faith the size of a mustard seed is required for prayers to be answered. So what could bold faith do? What if you took the limit off, what would the Lord be capable of in your life? Well, enter back into that scene at Lazarus' tomb. Martha is there as well as a crowd and they all witness the dead man who is still wrapped in burial cloth. Like a mummy, he came walking out. He had been raised, remarkable!

Saints Live with the Promise of Heaven

That same power of Christ who raised Lazarus and gave him a new chance at life is living inside of you. The Saint must have a bounce back mentality. No matter what he or she wards off in this lifetime, the fight does not mean so much if the attitude and receptivity to grace is not there. Think about which character you relate most to in this victorious story. And then there was Mary. We haven't even

---

[156] John 11:24-26
[157] John 11:40

considered what is going on with her yet. Mary was at home, full of despair, and her grief overwhelmed her. Later on she was filled with joy because her dead brother was alive again. So who do you see yourself in when reflecting on this powerful example of love conquering all things in the Gospel? Furthermore, are you pursuing holiness as a Saint? If so, keep carrying on with great vigor and valor. If not, it's time to ask the Lord to show you how to believe in his grace and redemptive power.

Lazarus was dead, fully dead. It was faith that saved him and not even his own, but the prayer and faith of others. That is immensely powerful. Our faith is all that we have at the end of our lives. It is up to you and me to trust and to believe. The reward for those who do believe equates to resurrections and comeback stories like we saw with Lazarus. When Saints experience this it changes them and it impacts the people who are around us. These victories and triumphs now remind us that God alone can win the eternal prize of the newness of life that comes to full fruition in our eternal salvation through Jesus Christ. Martha saw the glory of God thanks to her great faith. Mary's sadness turned to rejoicing and Lazarus was given another shot at life. The same holds true for each Saint. God's majesty shines when faith abides.

The boldness of faith is God's ask of us as his Saints. Jesus asks us what we want him to do for us. Throughout the Gospels, scripture is filled with our Lord asking people what they desire. He mentions continuously that true faith, void of any doubt, is the recipe for prayers being answered. Bartimaeus is a prime example of what persistence and faithfulness can do in our own lives. He was blind and kept showing up begging in the city center, hoping, and waiting for a healing. Bartimaeus believed in miracles and had heard of Jesus, yet there was no telling if the Lord would ever come that way when he was there in the streets. Day after day the crowds of people told Bartimaeus to stop begging and to go home. He could have easily grown discouraged, given up, and went his own way.

Yet, something made Bartimaeus cling to hope, actually it was someone—Jesus. The Lord knew that Bartimaeus would be there begging on the street corner as Passover was drawing near and he was on his way to Jerusalem. So in true Christ fashion, he purposely went that way to meet the blind man. As soon as Bartimaeus hears of the caravan coming because so many Jews were following Jesus from Jericho, he keeps shouting, "Son of David, have pity on me!" This persists until Jesus is close enough to hear his voice and the Lord summons Bartimaeus. The blind man gets up quickly and runs toward the crowd where Jesus was. Now, he still can't see, but he was called by name and this alone provides the necessary courage to encounter the Lord. Jesus asks him, "What do you want me to do for you?" The blind man replied to him, 'Master, I want to see.' Jesus told him, 'Go your way; your faith has saved you.' Immediately he received his sight and followed him on the way."[158]

Imagine how Bartimaeus must have felt when Jesus opened his eyes. The sheer joy and excitement must have been overwhelming. It was great faith that brought Bartimaeus to Jesus and the bold ask of God that healed him. What is most magnificent and moving is not only did the blind man come to see, but he then would follow Jesus as a disciple. For you and me there is a ton to learn from this story. Unwavering faith is certainly what the *everyday Saint* must strive for. Amidst things that can blind us, we have to persevere and stay the course. Ask God what you want him to do for you because if it is his will and for your good, your prayer will be answered. And as always, keep showing up. Drown out the crowd and naysayers by listening to Jesus who speaks to your heart. Finally, when you are healed or receive a prayer that is answered, give all the glory to God by sharing the good news with others. It's in our faithfulness to follow, especially during great uncertainty that the Lord draws nearer to us and we are able to provide a steadfast example of discipleship for the world.

In this technologically advanced world it is very easy to get caught up in various diversions. We live in and are consumed by a culture that needs results instantaneously. There are countless stimuli that infiltrate our mind and hearts on a daily basis. Like an all-out blitz on the football field where the quarterback just throws the ball away, we can't just give in so easily. Instead, we must stay in the pocket and deal with the pressure we face. Through buying a little more time we are able to connect with God who is our greatest receiver of our love. When the ball of faith is thrown to him instead of bailing, we are

---

[158] Mark 10:51-52

protected. With him on our side we score touchdowns for team Jesus by the way we conduct our lives. Much of the "noise" we stand up against in society is not for our benefit and it often distracts us from what is most essential and life-giving. Maybe you can't silence the crowd, but you have to at least try to tune them out.

This life is important, but remember, you were made for more. God created you to spend time with him. You were made to be with God forever. Since we are called to be Saints we are indeed workers in God's vineyard, as we have discussed throughout our journey together. By reminding yourself regularly that you are living for a Kingdom that is not of this world, it can ease the meaningless burdens faced and illuminate the calling God has placed on your life. The mission you have to fulfill becomes more tangible. It ultimately comes into clear focus because it's a mission of love. God brings clarity through the whispers of his Holy Spirit in our lives. Evidently, we have an important role and calling on this earth. However, the voyage doesn't cease in this lifetime. Therefore, never lose sight of Christ and keep him at the center. When Jesus is the center of your life you are complete. The stuff, the tasks, the material desires, as well as the agendas can be dealt with. The responsibilities and even balancing our relationships becomes lighter. This doesn't make these things and people unimportant at all. Christ actually enhances them and desires to be by your side through them all.

Saints Continue to Practice Heaven Daily

Not only will Jesus help you to survive, but our Lord will allow you to thrive. I often wonder why our Lord decided to come and live as God among us for a mere 33 or so years. Jesus could have stayed on the scene for much longer. He could have done even more miracles or at least started them sooner. Christ's great work on earth and his impact could have continued with his personal public ministry. Although he died, Christianity lives on. As the Son of God, Jesus knew well that the Kingdom is not of this world. It's interesting because at the same time Jesus did say, "nor will people say, 'Here it is,' or 'There it is,' because the kingdom of God is in your midst."[159] Now that might make you

---

[159] Luke 17:21

think, *What did our Lord mean?* Faith has led me to believe that he told people this for a reason. We will have slices and pieces of the Kingdom revealed to us here in the now, but it won't come to complete fulfillment until we meet our Lord face to face in Heaven. It is interesting that Jesus lived a fairly average life as a carpenter's son for three decades and then in his final three years or so he dedicated it to ministry. It was in the former that he was preparing and in the latter that he changed humanity forever.

It's in the daily grind of life and within the seemingly average moments where we meet our Lord on the road to holiness and take steps forward to Heaven. So often you have heard people say things like, "You become what you eat," or "You become who you center yourself around." Well, when you and I must center our lives upon Jesus and realize that this pilgrimage on earth is a single stop. At birth each of us set sail, but even with death there truly is no end for the Saint who believes. The burdens are made lighter and the yolk not as heavy when Jesus is your friend. Then we can focus on what truly matters and have an eternal outlook. As you go into the hustle and bustle of the week, keep your eyes on the prize and fix yourself on Jesus.

In the words of the great 13th Century poet Rumi, "If light is in your heart, you will find your way home." The light we follow to Heaven is Christ. The Son will raise you up this day and on the last day when you appear with him in glory as Christ promised us through his love on the Cross. The words of Jesus give us hope and point us in the direction we must always go. Jesus spoke and it's time to prayerfully listen as he said, "My Kingdom is not of this world. If my kingdom were of this world, my servants would be fighting so that I would not be handed over to the Jews; but as it is, My Kingdom is not of this realm."[160] Earth and life are our reality, but as Saints, so is Heaven. That is what we were created for. We were made to be in an eternal relationship with God the Father, Jesus Christ, and the Holy Spirit. Heaven is the true place we call home. Until we arrive, we must practice Heaven by being *everyday Saints* here on earth.

---

[160] John 18:36

Challenge 18
Stop, Be Still, Listen & Journey On

This week or in the near future, when you are feeling the weight of the world and are becoming distressed, stop. Close your eyes and ask God to help you to be still and to listen. Rest at the Lord's feet as Mary did and allow Jesus to calm your anxious heart. Call to mind that "this too shall pass," and the thing that you are currently facing, as challenging as it might be, can be lightened when you lay it down at the Lord's feet. Keep persisting as Bartimaeus did and don't lose faith because God is listening. You are always in the holy presence of the Lord. Jesus desires to calm your restless heart and he wants to know what you want him to do for you. Most of all, remember you were made for life. Your journey, as challenging as it is, doesn't end here. True life and a relationship with God reaches its surest and purest fulfillment when we are in his presence.

MARCHING IN
CHAPTER 19

"Every great dream begins with a dreamer. Always remember, you have within you the strength, the patience, and the passion to reach for the stars to change the world." – Harriet Tubman

Pilgrim's Walk

You now know that life is a real pilgrimage. Assuredly, the mission of a Saint never ceases. It simply comes to full richness when we arrive home. For God's faithful people, we continue to listen and understand that our presence on earth is defined in our universal call to become Saints. This is what God desires and who he created us to be. The story of your life is still being written and what a beautifully powerful adventure it is. Nobody knows what life will bring next nor can we even begin to imagine all that God will lead us to during our lifetime. No matter what we do, what we are called to, or where we go, God is with us and he is for us. Whether you and I live for a very long time or if our stay here on earth is quite short, God's love never ends. Every Saint's trek concludes with crossing the finish line of faith, as we enter into paradise with our Creator. The great commission of the Saint is a matter of the heart. Having our minds and lives fixated on the things that are above, namely God, and leading a life worthy of our calling is most essential. So many great Saints have paved a way for us. The pattern of their lives gives you and me an example of what a holy life on earth is about—love.

St. Thomas Aquinas was someone who worked and taught others both intellectually and spiritually. His desire to seek God and pursue happiness truly rested in the fact that it's not enough to merely know of God. We must know God intimately. Even knowing him is not enough, but it's a start to what will lead us to the greatest and only sustaining joy in our hearts. Evidently, we arrive at complete fulfillment when we fall madly in love with God. It is not a matter of the head, but all a matter of the heart. The Father made us in love to love so that we could be consumed by his love for us. This love we receive then leads you and me to share God's love with the world. Through this beautiful love affair with the Lord we consecrate ourselves to Jesus by building a relationship with him. A friendship with the Lord that is founded on love leads us to ultimately pursue God's will for our lives. In doing so he uncovers in us real virtue—sanctity and holiness abound.

Sainthood is love lived out with the greatest intensity in order to share the joy and fruit of the spirit that comes through deeply knowing God and falling in love with him. Becoming a Saint on the road to Heaven is about humility and lowering ourselves so we can be raised up by Christ to abide in him and in the Father. We are made one with them in complete unity of body, mind, and soul. For those who do not fall in love with God, they are not filled with pure joy. As a result, countless people are always on the chase of something to fill the void left in their soul. However, they fail to realize that no earthly or material thing, no pleasure or fortune will fill that hole in their heart. Only God and his love can. The craziest part is that there is no standard or requirement besides for you and me to receive God's love. We must be humble enough and open ourselves to him. People have to want it and that is a matter of our hearts saying "yes" to God when he seeks us out. When he does you have to be willing to at least crack open the window of your soul for Jesus to enter in. When you do, your life is forever changed and the path to Sainthood becomes quite easy. This is because it is not about us at all, but it's all about our loving God living in us.

Saint Thomas Aquinas lived out this message of love and joy with substantial authenticity and vivaciousness. He was a great teacher of the faith and worked arduously to lead the hearts of men and women to Jesus. My "esperanza" (hope) as we say in Spanish is that we can heed the example of Aquinas who said, "No man truly has joy unless he lives in love. To love God is something greater than to know him. Happiness is secured through virtue. It is a good attained by man's own will. Man cannot live without joy, therefore when he is deprived of true spiritual joys he becomes addicted to carnal pleasures." As God remains on the hunt for your heart, don't run away from him. Be there, be still, and allow Jesus to love you. Not only will he become your friend, he will unlock the joy that is inside of you that will gush forth like a raging river. You will be filled with lasting peace. The light of Christ that illuminates your soul will shine so brightly that others will be attracted to you in such a manner that they will desire to gain what you have. But soon the people in your life will realize it has never been what you have, but who you have—God and his Son Jesus abiding in you with the Holy Spirit directing your life.

Saints are Quenched by Jesus' Sacred Heart

Alone you and I will always thirst and our hungry hearts will never be filled. Meanwhile, when we find true holiness which comes from opening our heart to God and being consumed by the Sacred Heart of Jesus, we are quenched. The living water that flows inside of us is the same water that sanctifies every Saint at their baptism in Christ. The well springs of God's love and joy lead us to inner peace that nobody and nothing can take away. John articulates this love affair and being one with God so eloquently in his Gospel. He shows us that we are in the world, but the Lord is calling us to not be of the world. Saints are different and they are consecrated to the truth—the way, the truth and the life, who is Jesus Christ. Intense, yes. Profound, yes. Some would argue that it is difficult to comprehend. What it comes down to is love. Are you willing to allow God to love you fully and can you imagine his love flowing through you daily? This type of unifying love brings us to the Heart of God. Rest in the words of Saint John who shares the prayer of Jesus to the Father:

> *I pray not only for them, but also for those who will believe in*
> *me through their word, so that they may all be one, as you,*
> *Father, are in me and I in you, that they also may be in us, that*
> *the world may believe that you sent me. And I have given them*
> *the glory you gave me, so that they may be one, as we are one,*
> *I in them and you in me, that they may be brought to perfection*
> *as one, that the world may know that you sent me, and that*
> *you loved them even as you loved me... I made known to them*
> *your name and I will make it known,* that the love with which*
> *you loved me may be in them and I in them.*[161]

You, the Saints of this world, must not forget that perfection is never the key. Instead, it's a perfect and lasting pursuit of God with a heart-filled desire to enter into a loving relationship with him that is. Aquinas, John, and the apostles showed us this. Popular Saints like Mother Teresa, Cabrini, Francis, Ignatius of Loyola, Thérèse of Lisieux, Augustine, and you—the *everyday Saints* shower the world with the tender love of God. By radiating the joy of Jesus through the gospel lived out by our lives we are holy. The human heart is undoubtedly complex, but when God is abiding in us and we rest in him, our hearts are satiated. A full heart is able to love others as we are called to do. God first loved us, now you and I are asked to love.

Certainly the word love is completely overused and illegitimately attached to everything under the sun. That kind of "love" is not a matter of the heart. The love we are talking about and pursuing on our road to Sainthood is. Perhaps this book is a love manual and has articulated a little bit clearer how love, a four letter word, truly does encompass what this life of faith is about. Love encourages us to do radical things in building up the Kingdom. Love causes us to sacrifice and to pour into the lives of those we encounter. Love leads us to forgive, even when our minds don't want to. Love brings us to the foot of the Cross to surrender our broken selves. It urges us to pray for our family and friends, and inspires us to spread peace. Love is hope and it shines brightly as we spread the joys of our heart by serving others. Love is the anthem of the Saint, the rhythmic drum beat we march to on our way from this Earth to Heaven. It's the sound that soothes our

---

[161] John 17: 20-23, 26

weary souls and satisfies our restless hearts when someone who tenderly cares for us says, "I love you."

And love is who Jesus is, the incarnate joy of the Father outpouring his blood on the Cross at Calvary for the salvation of the world. Love is the ticket to Heaven and the surest and purest path to Sainthood. Without it we are mere bodies walking around lifeless. With it we are truly alive. With love we receive the gift that leads us to the fullness of joy. It's to be treasured always. For the Saint, love begins here on this planet. It's discovered, received, and shared and it becomes who we are. Love takes us to the highest of heights. When we enter into the completeness of God's love, our soul soars. When we are filled with love we find who we are truly created to be—Saints. Love is the key as we are blessed by God. Love unlocks our hearts leading us to eternal life.

Like the chorus of that classic upbeat song, "The Saints go marching in," you will indeed go marching in and it starts each day with love. To all my readers and the Saints in the making out there, thank you for taking time to journey along with me on our road to Sainthood and to invest in the Kingdom. Know that I am praying for you and ask that you pray for me. Please keep your brothers and sisters in faith in prayer also. Your life matters and the impact you have on others is profound. Each of you has a sphere of influence with weighty paramountcy. The small stone of your life when thrown into the river of the world and lived with great intentionality will cause a ripple throughout the Earth. As a believer myself, striving to become a Saint, I appreciate your faith, time, love, and support. I hope you are encouraged, inspired and motivated by this message God has placed on my heart. My prayer is you are fired up to continue to receive the love of Jesus and share your beautiful heart with every person you meet. Undoubtedly we were created to be in relationship with God and one another. In faith we can have a full life on earth and we rest in the eternal hope of being with our Lord where perfect love has no end. But before that day comes, we, the *everyday Saints,* have some unfinished business to attend to.

Challenge 19
Eyes on the Prize

This week I encourage you to do an overall reflection of your life. Where have you experienced and practiced Heaven? In what ways have you lived with love as your anthem and how can you focus more on what really matters? How has God touched your heart through your experiences, trials, and blessings? Listen to the Lord and pay attention to the ways you can walk faithfully amidst the business, family responsibilities, and things that require your time. Ask Jesus to give you his eyes and heart so that love is always your main objective. This will help each of us keep our eyes on the prize and not get caught up in the stresses of this world. Never forget, someday soon you will be marching in to receive the fullness of God's love with all his holy people and Saints in Heaven.

UNFINISHED BUSINESS
CHAPTER 20

"I don't stop when I'm tired, I stop when I'm done."
- David Goggins

Saints Don't Stop, They Live on Forever

As I look at myself in the mirror today, I see someone far different than a decade ago. You probably can say the same. I expect something far greater as well. It's because the longer I'm on this journey through life, more is learned and the fonder my heart grows to do what is left— to live out this mission to love. Ideas and desires have become manifested because time and our choices of what we use each day adds up to become the reality of our lives. For me, I know there is so much unfinished business. The goals that have been set and the dreams I once had no longer are merely far off fantasies that pass like the whoosh of the wind. Instead, these fire me up in the morning, get me out of bed with enthusiasm, and make me take on the day to make it my masterpiece. I share this with you because no matter how old or young you might be, as long as your heart is beating and you have air in your lungs, there is unfinished business for you to complete. What is ultra-important is that our unfinished business that we work hard on daily be done lovingly for God. Hugh of St. Victor said, "I know, my soul, that while you are loving anything, you are transformed into its likeness." Each of us has unfinished business to love and when we do we are transformed each day into the person God created us to be. It's not about how you start, it's about how you finish.

The journey to Sainthood and living out your faith through discipleship comes down to hearing and accepting the call God places on your life. You have been called. The task is great and involves a large responsibility. But know that like the scriptures so powerfully proclaim, "being confident of this, that he who began a good work in you will carry it on to completion until the day of Christ Jesus."[162] Certainly we have unfinished business to take care of. There is great possibility and opportunity ahead. The road to life is at stake and we have been commissioned as the Church—namely the Body of Christ, to go out and to tell the world the good news. That is the primary reason why this book was written and why you have read it to the end.

At times you might feel that this extremely challenging assignment is burdensome due to its significance. Human nature might even think it's too heavy to bear the weight of the Cross and continue to aid in the fight for souls. Yet, you and I must not grow tired of doing good because souls are thirsting for the Lord and he is searching for the hearts of his beloved. On this road to Sainthood we have uncovered what a life of holiness involves. Love is the greater way. Practicing Heaven is what we are to do by loving because where love exists, God dwells abundantly. The *everyday Saint* spreads Christ's love through heartfelt compassion, forgiveness, and selflessness. These are part of the call God places on our lives. The apostles were fishers of men and so are we today. Cast out your line, you will be surprised what you catch. The Lord has something beautiful for you to reel in. There is a chance that your "nets" will overflow in abundance like the disciples experienced when Jesus told them to toss out the line one more time.

Furthermore, charity, prayer, iron discipleship, and trust all play

---

162 Philippians 1:6

a serious part in our own spiritual growth as God molds us into his masterpiece. The Lord continues to prepare you by working on your heart so that you are well fit with his armor to go into the world and impact those you meet. Lastly, his grace is necessary as he fills in gaps. We know that the treasure which satisfies the soul is found only in the mystery of the Cross, which came to its full completion through the love of Jesus. And so we walk faithfully on the road to Heaven. I implore you to listen to the words of the humble servant Saint Angela of Merici, who was the foundress of the Company of Saint Ursula. Angela started the first teaching order of the women religious in the Church and said:

> It will be impossible for you not to cherish them day and night, and to have them all engraved in your heart, one by one, for this is how real love acts and works. And this charge must not be a burden for you; on the contrary, you have to thank God most greatly that he has designed to see to it that you are among those he wants to spend themselves in governing and safeguarding such a treasure, his own. Grace is certainly great and destiny inestimable, if you are willing to recognize it. Have hope and firm faith in God, for he will help you in everything. Pray to him, humble yourselves under his great power because without doubt, as he has given you this charge, so he will give you also the strength to be able to carry it out, provided you do not fail for your part. Act, move, believe, strive, hope, cry out to him with all your heart, for without doubt you will see marvelous things, if you direct everything to the praise and glory of his Majesty and the good of souls.[163]

Trust and be faithful to the Lord. My journey has not been easy and I am sure yours has had its fair share of valley moments. Know that you have what it takes and as long as you stay firmly planted and continue to share love with others, your mission will be fulfilled. God has placed such great and important things on your heart for a reason. Your life and your call to Sainthood will greatly impact the lives of each person you encounter. Know that Jesus provides his Holy Spirit

---

[163] Magnificat, January 2021, Vol.22, No. 11, pgs 380-381

which gives us the wisdom to understand all things. This is especially true during your times of need. As long as you go and show up, the fruit will be ripened as the harvest is abundant out there. Don't hold back, *Everyday Saints*—that's who you and I are called to be. It's who we are because we are the new-age disciples of Jesus.

What awaits you and all souls out there for that matter is eternal life; complete and perfect union with God. The gates of Heaven are being polished as the angels are eager for your entrance. The scriptures clearly outline this by promising us what the Lord will say to his faithful servants, "Well done, my good and faithful servant; you were faithful over a few things, I will put you in charge over many things. Enter into your master's joy."[164] Our commission is to be the sower. You and I are to plant the seed of faith wherever we go and to allow God to cause the growth. True and lasting happiness comes through the soul connection that we have with our Lord and with our fellow human beings.

That is why I go out onto the streets and greet strangers with a smile. This is the thing that excites me when my alarm clock rings at 4 am to take on another day. Today is the gift given to us and who we love and how we impact people we encounter is our gift back to God. What draws me to the chapel each morning for quiet time with our Lord is his love for me. This love fills my heart and allows me the capacity to go out into a broken world and love others more. Certainly, my failed attempts and efforts will always be far less than perfect. However, at the end of my lifetime I want to be able to have peace in knowing that I did all that I could to love people and share hope, peace, and joy that comes from knowing Jesus.

At the end of the age it will not matter how much money we had, what our occupation was, or the fame or notoriety we acquired. Only one thing will matter and that is how we loved God and that we shared the Lord's love with others. Our life mission comes down to Sainthood, which is found in our universal call to listen to God so that we continue to build up his Kingdom by sharing the heart of Jesus with the world. In the words of the famous Christian athlete, great servant of God, and philanthropist, Tim Tebow said, "The purpose of life is not to be happy. It is to be useful, to love God and people, to be

---

[164] Matthew 25:31

honorable, to be compassionate. To have it make some difference that you have lived and lived well." So how will you live and live well? You are destined for greatness! Your call to be a fisher of men and a Saint is an everyday calling. It starts with a small "yes" in the morning when your eyes open to a new day full of possibility. Our Church needs you. Our brothers and sisters throughout the earth need you. Today and each moment is the right time to go out and to spread the good news. You are a Saint and your life with God living within you can truly change the world!

Victory Awaits God's Saints

As we near the end of this journey together, it's important for us to keep in mind the words of the great St. Padre Pio who said, "My past, Oh Lord, I entrust to your mercy. My present to your love. My future to your providence." It's time if you haven't done so already to forgive and to let go of the things that are holding you down. In the present moment of life it is about loving everyone we can and sharing God's infinite love without judgment or reservation. Try not to worry too much about the future and what it holds, while always reminding yourself of who holds your future. It is good to contemplate what Heaven will be like. Will it be worth it when we get there? I believe wholeheartedly the answer is an emphatic and unanimous YES!

Although we don't get more than a mere glimpse from the scriptures about life after death, we do have one very strong indication from the Lord through John's Gospel as it says, "Now this is eternal life: that they know you, the only true God, and Jesus Christ, whom you have sent."[165] The more we get to deeply know the Lord and enter into communion with him, the clearer the picture becomes of what Heaven will be like. Joy is at the center of it all. Joy is what you and I have been promised in this lifetime and joy is the reward that awaits us in eternity when we answer the call to become Saints. Wholeness and completeness occurs when we enter the gates. Imagine being there and arriving home. Jesus will be standing in your place and the Father will see you, his son, his daughter, as a reflection of Christ.

---

[165] John 17:3

Then you and I will be made fully holy because he is holy.

For now, we journey on and have some unfinished business to take care of. What that completely involves and where we will ultimately go, only God knows. What we do know is that Saints are made for greatness. You and I are here to impact the hearts, minds, and lives of others. Souls are searching. Cast out your net of love and keep forging ahead. The road to holiness happens "poco a poco"—little by little. Your life is the living gospel and you are a tremendous witness to the faith. You are to be like Saint Barnabas who built community and chose to *Be Church*, as he was deemed the son of encouragement. You are the messenger of hope that people so desperately need. You are the modern day John the Baptist who professed the ancient words of the Prophet Isaiah, "Prepare the way of the Lord."

Believe and continue to live boldly. There is nothing that God cannot do and it starts with you. Hear and strive to live by these powerful words of St. Paul. I believe he sums up our lives as Saints very well by saying, "So that Christ may dwell in your hearts through faith; and that you, being rooted and grounded in love, may be able to comprehend with all the Saints what is the width and length and height and depth, and to know the love of Christ which surpasses knowledge, that you may be filled to all the fullness of God."[166] Receive God's fullness and share that fullness through your life.

My hope is that you will keep striving with me and our faithful brothers and sisters toward holiness. I pray that your road to Sainthood will be paved with unwavering faith and that you will feel the love of God every step of the way. It excites me to think about all the possibilities out there and what the Lord has planned next. I believe that life enthusiast, David Goggins, articulated what you and I must do now. He summed up the journey on earth and made this message a mantra to live by in stating, "I don't stop when I'm tired, I stop when I'm done." We are done when God says so. Only he knows the day and the hour. So we trim our lamps and keep shining brightly to bring him honor and glory. Until then, you and I, along with the *everyday Saints* of this world, have unfinished business. There is a mission to complete. Let's go out into the mission field and carry the

---

[166] Ephesians 3:17-19

Cross by sharing the endless love of God and lead souls to Jesus. By professing the gospel by our lives we will finish the race of faith.

The world needs change and you and I are called to be agents of that change. How we practice Heaven by living love is a radical shift that we will initiate. If not us, then who? If not now, then when? My only ask is that you would continue to be true to who you are and the call God placed on your life. Allow the Holy Spirit to show you the way. I urge you to live with unwavering faith and to do all things with great love. Run your own specific race and always keep fighting the good fight. St. Paul reminds us that we are amazing spiritual athletes on the hunt for the ultimate prize! He says, "All this I do for the sake of the gospel, so that I too may have a share in it. Do you not know that the runners in the stadium all run in the race, but only one wins the prize? Run so as to win. Every athlete exercises discipline in every way. They do it to win a perishable crown, but we, an imperishable one. Thus I do not run aimlessly..." [167]

Most of all, never give up. The Saint stands firm and receives God's love allowing this great gift to flow to others from their heart. No matter how hard the battle is, keep marching. *Everyday Saints* carry on. Understand that you are made in the image and likeness of God. You are called to share him with the world. If you gained anything positive out of our time together, please pass this faith-filled message along to someone you love and believe in. God bless you and know with full certainty that the power of Jesus Christ is living in you. Keep spreading hope, love, and light wherever you go. Always remember, it happens one person, one encounter, and one act of love at a time. You and I are the Saint next door and it's time we recognize the Saint in one another. Together we are Saints who will renew the face of the earth!

Challenge 20

Over the next few weeks take some time to reflect on the larger picture of life. What unfinished business do you have? What has God put on your heart? Think about the things that make you the most joy-filled

---

[167] 1 Corinthians 9:23-26

and allow your spirit to soar. For some of you it could mean that change is on the way. Don't resist it, but listen. Allow your soul to receive the love of Jesus fully so that you can work in unison with God to fulfill your personal destiny.

Finally, pray about who you are to share this message of love and hope with. When God puts a special person on your heart, listen to him. Pay it forward to that individual by passing this book along. In this small manner you will invite your friend, family member, or someone you just met to take the next step with you on the journey toward Sainthood. Heaven is to be practiced here with one another because love has an eternal reward. Holiness lives in you. All it takes is a small crack to open the door to invite a person to receive the goodness of God. Believe in the power of Christ and believe that you are a Saint.

CLOSING PRAYER

Lord God, through the power of your risen Son, Jesus Christ, and through the working of your Holy Spirit, as well as the holy intercession of the Blessed Virgin Mary, consecrate my life and call to Sainthood to you. Guide me and inspire me to be encouraged along the way and to aid the journey of others by heeding the example of the great Saints and holy people of your Church. Through your power, live in my heart and give me the grace to live out the call to Sainthood that you placed on my life. Grant me your most pure heart, oh Lord, and keep me in your heart that I might be connected to your Son. Help me to never be separated from you. Sanctify me and allow me to die to self, offering up my entire life to you. Bring me to holiness in body, mind, and spirit so that I am connected to and given the Sacred Heart of Jesus. Oh Mother of God, lead me ever closer to your Son each day through divine intercession and protect me. Guide me and show me the way to the Lord so I can have the same trust you had in God's plan for my own life. Lord Jesus, lead me and transform my heart so that I live to do all things with great love in order to build up your Kingdom by bringing others to you. Heavenly Father, give me the strength, words, thoughts, and the actions of eternal life so that I live out my baptismal call and become a Saint for your Church. Amen.

"Love is the most powerful force in the universe. Sainthood isn't about achievement or what we can do on our own. It's all about allowing Jesus to work in and through our lives. As disciples we were made in God's image and likeness, called to humbly serve. You have limitless potential and those you encounter need you. Your journey is the living gospel. Each day is an invitation to go deeper with the Lord as we walk with one another carrying the cross. *Everyday Saints* are among us. Look around and recognize that your own presence, time, treasure, and life are gifts. I encourage you to meet people where they are. Grace allows us to have eyes that look through a lens of love, rid of judgment. Then we can see the beauty shining inside of our brothers and sisters. Many think one person can't do much to change a world with countless problems. However, Saints believe each act of love matters. It might be a small drop in the ocean, but like Mother Teresa showed, how far lass would that ocean be without that single drop. Give your best, don't quit, and strive to practice Heaven. In doing so we gain increased freedom, receive happiness, and radiate Christ's joy! There's only one way to live and that's life to the fullest. Together we will do beautiful things with God."

- Dan Jason

REFERENCES

Ames, Mark Mary & Father Angelus (Franciscan Friars of the Renewal). *Poco a Poco [Podcast]*, "You're Not an Outsider." Episode 53, April 21, 2021. Available at: https://www.franciscanfriars.com/pocoapoco

Burke, Kevin. *"Pedro Arrupe: Essential Writings."* Maryknoll, NY: Orbis Books 2004.

Campbell, Jim. "20th Century Ignatian Voices: Pedro Arrupe, SJ (1907-1991)." A Service of Loyal Press (March, 2021) http://www.ignatianspirituality.com/ignatian-voices/20th-century-ignatian-voices/pedro-arrupe-sj/

Catholic Online. "Saint of the Day: St. Faustina Kowalska." 2020. https://www.catholic.org/Saints/Saint.php?Saint_id=510

Cutler, Howard C. (Dalai Lama). The Art of Happiness, Easton Press, 1998.

Dumont, Pierre-Marie. "Magnificat", Volume 22, Number 11. (January, 2020): pages 380-391.

Franciscan Media. "Saint of the Day." 2020. https://www.franciscanmedia.org/Saint-of-the-day

Gaitley, Michael. *33 Days to Morning Glory,* Marian Press, 2011.

Illigabiza, Immaculee. *Left to Tell,* Hay House Inc., 2006.

Ilibagiza, Imaculeeabout. "Surviving the Rwandan Genocide." Seek 2021 FOCUS Conference, February 5, 2021.

Jason, Dan. *Fire Burning Within: Fiercely Taking on Life With God Leading You Every Step of the Way,* author'sHouse Publishing, 2020.

Kowalska, Maria Faustyna. *The Diary of Saint Maria Faustina Kowalska : Divine Mercy in My Soul*, Marian Press, 2003.

Martin (SJ), James. *My Life With the Saints*, Loyola Press, 2016.

Mary, Francis. (Franciscan Friars of the Immaculate) *A Handbook on Guadalupe*, Ignatius Press, 2009.

New American Bible, Revised Edition (NABRE), Saint Benedict Press, 1983.

Pope Francis. Apostolic Exhortation: *Gaudete et Exultate on the Call to Holiness in Today's World*. Vatican, 2018.

Pope Francis. *The Right to Hope*. "Magnificat", Volume 23, Number 1. (March, 2020): pages 261-262.

Pro Football Reference. "Drew Brees." Pro Football Reference, 2020. https://www.pro-football-reference.com/players/B/BreeDroo.htm

Robinson, Sharon. *Promises to Keep: How Jackie Robinson Changed America*, Scholastic Inc., 2016.

Scharfenberger, (Bishop) Edward. (2021) "Fear Less and Love More." *The Evangelist*. March 11, 2021.

Scharfenberger, (Bishop) Edward. (2021) "Practicing Heaven." *The Evangelist*. March 18, 2021.

Teresa, Mother & Kolodiejchuk (M.C.), Brian. *Mother Teresa: Come Be My Light, The Private Writings of the Saint of Calcutta*, November, 2003.

Walsh, Fr. Jim, "Trusting in God & Jesus as a Magnet to the Hurting." St. Pius X Parish. Albany, NY. (January 31, 2021).

ACKNOWLEDGMENTS

I am deeply humbled and overwhelmed with gratitude with being able to share this message of hope and love with the world. Writing is a tremendous blessing. What a gift to receive such an amazing opportunity to author another faith inspired book. This would never have been possible without the grace of the Lord Jesus and so many supporters. The backing of beautiful people in my inner circle and my readers has been tremendous. Your prayers are truly felt and encourage me daily. I wish to extend my utmost gratitude to Bishop Edward Scharfenberger of the Roman Catholic Diocese of Albany for endorsing this book. His willingness to contribute to this literary work and unwavering support has been inspiring. I am forever thankful to him for believing in me. As a magnificent and dynamic leader of the faith, Bishop Ed has been a remarkable shepherd of the flock. Our diocese is blessed to have him as our guide and teacher.

I continue to be blown away by Bishop's efforts to champion the things God places on my heart. Bishop Ed's commitment to journeying alongside people and his vote of confidence provide so many parishioners with a spark that is powerful beyond measure. I am so blessed to call him my friend. I am thankful for the support of my family. It was special to have grown up in a loving home and to have experienced the presence of the Lord in profound ways early on. Faith has mattered greatly to me from the start and my hope has always been to share the light of Jesus Christ with the world. My baptism into the Church was the greatest gift I could have ever received. My faith filled friends and the brothers that I work with have all supported my endeavors over the years and they give me endless strength.

Faith is the bedrock of my life. The small seed that was planted during my childhood years has bloomed thanks to God's amazing grace. Throughout the course of my spiritual journey, I have gone through some very difficult circumstances. For those of you who have read my first book, *FIRE Burning Within: Fiercely Taking on Life with God Leading You Every Step of the Way,* you know that I hit rock bottom during my teenage years and my life came close to ending. However, by the grace of God I am here today and I am grateful for where the Lord is now leading me. I could not have gotten this far or survived the toughest times without my faith. I am who I am because of all that I've endured. Jesus continues to be my guiding light and He keeps chipping away at my heart. The Lord has blessed me with many divine connections, friendships, and encounters over my three decades on earth. These have challenged, motivated, and galvanized my faith leading me to heed God's call in an even greater manner as life unfolds.

Like you, I have had ups and downs, as well as my share of struggles. There have been mountains that have seemed nearly impossible to climb. Yet, God has kept me in the palm of his hand and I believe that he continues to keep you close to his Son. We know that the Lord guides our paths and directs our ways. As a result of faith and trust in Jesus, we are able to summit to new heights. I am very thankful for every person who continues to cheer me on by supporting my ventures for God. Through the writing of these books, the building of my faith based foundation *EF3 LIFE*, and my call to mission, I have grown closer to Jesus each day. I am forever grateful for this faith filled journey that has provided me with wind for my sails. Most of all, thank you for sharing this beautiful faith we have because ultimately we believe in Jesus who is everything.

I appreciate you taking the time to read this book. I am excited to journey with you as we work together to discover the Saint that is inside each of us and all that we are called to be. Thank you for investing your time in building up the Kingdom of God. I am grateful for your willingness to listen, to pray through this book with me, and hope that you are left inspired. My hope is that the Lord will powerfully infiltrate your life and open up your heart to his call.

Remember, we each have a distinct purpose and a unique mission.

Our God calls us by name. May the peace of Jesus Christ and his great love fill your soul as we journey on together in this world until the glorious day when we are called home. God bless you and your family and know that I lift you up in prayer. I pray that you always strive to impact the lives of others and know that you can have that inner peace by walking with the prince of peace. By the grace of God and through his mercy I believe that we can share the greatest gift, God's love, and the joy we receive with the world. Let us remember that this is hard work, but we win the discipleship mission by not quitting and by going faithfully to wherever Jesus leads us. The love of Christ must be shared, so let us go out and tell the whole world the good news.

– Dan Jason

ABOUT ATMOSPHERE PRESS

Atmosphere Press is an independent, full-service publisher for excellent books in all genres and for all audiences. Learn more about what we do at atmospherepress.com.

We encourage you to check out some of Atmosphere's latest releases, which are available at Amazon.com and via order from your local bookstore:

The Swing: A Muse's Memoir About Keeping the Artist Alive, by Susan Dennis

Possibilities with Parkinson's: A Fresh Look, by Dr. C

Gaining Altitude - Retirement and Beyond, by Rebecca Milliken

Out and Back: Essays on a Family in Motion, by Elizabeth Templeman

Just Be Honest, by Cindy Yates

You Crazy Vegan: Coming Out as a Vegan Intuitive, by Jessica Ang

Detour: Lose Your Way, Find Your Path, by S. Mariah Rose

To B&B or Not to B&B: Deromanticizing the Dream, by Sue Marko

Convergence: The Interconnection of Extraordinary Experiences, by Barbara Mango and Lynn Miller

ABOUT THE AUTHOR

Dan Jason is a passionate Christian author who wants to journey with you on the road to Heaven. Dan hopes that his faith based works of literature motivate and inspire each of his readers. As a part time Christian missionary and leader in the faith, Jason's second book entitled *The SAINT Next Door* is an invitation to recognize Jesus in our neighbor, as well as God's holiness in ourselves. Jason's latest text is a sequel to his first nonfiction work: *FIRE Burning Within.* As an author and disciple, Dan believes that everyone has greatness inside and God calls each of us to be Saints. Book proceeds will help benefit Jason's work of global outreach and missions of serving the poor around the world.

CPSIA information can be obtained
at www.ICGtesting.com
Printed in the USA
LVHW041621101221
705869LV00014B/398/J